The Cultivation of
Hardy Perennials

The Cultivation of Hardy Perennials

RICHARD BIRD

B.T. Batsford Ltd · London

For Sue Martin

Photographs by Richard Bird
Line drawings by Duncan Lowe

First published 1994
© Richard Bird 1994

Typeset by Goodfellow & Egan, Cambridge
and printed in Great Britain by
Butler and Tanner, Frome, Somerset

Published by
B.T. Batsford Ltd
4 Fitzhardinge Street
London W1H 0AH

A catalogue record for this book is available from
the British Library

ISBN 0 7134 7061 5

Contents

Introduction

There can be no doubt that if you wish to have an attractive garden you have got to work at it. In spite of numerous books and articles to the contrary there is no such thing as the instant garden. You might end up with a designed space with a few boring plants but you will not have a living, breathing garden that changes with the seasons and that is full of satisfying colour, shapes and textures.

In order to make a garden worthy of its name, time and energy are needed. There are no short cuts. However, if carried out in time and in the right sequence, many of the tasks are less onerous than many non-gardeners would believe. The key to gardening success is being in control and that, basically, is what this book is about. It is not concerned with aesthetics but the more practical side of getting the best out of your conditions and your plants.

The main part of the book is an A–Z of all the genera of perennial plants that are likely to occur in a garden. Each entry provides cultural requirements, including any special treatment or conditions. Very few books carry this kind of information and this is the first ever to provide it so thoroughly.

Remember, there is no right or wrong way to garden. What will work in one garden for one person may not work for another. There are so many variable factors, particularly local soil and weather conditions, even within a particular garden, that it is impossible to give specific advice for each and every situation. Even the gardener's temperament and lifestyle influence the way plants are tended. So, while this book sets out to offer as much advice as possible it must be remembered that it is only a guideline. If things work for you contrary to the following advice, do not change your methods.

There is generally a time for everything in the garden. If the borders are prepared properly in the first place, much time and effort will be spared later. Similarly, if borders are given attention throughout the winter and in the early spring, life will be easier for the rest of the year. If you do not start gardening until the weather warms up enough for you to do it in a sun hat and shorts, then the weeds and pests will be in control and it will be

7

an uphill struggle. On the other hand do not get over-anxious if you have ignored certain jobs or if time is running out. There is always another year. While writing this I looked out of my window and spotted a large clump of *Iris unguicularis* that should have been cut back in the summer. It is now too late, but all it means is that it will not be so easy to see the flowers this winter because of the amount of old leaves. Perhaps next year I will remember it.

If you can, try to plan your day in the garden. Decide as you go out what you are going to do and stick to it. It is so easy to fritter away a day moving from one little job to another, as each takes the eye. You start in one border and while fetching a wheelbarrow notice another task, and so on so that the wheelbarrow and the original border is forgotten until it is time to pack up. Personally I love nothing better than doing this, but at the end of the day it can be surprising how little has been achieved. Whereas if you decide to concentrate on one bed, nothing will be missed and the tasks that you detest, tying up roses perhaps, will not have been overlooked in favour of more preferable tasks on the other side of the garden where the sun is shining. This may sound fanciful but all experienced gardeners will know what I mean.

However, not all available time should be spent with your head buried in the border. The whole purpose of a garden is to provide enjoyment and time must be allowed for standing and staring. A gentle stroll around a garden or a rest on a favourite bench is absolutely essential. As well as giving a great deal of pleasure, such activities will also allow you time to look at the plants. When working on a border you can be too close to notice what is going on. Every gardener will have experienced giving a border a really thorough weed only to walk past ten minutes later with a guest and spot a giant stinging nettle growing right in the middle.

Standing back and staring will show you what needs to be done, it will often give you forewarning of problems as you will notice plants that are beginning to wilt through lack of water or pests beginning to accumulate. If you are methodical you will carry a notebook and jot down what needs doing. If you are human you will commit it to memory instead, and promptly forget about it until the next time you walk round. Eventually, however it will get done.

I hope this book proves useful to all its readers. It is unique but also far from complete; no one book on such a huge topic ever could be. Please forgive any shortcomings. It would be nice to think that they may be rectified in some future edition, when both the author and his readers have learnt more about this vast topic.

Richard Bird
Rogers Rough

Border Siting

Although this is not a book about design or garden aesthetics there are still a few crucial, practical points about the siting of the border which are of a practical nature.

It is important to consider the types of plants that you want to grow when laying out the garden. It is no good hoping to grow sun-loving plants in a part of the garden that is constantly shaded from the sun. Similarly if you want to specialize in plants that are on the tender side then a border in a cold or exposed position spells disaster. Instead, if you decide to grow tender plants then it would be sensible to forgo a patio immediately next to the house, creating a border there which will benefit from the warmth of the walls in winter.

As implied above, weather is one of the most important considerations when siting a border. There is little you can do about the weather itself, although one drastic solution is to move, but it is possible to make one or two modifications to the garden that will change its effects.

One of the most frequent problems is the wind. This is liable to have two effects. The first is to damage plants by blowing them about, causing them to flop over or to spoil the leaves and blooms. The second is to chill the plants in winter and desiccate them in summer. The most obvious solution is to create a shelter belt.

If the wind is channelled between two buildings or trees a couple of shrubs may be the remedy. On the other hand the whole garden might need protecting, in which case a hedge is required. Hedges are the best form of wind breaks. Not being solid they allow the wind to filter through, thus decreasing its speed. A wall or a solid fence simply blocks the wind, which is then forced over the top, creating tremendous turbulence which often does even more harm to the plants than the original wind. When planting a hedge it is a good idea to use a temporary wind break of plastic netting that can be purchased especially for the job. This will not only give shelter to the garden, but also protect the hedge while it is growing.

Another aspect of wind is the staking and support of plants but this will be dealt with in a later chapter.

Shade must also be seriously considered. To have a wide range of plants there must be areas of the garden that provide shade as well as those that are in full sun. There are many very attractive woodland plants that will only survive if shielded from the sun. Most gardens have some areas of shade. Many gardeners despair of such places but there are many plants well-worth growing that find these conditions ideal. If you have not got such an area it is worth growing one or two larger shrubs, which will provide deepish shade directly beneath and a moving, lighter shade around them.

Little can be done about the amount of rainfall that a garden receives. Sometimes it is possible to put covers over certain plants or parts of the border during the winter months. This is unsightly but it does allow the range of plants grown to be extended. Any such cover should be open at the sides to allow the air to circulate freely, otherwise the plants will be in danger of fungal diseases. Obviously if the garden slopes it is a good idea to create borders at the top where water does not accumulate. The lower, wetter areas can either be drained or advantage taken of the moisture and a pond or bog garden created. Creating a water feature increases the variety of plants that can be grown and thus makes the garden infinitely more interesting. Improving the soil, as will be seen in the next chapter, also helps to increase the drainage and is essential in gardens that receive a high rainfall.

Cold, particularly in the form of frost, is a problem that most gardeners know only too well. Certain areas of the garden may act as a frost hollow, allowing cold air to accumulate. This is a bad position to create a border but for various reasons there may be no option, it might be possible either to divert the cold air as it comes down the slope by building a wall or hedge, or to make a hole at the bottom of the slope to let it drain away. Even a small gap created at the bottom of a hedge will be sufficient to allow the cold air to pass through, warming that part of the garden by several degrees.

Some parts of a garden are usually warmer than others, and it pays to discover where they are. Certainly borders in front of south-facing walls hold the warmth. Rock in a rock garden can have the same effect but on a more limited scale. Fences, trees and shrubs can all form sheltered areas in which the more tender plants may survive. Some plants, mainly bulbs, can be lifted for the winter and stored in peat or sand in a frost-free place. Others can be left outside and given protection of some kind in the border itself (see page 40).

Not all of the above stem directly from the position of the border but the weather is one of the most important considerations when considering its siting. Another is the soil. It is a waste to use the area with the best soil as a lawn and then struggle with heavy conditions for the borders. Aesthetic considerations may dictate that this is the only sensible thing to do; in which case you may have to bite the bullet and move the soil around. This is a tedious job, but hiring a mechanical digger will make it considerably easier. Small ones are now available that are capable of passing along a narrow path beside a house, so access is no longer a problem for most gardens.

Border
Preparation

One of the keys to good gardening is thorough preparation of the borders. If the soil is in good heart and free from weed the plants have a chance of getting off to a flying start, and you will not have to spend the rest of the summer battling with the weeds.

The first thing to do is to remove all perennial weeds. If you have a light soil then this can be carried out as you are digging, simply by removing all bits of root by hand. If you leave the border for a month or more after this any new pieces of weed that appear usually come out very easily.

However, if your soil is heavy this process is not at all easy as pieces constantly break off and remain hidden in lumps of earth. The only practical solution is to resort to a chemical weedkiller. Many gardeners are quite rightly now against excessive use of chemicals. However, if they are used properly it should only be necessary to clear the ground once of weeds in this way, after which they can be controlled by hand as they appear. Alternatively, it is possible to cover an area with polythene or an old carpet to rid the soil of weeds. This works well with annuals but takes a very long time to be effective with tough perennials, especially any whose roots extend well beyond the affected area.

Whichever method you use it is useless if weeds are allowed to remain in an adjacent area. For example you can remove all the bindweed from a border, but if the border fronts a hedge that still contains it the problem is bound to return within a couple of months.

It is important that all borders should be free of standing water. Even plants that require a moist soil do not like to have stagnant water around their roots. Conditions can be improved considerably on heavier soils by the addition of grit and well-rotted organic material. This increases the porosity and allows much better drainage. In really wet soils it may be necessary to lay a drainage system of some sort. This may flow into a convenient ditch or, more likely, a soakaway has to be constructed. This is a large hole of at least a cubic metre (cu. yd) in capacity, which is filled with rubble. Water is directed into it through the drains and slowly seeps away into the surrounding subsoil, well away from the roots of most plants. Another alternative is to direct the

11

water into a pond or a bog garden, where wet-loving plants can be grown.

When digging it is always important to incorporate as much well-rotted organic material as possible. This has many beneficial effects. It improves the quality and texture of the soil, it feeds the plants and it provides a reservoir of moisture.

The last is very important. You will often read or hear the apparently contradictory statement 'a well-drained, but moisture-retentive soil'. This means that the soil should have the ability to shed excess water so that there is none lying stagnant between the particles, but that sufficient moisture should remain, held in the fibrous organic matter, to supply the plants' needs.

A plant needs oxygen at its roots in the same way as it needs it around its leaves. If the roots are in water they cannot get the oxygen they need. Surprisingly, many plants that cannot tolerate stagnant water can survive short periods of moving water. This applies particularly to mountain plants where snow-melt quickly passes by, aided by the sharp drainage of the stony terrain. Pulsatillas, for example, prefer a well-drained soil, but will tolerate short periods of excessive wet weather as long as the water does not hang around in the soil.

Organic material can be obtained in many forms. The most obvious is garden compost. All weeds and other organic material from the garden and kitchen are composted either in a container or in a heap, and when rotted are returned to the soil. Avoid plants that are in seed because although it is often said that if composted correctly the heat will destroy all weed seed this rarely happens in practice. Also avoid any kitchen waste that has been cooked or is otherwise likely to attract vermin. Material that will not rot down quickly, such as thick hedge trimmings or cabbage stalks, can be passed through a shredder, before being added to the heap.

Another source of material is animal manure of various kinds. Horse, cow, sheep, pig, and chicken are all very good but they must be allowed to rot down and, in the case of the last, to weather. Chicken manure should never be used directly on the border as the ammonia contained in the urea will kill many plants, but once this has evaporated it makes a very potent manure fertiliser. Never use the faeces of cats or dogs as these contain bacteria that are harmful to humans.

Leafmould makes an excellent addition to the soil. It is especially useful when trying to create a woodland-type soil for those plants that come from this kind of area. Collect leaves and compost them in a wire netting container. Several containers may be needed as leaves do not break down very quickly. Do *not* go down to the local woods and help yourself as this will impoverish the soil there and break the natural cycle, thus adversely affecting the trees.

Peat is no longer a suitable material for adding to the soil. It is doubtful if it ever was, and few experienced gardeners used it for this purpose. Although it is generally sterile and thus contains few weed seeds it is also nutritionally dead, offering very little to the plants as it rots down. Peat also breaks down so fast it does little to improve the soil. Through over-extraction, many peaty wetland areas are under threat, and it is no longer environmentally sound to use it in any quantity and certainly not in this wasteful way.

In the traditional garden peat beds for growing ericaceous plants, leafmould and pineneedles make excellent substitutes. Another good alternative is shredded or composted bark. The old name of 'peat beds' is retained throughout this book but it is not meant to imply that they are still constructed of peat.

Bark in its various forms, shredded, chipped or composted, is a very valuable material. It can be used for improving the soil although its nutritional value is quite low; generally it is best used as a mulch (see page 34). Some gardeners have been using it for years, particularly where local supplies have existed. If you have the space to store bark buy it by the lorry load rather than by the sack as it will work out very much cheaper.

There are various other materials that may be locally available. Hop waste from breweries has always been a favourite. Spent mushroom compost is another. This consists mainly of chopped straw or bracken and horse manure but it also contains some chalk to keep it sweet. This means that it should not be used on soil where ericaceous or lime-hating plants are grown.

One substance that many people find surprising when used to improve the soil is grit. This is extremely useful on heavy soils as it does much to increase the porosity. Flinty grit that has been crushed thus presenting a number of faces and angles is the best; the rounded peabeach is not so effective. If you burn pernicious weeds the baked pieces of soil that cling to their roots are also a very good addition. In effect this turns to pottery and cannot be re-wetted and helps break up heavy soil.

It is important to keep working heavy soil, adding as much material as you can. Over the years it will break down. I know a garden in which, during my gardening lifetime, sticky, yellow, wealden clay that was backbreaking to dig has changed to a loam that can be dug with a fork in mid winter.

When preparing a border it is a good idea to dig it as deeply as possible, double-digging if you can manage it. Adding organic material to the bottom spit is a great benefit. In the first year of the recent droughts that the south-east of England has endured the author started a series of new beds, all of which had farmyard manure dug into the lower spit. In spite of the severe drought no extra watering was required after the initial planting, and all the plants got away magnificently. They stretched their toes down to the moisture in the lower spit where the organic material was and never looked back. Elsewhere in much older beds where the soil was tired and no such material remained, the roots developed towards the surface to capture what little moisture fell and then died as the drought increased in severity; many plants were lost.

If the bottom spit goes into the subsoil, avoid mixing it with the upper topsoil.

The best time to prepare a border is in the autumn. This gives it a chance to settle down before planting commences in the spring. The weather, particularly the frost, breaks down the soil, making the final preparation much easier than if it all has to be done by hand. As the soil breaks down, eggs and larvae are exposed and birds will help eradicate these pests. Another advantage for leaving it so long is that any pieces of perennial weed that were missed will come into growth and can be extracted before they have time to regather enough strength to start spreading again.

In the spring go over the border with a hoe and break down any remaining lumps of earth to create a good, friable, planting medium. Try not to heap the border up too much above the surrounding area, whether it be a path or lawn. It looks slightly ridiculous if it is higher, especially the slope around the edge which will inevitably be steep. This makes it difficult to plant and soil keeps washing down into the gully making it difficult to trim the edge of the grass. Over the years as more organic material is added, not to mention the potting compost around the roots of plants, a border slowly increases in height and it becomes necessary to remove some soil. If you have the strength and the will-power (and it is the most horrendous of jobs) rake or dig back the topsoil – do not waste it – and remove the excess from the subsoil, being careful not to mix the two.

Acquiring Plants

Always choose the best plants you can find. They should be healthy, show signs of vigour and be free from pests. Never buy plants that are pot-bound or showing signs of distress. It is not a good idea to go for the biggest; choose a medium-size plant that is well developed with lots of growth potential. Such a plant will soon catch up and overtake a larger plant.

As you become more experienced so you will become a better judge of what to buy; occasionally it is possible to buy a plant that is pot-bound or only a slip of a plant and make something of it.

As well as checking for signs of pests on the parts above ground, some gardeners like to knock the plant out of the pot and remove all soil so ensuring that no soil-born pests such as root aphids or vine weevil come in with the plant.

Another reason that some gardeners like to remove all the soil is so that they can put the plant into their own compost. Most garden-centre plants are in a soilless compost, and many plants find difficulty in making the transition between this and the loam of the border. The roots often stay in the compost rather than venture out into the soil. At other times the soilless compost dries out and becomes difficult to re-wet whereas the surrounding soil is actually quite moist, in which case the roots die. Most gardeners have experienced digging up a plant, sometimes years after it has been planted, only to find that the roots have hardly spread. Plants grown in a loam-based compost do not seem to have this problem to the same extent.

If you buy plants through the post there are several things to remember. If you are going to be away during the delivery time tell the nursery not to send them until you return; a packet of plants that has been sitting on the doorstep in the sun for a fortnight is not a pretty sight. Open the packet as soon as you get it. If the plants are in pots water and stand them in a cool place, preferably in a shaded coldframe. If they have been bare-rooted pot them up and then put them in a similar position. Slowly harden them off and when they look as if they are happily growing away plant them. Do not plant them straight from the packet or you will have a lot of failures on your hands.

If the plant comes from a local plant sale or from a friend check it carefully. Often hidden in the roots will be a piece of ground elder, couch grass or some similar weed that if left will quickly infest your own border. Perhaps this may seem a harsh thing to say about friends, but it is surprising how often it happens, even from experienced gardeners.

If you are offered a piece of a plant from a friend's garden there is always the question of whether it is the right time to accept it or not. Most gardeners' experience says take it then rather than wait for the right time. If you wait either you or they will forget about it. If the soil is dry water it and come back for it when you have looked around the garden. Dig up the piece and place in a polythene bag. As soon as you get home pot it up or plant it out in the border, whichever seems the most appropriate to keep it alive. If it is hot and dry then it is better to pot it, possibly splitting it up into further pieces, as you will be able to give it better attention in a coldframe. Again check that there are no pernicious weeds coming in with the plant.

As soon as you get any plants home, if you do not know anything about them, check them out so that you can give them the right conditions. Sometimes they give some directions on garden centre labels, but they are usually very vague and sometimes inaccurate.

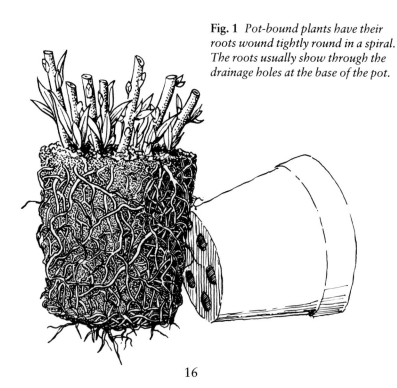

Fig. 1 *Pot-bound plants have their roots wound tightly round in a spiral. The roots usually show through the drainage holes at the base of the pot.*

Planting
the Border

The positioning of plants within the border is mainly an aesthetic consideration. Although this is of no concern here, there are other aspects that should be discussed.

Planting should only take place when the weather allows. This means avoiding periods when the ground is frozen, the wind too cold or too desiccating, the ground too dry or too wet, or the sun too hot. All these extremes will make it difficult for the plant to establish itself. The ideal weather conditions are overcast with slight rain so that the moist atmosphere keeps the plant turgid. The best time is generally in the autumn or spring. In colder areas the spring is the better alternative.

Autumn planting, while the soil is still warm, will allow the plant to establish itself before winter sets in. Spring-flowering plants are often best planted or transplanted at this time so that they are ready to flower the following year. Autumn generally does allow plants to settle down quicker and achieve an extra season's flowering. However, spring is a safer time to plant, especially on cold, wet soils. A newly-planted, inactive plant that has not established itself in autumn is bound to suffer during the winter from either the cold or the wet, even both. A spring-planted specimen will soon move into growth, the hostile conditions will be left behind, and the hot, dry summer conditions are still some way off.

Since you do not disturb the roots, container-grown plants can, in theory, be planted at any time provided the weather is not extreme. More attention should be paid to aftercare if they are planted in summer as conditions may not be ideal for the plant to look after itself.

Another aspect of timing concerns the soil rather than the plants. Do not work on borders when they are wringing wet or liable to be compacted by your weight, as you will do a great deal of damage to the soil structure and the border will never be totally satisfactory. If the soil is still too damp to work on but suitable for planting, use a long plank to spread your load. Once planted make certain that a plant does not dry out and that it is protected from any hot sunshine by light shading. When growth has been established the plant can be weaned off this aftercare.

Some plants can be moved even when they are in flower without their seeming to notice it. However, there are a large number of plants that resent being moved. These are mainly those with deep roots, especially tap roots. Make certain that these are planted in the right position from the start; changing your mind later on may mean the death of the plant. If you do have to move such a plant dig it up with as large a rootball as possible so that the roots are left undisturbed.

Not all plants are happy with a certain position. They will languish, even sulk, and look most unhappy. If this happens and you can think of no obvious reason for it, dig it up and move it elsewhere. This often does the trick even if it is only a short distance. It may be that the local conditions of the soil were not to its liking; there may have been a concentration of something it disliked, or the lack of something it needed. Even with sophisticated soil testing kits it is impossible to tell exactly what is happening around a plant's roots. For example, in old cottage gardens one often comes across the remains of old radio and torch batteries. God knows what these may let into the soil, even in very small quantities, but they could affect a plant. In newer houses a plasterer may have emptied his bucket in a particular place making it much more limy than elsewhere, without the gardener ever realizing. It is surprising how frequently a plant can be revived by moving it.

Fig. 2 *While working on damp soil, spread the load by standing on a plank of wood.*

Fig. 3 *Do not cover the rhizomes of irises with soil; they need to receive sunlight.*

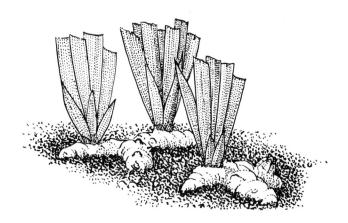

When planting out the best depth is that at which the plant was set in its pot or the nursery bed. There are a few occasions when it is necessary to plant deeper and they are mentioned in the A–Z part of this book. In some cases, peonies for example, it is very important not to plant them too deeply. Again this information has been given. Rhizomatous irises need to be planted with their rhizomes only partially covered with soil so that the sun can reach them. Bulbs vary in their planting depth and again all information is given. However, as a very rough rule of thumb, bulbs should be planted about three times the height of the bulb.

The distance between plants is always very difficult to assess. The rule of thumb here is that they should be half the eventual height away from the next, but this can vary considerably depending on local conditions. Spreaders should be planted further apart so they have room to develop, whereas those with only a few stems or that are clump-forming can be closer together.

Some gardeners like to plant close together so that the border soon looks full. They then thin as the plants thicken up. Another reason given for doing this is that closely grouped plants help to support each other and therefore need less staking, while the thick cover of foliage helps to suppress weeds.

Others like to leave plenty of room right from the start so that the plants can freely develop. They like space to move between the plants so that they can tend them. In wetter areas many gardeners like this extra space so that air can circulate freely between the plants thus reducing the chances of mildew and botrytis. Finally, many gardeners like the look of the freshly-dug earth between the plants.

Be careful about siting plants that spread vigorously either by self-sowing or vegetative means. This is dealt with more fully under 'weeding' on page 31.

The choice is up to individual gardeners and the best advice is to suggest that you do what suits you and ultimately your plants. I tend to vary according to what I am planting and the kind of border I am creating. Unfortunately this is intuitive rather than down to any prescribed plan or reasoning, although it is mainly based on a mixture of the reasons given in the last two paragraphs.

When planting a whole border it is a good idea to place all the plants if they are in pots in position so that you can see that they all fit and so that there will be no need to dig some up and replant them if they are incorrectly positioned. Larger areas of one plant can be marked out on the border with lines of sand or canes (be careful if you use the latter method as it is possible to cause eye injury on them while bending over to plant).

Fig. 4 *Lay out the plants in their pots before planting so that you can get an idea of how the arrangement will look.*

Fig. 5 *'Draw' on the soil with sand to get some idea of where clumps of plants will go.*

When putting the plant into the soil always dig a hole that is big enough to take all the roots when they are spread out. Try and avoid the situation where you are cramming them into an insufficient space. Some plants, such as bulbs, like to have extra sharp drainage around the roots in which case these can be placed on grit or sharp sand. Another advantage of this method is that it deters slugs to a certain extent. Some plants, eremurus for example, like to be planted on a slight ridge with their roots running down either side.

Plant firmly, pressing the soil around the plant with the knuckles of the hand or the heel of a boot. However, do not compact the ground. Some gardeners like to leave a slight depression around the plant to ensure that when watering the water remains round the plant rather than running away sideways. By the time the plant becomes established any such depressions will have vanished, filled in by the action of weeding or forking over the border.

Some gardeners like to label, others definitely do not. There are two reasons for labelling. The first, and most obvious, is so that the plant can be identified. In a small garden where the gardener knows all the plants this might not be necessary. In a large garden, however, where there is a constant

Fig. 6 *Always dig a hole larger than the plant so that the roots can be spread out.*

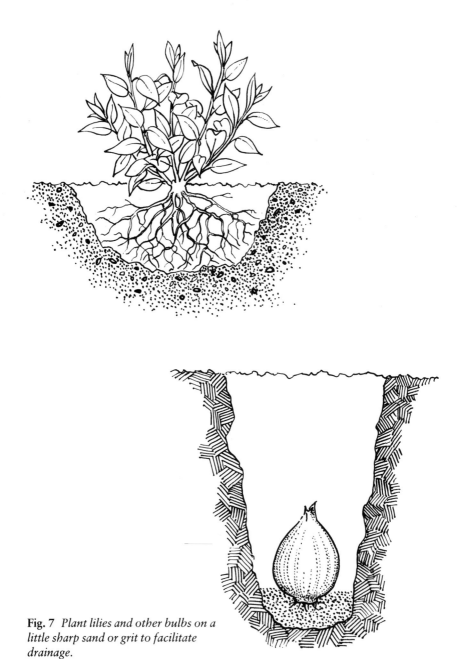

Fig. 7 *Plant lilies and other bulbs on a little sharp sand or grit to facilitate drainage.*

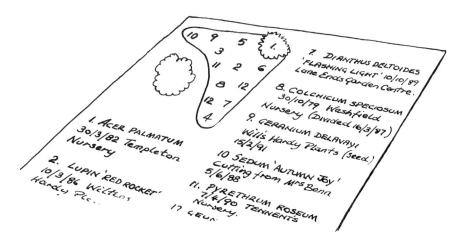

Fig. 8 *A typical page in a planting record book.*

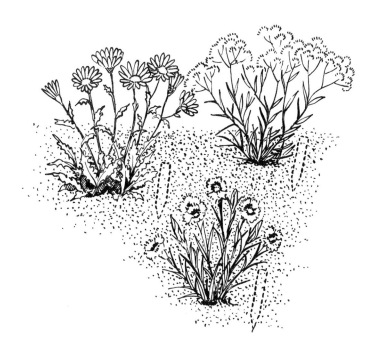

Fig. 9 *Always place the label in the same place relative to each plant.*

introduction of new plants and new forms, it may become necessary. I like to include other information on the label, such as when it was planted and from whom it was acquired.

An alternative is to keep all this information in a book. I draw a plan of the border, placing a number at the site of each planting and then list the plant names and information against that number below. It is simple and effective.

The second reason for labelling plants is to know where they are. Many retire below ground early or appear late. For example *Cosmos atro-sanguineus* does not appear above ground until early summer and it is quite easy to disturb it accidentally in spring while weeding, or even over-plant it, thinking that the space is empty. It is always a good idea to put the label in the same position relative to the plant or group of plants it refers to. I always place my label in the upper right hand corner, between one and two o'clock.

If your objection to labels is that you do not like to see them sticking up like tombstones, you can always bury them, as long as you put them in the same place each time.

Maintenance

Once a border has been prepared and planted it must have constant maintenance to keep it in good shape. This need not be arduous. 'Little and often' is best. For those in a position to do so, an hour a day achieves a great deal over the course of the year (and also helps to keep you fit). This is not too difficult to achieve in summer when the evenings, or mornings if you are an early riser, are light, but it is not so easy for many to achieve during the winter. However, a few hours at the weekend works wonders provided the time is used wisely and not frittered away.

I will come to the seasonal maintenance later, but for the moment it must be said that if the bulk of the tidying and ground preparation is done between the autumn and early spring, then maintenance throughout the rest of the year is much easier. Leave it to the spring and you will have problems catching up, especially if it has been a mild winter and weeds have continued growing.

The winter work consists of cutting back the previous year's dead growth, top-dressing with organic matter and forking it in, and weeding and mulching if necessary. Any splitting of plants can be done towards the spring when the soil and weather is suitable, as can the training and staking of plants for the forthcoming season. From spring onwards the main tasks are weeding, tying in, deadheading, watering, and keeping an eye out for pests. Each of these tasks will be dealt with later.

As well as routine tasks there are also others that occasionally crop up. Sometimes a pernicious weed gets into one area of the borders, or a group of plants begin to look a bit tired. The plants in that area can be removed, the soil cleaned or rejuvenated, and then replanted. This is best carried out in autumn or in spring. Sometimes the whole bed needs renewing. This is a big undertaking and needs space to store temporarily the plants that are removed.

In effect this is nothing more than the preparation of the border from scratch, except that the plants must first be removed. Sometimes it is possible to leave some of the plants that do not like being disturbed where they are and work around them. In the case of bad weed infestation it is probably best

25

to take everything out otherwise the pieces of weed that are bound to be left in the remaining plants will only spread out into the border again.

With tap-rooted plants, and many others that do not like being disturbed, it is often sensible to start again with fresh young plants. However, many of the other plants can simply be divided and replanted, throwing away the older, woodier, central parts.

STAKING

Herbaceous and perennial plants do not always have the strength to stand upright and often flop untidily over their neighbours. The reasons for this are several. The most common is that the border is in a windy or turbulent site and the plants simply get blown over. Another is that the heads might be too heavy for the plant. This is especially true of double flowers, such as peonies, when weighed down with rainwater. Some plants are naturally floppy and need some form of support. Unfortunately many relatively modern cultivars have been bred for the colour and size of their flowers, often at the expense of the strength of their stems.

There seems to be two current philosophies about staking. Either you are positively against it, or you strongly defend the case for doing it. Those that argue against it feel that it takes a lot of time and effort and looks unnatural, while those for it, support it on the grounds that it improves the look of the border beyond any cost in effort.

Those who do not stake employ two tactics. The first is simply to reject any plant that needs to be supported, only go for the stronger forms. This, unfortunately, is very restricting on what they can grow, especially if the garden is somewhat exposed. The other solution is to plant everything so closely together that the stronger support the weaker. This can work but it can also make the border a bit of a jumble. Another problem is that it reduces the amount of air that can circulate between the plants creating a close, damp atmosphere that is much beloved by fungal diseases.

It does take time to stake but it is usually time worth spending as the overall effect of the order is much enhanced. If done early enough and properly the supports should not show. The staking that does show is that which is applied *after* the plant has collapsed. One of the most horrendous examples I have seen was a large *Crambe cordifolia* that had a piece of wire sheep-netting tied around it and pulled tight like a giant corset.

Staking should never hold the plants rigid; they should be allowed a certain amount of natural movement but prevented from flopping over. For bushy plants the support should be about two-thirds of the height of the bushy part of the plant (flower stems may well over top this). The staking should be applied just before the plant reaches the height at which it is to be supported. In this way the support is quickly covered with foliage and is hidden. The few days that it remains visible, usually in spring, is really insignificant.

There are several methods of staking. My preferred technique with most herbaceous plants is to use pea-sticks. Any brushwood will do but hazel boughs are the best as they tend to fan out in just one plane, ie they are flat. Cut them in winter before leaves appear on the bushes. Push a few sticks into the ground tight to the plant to be supported. At the height at which support is required, bend over the sticks and entwine the twigs or tie them together so that they form a network or mesh just above the plant. Very quickly the latter will grow up through this mesh and out sideways through the upright sticks, completely covering them, but at the same time obtaining perfect support.

Fig. 10 *As a support use bent-over peasticks to create a mesh through which the plants will grow.*

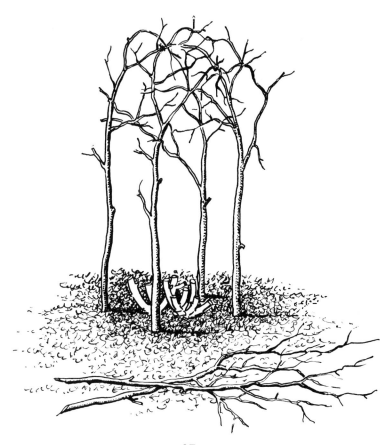

Most other methods follow the same principle of creating a framework through which the plant grows. Further home-made techniques involve putting several stakes or canes around, and even in, the plant and then weaving a cat's cradle of string between them to form the support. For large areas a sheet of large, mesh wire-netting can be suspended above the plants from a number of stakes. If done well it cannot be seen and gives very strong support.

There are commercial forms of staking. Some simply involve a metal or plastic hoop on three legs which is pushed into the ground around the plant. This then grows up through the hoop. More refined hoops have cross-wires to give added support. Another method uses inverted L-shaped pieces of wire which interlink to form whatever configuration you need. It can simply go round the edge of the plant or a few can be linked across the plant for added support. This method is particularly useful for rescuing plants that have already flopped over.

Fig. 11 *Use canes and string to create a cat's-cradle to support the growing plant.*

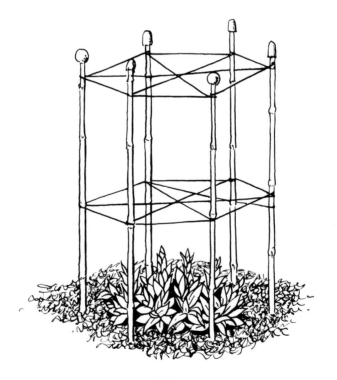

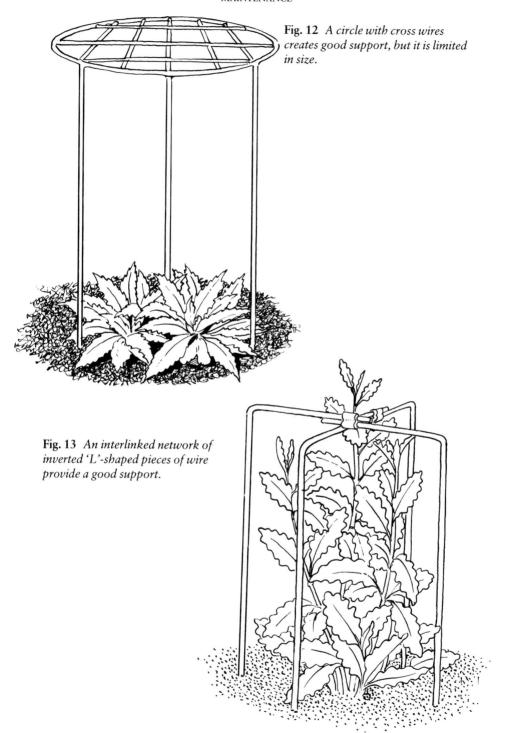

Fig. 12 *A circle with cross wires creates good support, but it is limited in size.*

Fig. 13 *An interlinked network of inverted 'L'-shaped pieces of wire provide a good support.*

So far only clump-forming plants have been considered, but there are a number of plants, such as delphiniums, that put up single flowering spikes and for which the above techniques are not suitable. These require individual stakes for each spike. A large cane should be inserted into the ground behind the stem and fastened to it with soft garden string. A commercial alternative is to buy wire stakes which have a plastic or wire hoop on them that clips round the stem. Both methods need to be carried out carefully or they will show, to the detriment of the plant. Fortunately most plants requiring this kind of attention are placed at the back of the border because of their height and therefore the stakes are not quite so obvious.

Information on those plants that need staking, and what form it should take, is given in the A–Z section of this book.

Fig. 14 *Tall flower spikes can be supported individually by being tied in to canes.*

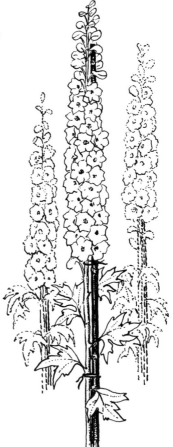

WEEDING

This is a chore that most gardeners hate but it can actually be a very interesting and peaceful task. By the nature of the work you are down amongst your plants where you will notice things you have not spotted before. Some will be of interest or beauty, others will be of a more practical nature. You are much more likely to spot the beginnings of disease or a clump becoming congested if you are close to the plants rather than peering from the border's edge. Weeding teaches you a lot about your plants.

If the border has been prepared properly weeding should not be too much of a chore. Make your first assault in the early spring and remove any weeds that have appeared during the winter; if you leave it until the weather has warmed up then the weeds will have become established and much more difficult to remove. After this first effort go round the borders as frequently as possible removing the odd weed as it occurs. At the same time cancelling out other tasks such as deadheading.

Some gardeners remove weeds by hoeing. I might do this when a border is first laid out and when there is plenty of space, but I have great difficulty in manoeuvring a hoe between the plants and inevitably chop off some valuable individual plant. I much prefer to work through the border with a border fork, tickling over the surface as I go and removing any weeds completely with a digging action. The advantage of this is that you get out all the weed, including the root. Hoeing off the top of a perennial weed simply means that it will be back again the following week.

When the soil in a border is all loose I might well remove single weeds with a trowel or another of my favourite pointed implements that I use specially for the purpose. Again remove the whole weed. Never just pull it up without first loosening it, as it is just as likely to snap off leaving the roots and the base behind to re-shoot.

Whichever method you use be careful around plants, such as *Monarda*, that have shallow roots. These can easily be damaged by over-vigorous weeding with either a hoe or a fork. It is best to hand weed, using a thin trowel or other pointed weeder, that will not disturb more than just the immediate area in which the weed is growing. Some plants die back prematurely. These should be carefully marked so that they are not disturbed when weeding. Avoid using weedkillers in a border. They should not be necessary if it was properly prepared in the first place. Sometimes perennial weeds do creep in and the best thing to do is to take out that area entirely and replant after freeing it of weed.

Bindweed, *Calystegia sepium*, can be a major nuisance as it will soon infect a whole border. It is sometimes possible to remove it by painting its leaves with a weedkiller. Certainly never try spraying herbicides in a border as even the smallest amount of drift will damage plants other than the weeds.

31

We will come to mulches later but for now it is worth noting that they are very useful for the suppression of weeds. They bury the weed seed too deeply in the soil for them to germinate. Mulches will be no good whatsoever for perennial weeds that already exist in the border; indeed it is likely to improve conditions for them.

It is worth remembering that weeds are plants that are in the wrong place and it is just as important to remove any seedlings of border plants as it is to eliminate those more commonly recognized as weeds. Some seedlings are worth keeping, either where they germinate or by removing them elsewhere, but there are many others that will become a nuisance if left to develop. They will soon make the border spotty and top-heavy in certain species. Some have deep tap roots that make them difficult to remove once they have developed. *Cephalaria gigantea*, for example, scatters its seed far and wide and seedlings soon spring up everywhere. The longer they are left the more difficult they are to remove, especially those that send down their roots through the crowns of other plants.

Some ornamental plants spread rapidly by vegetative means with either above- or below-ground rhizomes or stolons. Some are gentle spreaders and their activities can easily be curtailed simply by pulling them up by the handful. Others are much more vigorous and tenaciously hold on to the territory they have gained. Be careful about planting any of the latter. If you must have them either plant in a wild part of the garden where they can ramp to their heart's content or fight it out with other thugs, or plant them in such a way as they are contained. For example mint, *Mentha*, can be planted in a bottomless bucket, or in a small border between, say, a wall and a concrete drive, where its spread is restricted. One or two can be restricted by digging them up every year and replanting just a portion of the plant.

Information on those plants that are copious self-sowers or that need to have an eye kept on them because they spread vigorously by vegetative means is given in the A–Z section of this book.

Perhaps the first season is the worse for weeds. There is still plenty of weed seed in the soil and the other plants have not yet formed an effective cover. After one or two years the number of remaining seeds in the soil is reduced, and the foliage of the surrounding plants begins to shade the border so that any germinating weeds are starved of light and die.

WATERING

Some gardeners, myself included, think that watering is one of the most boring of gardening chores. However it can be a necessary evil.

Watering can be reduced to a minimum by careful border preparation and mulching. Adding organic matter to the soil helps preserve moisture where the roots can get at it. Mulching helps to hold the moisture in by preventing evaporation. During the droughts of several recent summers, when water restrictions have prevented large-scale watering, these techniques have proved invaluable. If they have removed the need to water under these extreme conditions, then they will certainly obviate its necessity in a normal year.

If you have to water there are two possibilities. One is to water overall and the other is limited watering of individual plants. Whichever method you employ make certain that the ground is thoroughly soaked and not just dampened on the surface. Light surface watering can be very dangerous. Plants form roots just beneath the surface to utilise this easily obtained moisture but as soon as it is not available for any reason the plants lose their ability to search for water deep down in the soil. In one year in a recent drought we had a wet June which provided ample moisture for the top few centimetres but nothing deep down. Many emerging plants grew lush on this, but once July came, with no rain and a beating sun, the roots were unable to cope and we lost more plants than we did in years when there was no rain at all.

It is necessary to apply at least 2.5cm (1in) of water. If you use sprinklers place a few tins or jam jars in their range so you can gauge when enough water has been applied.

Many gardeners prefer the pulsating type of sprinkler as they give an even spread, but many others are just as happy with the oscillating kind. If you have borders of moisture-loving plants that need to be kept damp then it is possible to lay a perforated hose within the mulch. It can be left there permanently. Whenever it is connected up and switched on it will invisibly dribble water into the border.

Some plants need more water than others and it may be possible to water just one or two selectively. This can be done with a watering can. Again, be certain to water the area around the plants thoroughly. Rather than filling a can from a tap, it is usually quicker and more convenient to dip it into a butt. However, do make certain that there is a lid on it so that pieces of leaf and other rubbish do not get in, otherwise they are likely to clog the rose of the watering can.

FEEDING

You cannot keep plants on the same plot of ground year after year without feeding them. In the wild, decaying vegetation returns nutrients to the soil; in the garden we tend to cart off any spent vegetation to the compost heap or bonfire. It is essential to replace this if we expect to grow vigorous, healthy plants.

One way is to bring the rotted organic matter back again. Top-dressing in winter or early spring with compost or another organic material such as manure, working it into the soil, is probably one of the best ways of replenishing the nutrients. It not only provides a certain amount of nutrition but also helps to improve the quality of the soil.

The use of organic material has been discussed in Border Preparation (see page 12). When used as a top-dressing avoid using a material that might contain weed seed. It is acceptable to dig it deep into the soil where the seed will not germinate, but if left on the surface all kind of weeds can erupt.

Another way is to use organic and inorganic chemicals. A light dressing of a general fertilizer in the spring can be very beneficial. A further dressing in mid summer will also help. It will supply more nutrients than organic matter but it will do nothing to improve the soil in any way. Be careful not to bring it in contact with the plants' leaves as these could be burnt by the chemicals, and do not overfeed.

Slow-release fertilizers are better than those which are quickly leached from the soil. Bonemeal is ideal for flower borders but do not use a fertilizer that is too high in nitrogen as this will help create lush foliage growth at the expense of flowers. A potash-rich feed in early summer will help with the flower production and is particularly beneficial for bulbous plants.

If you so wish the summer feed can be applied as a liquid, either applied to the roots or as a foliar feed, sprayed onto the leaves.

Since this is of benefit to most plants the advice is not repeated after every plant in the A–Z section, except where special, or no treatment at all, is required.

MULCHING

Although mulching is a very old garden technique it is only relatively recently that it has become a widespread practice. Its benefits are several. It helps hold moisture in the soil by preventing evaporation, particularly when caused by sun and wind. Weeds are suppressed as their seed is buried too deep to germinate. Mulch usually helps keep the soil cool in summer and warm in winter. Some forms present a good uniform background against which to see the plants.

There are quite a number of different types of material that can be used. Peat used to be recommended but it should not be used, partly on the grounds that peatlands are destroyed in obtaining it and partly because it really is no good as a mulch. It breaks down too quickly, dries out and is very difficult to re-wet, and is so light it blows away in the wind.

Another material to avoid is plastic. This is often recommended as the ideal mulch but it always shows, even if buried, and does nothing to enhance the appearance of the border. If buried beneath a layer of soil weeds can grow above it. If a layer of bark is used, why bother with the plastic in the first place? The idea is that you cut holes for the plants, but most perennials expand and will soon outgrow the holes. If the holes are made bigger in the first place, then weeds will grow in them. Water cannot percolate through the plastic, and so although it holds the water in, it will not allow new water to reach the soil.

However, there are several materials that do make a good mulch. Bark in any of its forms is very good. Some people worry that it can introduce honey fungus but the spores of this are already in the air in every garden, so the risk is not much increased. The advantage of bark is that it is sterile and does not introduce weed seed, unless it has been stacked in an open position where nettle and other seeds have blown over it. Bark can be quite expensive if bought by the sack, but if you have the space, a lorryfull is the cheapest method of buying it. An alternative for those living near where it is produced is to buy it by the trailer and cart your own behind or in the car.

Spent mushroom compost is a marvellous mulch. It comprises either chopped bracken or straw, and rotted horse manure. It also contains chalk to keep it sweet. This is a welcome addition on acidic soils but can be a problem if you want to grow ericaceous or lime-hating plants.

Straw makes a good mulch but it is ugly and takes a long time to break down. One good idea is to use it at the back of large borders where it cannot be seen. Grass cuttings create a similar problem, and again should be used at the back of the border. Do not apply it too thickly, no more than 5cm (2in); more will heat up and burn the plants it is meant to protect. This rots down beautifully and helps to increase the fertility of the soil. It is especially useful if the border is backed by a hedge; the mulch helps feed the hedge which will not then rob the border of nutrients. Once rotted down the grass cuttings do not look too bad, and by this stage birds will have usually helped scatter it over other areas of the border. If the grass clippings mat down into a slimy mess, break them up with a fork.

It is a good idea to top-dress the border with well-rotted manure or garden compost, but it is not really recommended as a mulch unless you are certain that it is weedfree. Gravel is often recommended as a mulch and, indeed, works well but it does look out of place in an herbaceous or mixed border. Save it for the rock garden or scree beds.

One problem that organic mulches have is that as they break down they remove the nitrogen they need for the process from the soil, thus temporarily impoverishing it. One solution is to give a light dressing of a nitrogenous fertilizer to the soil before the mulch is applied. Once the mulch has broken down the nitrogen is added back to the soil. Another method is to top-dress the soil with a different well-rotted, organic material before introducing the thicker layer of mulch.

A further problem is that not all mulches allow water to percolate through them in an even manner once they have dried out. So never apply a mulch to a dry soil, always do so after a rainfall or watering.

Moles and birds can be a problem when using mulches. Because the soil is moist under the mulch, plenty of earthworms are usually present which attract the moles. These then bring the soil to the surface with their familiar hills. Soil on top of the mulch destroys its whole purpose so trap the moles and remove them elsewhere. Birds similarly search for insects that love the mulch and end up scattering it everywhere. There is not much you can do except buy a cat but this in turn will find an alternative use for the mulch. Once the plants have grown up both problems are reduced considerably.

DEADHEADING

After blooming it can be beneficial to remove either individual flowers or the complete flower spikes. There are several reasons for doing this. First, a plant without the dying remains of a flower is much tidier and can hold its place in the border as a foliage plant. Second, by removing the old head the considerable amount of energy that would have been spent on seed production is channelled into producing more flowers. This might mean that any flowers from existing buds will be larger, or that the plant will have another flush of blooms later in the season. A third reason is that deadheading prevents the plant producing seed which it may then scatter all over the garden, resulting in self-sown seedlings cropping up everywhere.

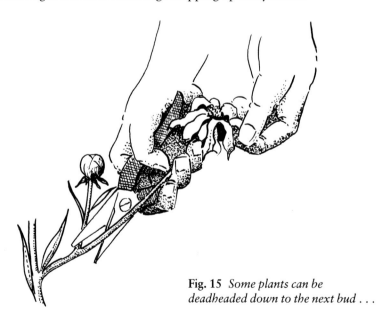

Fig. 15 *Some plants can be deadheaded down to the next bud . . .*

36

Fig. 16 . . . *or down to the foliage if the fading flower is the last.*

There are several different methods of deadheading depending on the plant involved. Individual flowers can be removed along with their stalk, down to the next bud or down to the foliage if it is the last or only one. The whole spike can be removed either down to the next flowering stem or to the foliage. A third method is to remove the flowering stem tight down to the base, leaving any foliage that rises from the base. Finally the whole plant can be cut to the ground.

The last method is valuable for lots of plants that begin to look tatty once flowering is over. For example some of the *Geranium* will put up a new flush of leaves that look brighter and fresher making an attractive foliage feature. The same will happen with *Alchemilla mollis*.

Some early-flowering plants, such as *Aubrieta*, need to be sheared over so that the plants stay neat and compact.

Not all plants need deadheading. Some have decorative seed or seedpods which enhance the border if left. You may wish to collect the seed for propagational purposes, from others. In this case leave all or just a selection of the stems.

Fig. 17 *With many plants it is best to shear them over close to the ground once flowering has finished.*

Fig. 18 *Shear over plants, such as* Aubrieta, *that need to be kept compact.*

During the autumn and winter clear-up, all the dead and dying vegetation of the perennials should be removed. This will be looked at in more detail under winter management (*see below*).

Try not to waste deadheading material; if it is taken before seed develops it can be composted and returned to the border when it has broken down. The more woody material can be put on a heap reserved for material that takes a long time to break down, or shredded before adding to the ordinary compost heap. It is a waste to burn it or take it to the refuse tip.

WINTER MANAGEMENT

Winter is one of the most important times in the garden. If it can now be prepared for the coming season while the majority of plants are dormant it makes life a lot easier. The work has three phases: tidying up after the past year, protecting plants against the winter weather, and preparing for the coming seasons.

The clearing up consists of basically cutting down all the dead and dying vegetation. It is difficult to generalize about the timing of this work. In some respects it is most sensible to do it when the weather is suitable. If left to spring bad weather might prevent you from finishing it before plants burst into growth. However, there are two reasons why some gardeners like to leave it to the end of the winter. First, the dead stems and foliage give the plants a certain amount of frost protection. And second, the birds and small mammals find food in the form of seed heads and overwintering insects.

Whichever approach you favour, it must be carried out before the spring rush starts and before plants burst into growth. It is very time-consuming cutting down old stems from amongst the new ones. Never work when the weather is very wet as you are bound to upset the structure of the soil, mainly by compaction. Work from planks if you think the soil is too wet or soft. You can work when the soil is frozen, and this is a good time for wheeling on barrows of compost or manure.

When removing dead stems cut them as low as possible. Old pieces of stem tend to collect leaves and rubbish in which pests such as woodlice and earwigs lurk. The old stems also make it difficult to weed in the centre of the plants should it be necessary. Furthermore you end up cutting just that bit higher every year to avoid the previous year's snags, eventually creating an impenetrable jungle.

Some vegetation that of *Geranium sanguineum*, for example, will pull away very easily if left until late winter. With other plants, even at this time of year, will still be firmly attached and the plant can easily be torn, allowing ingress for diseases. In such cases the vegetation needs to be cut away cleanly with a knife or secateurs.

Some evergreen perennials also need to be cut back and treated as herbaceous plants. Information is given in the A–Z section where this is necessary.

Winter protection may be needed against either the cold or the rain. Some tender plants, bulbs for example, can be lifted, stored in just-damp peat or sand in a frost-free place and then replanted in the spring. Others can be protected by giving them a winter mulch of bracken, leaves, or straw. It is possible to cover with polythene to keep the mulch dry and thus extra warm, but this usually creates a pool of stagnant air around the plant which can cause fungal diseases, so do use polythene with care. Sometimes it is sufficient just to heap ashes or more soil over the plant.

Protection from the wet can be achieved by placing sheets of glass or plastic over the plant and anchoring them with rocks or wire clips. Larger areas involving several plants can be protected by covering a frame with polythene. Avoid boxing in the plants completely as, once again, fungal diseases can be promoted in the damp atmosphere.

Preparation for the spring is an important part of winter's work. The beds should be gone through to remove any weeds and any surplus plants. They should be dressed with organic material, which can either be worked into the surface or left for the worms to incorporate. Any mulches can be applied once all else is finished.

Towards the end of winter and in early spring, if the weather allows, you can divide plants that are congested or transplant others. Some plants need to be regularly divided, sometimes as frequently as every other year or they will begin to lose their vigour. Always discard the woody central parts and replant the young growths from around the edges of the clumps.

Fig. 19 *Tender perennials can be mulched with bracken, leaves or straw during cold weather.*

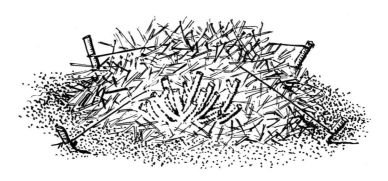

Away from the borders, winter is the time to cut your pea-sticks if you are able to collect your own. It is also the time to replenish your stocks of stakes and canes. One of the more pleasant winter duties is to browse through the mail-order catalogues and put in your orders so that they can be delivered in spring while there is still suitable planting time.

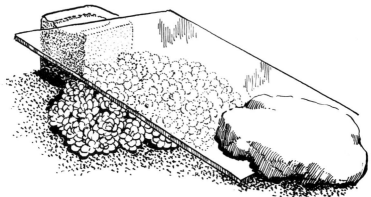

Fig. 20 *Individual plants can be protected with panes of glass anchored with rocks or wire clips.*

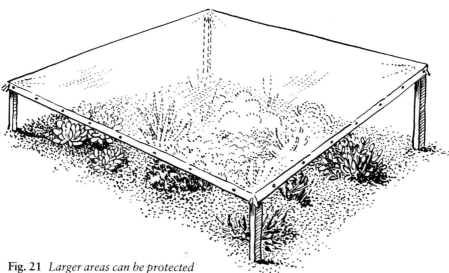

Fig. 21 *Larger areas can be protected by wooden frames covered with sheets of clear polythene.*

41

Pests and Diseases

One of the problems of gardening, inevitably, is having to deal with pests and diseases. If a few precautions are taken, however, growing perennials is safer in this respect than many other aspects of gardening.

The greater the diversity of plants you grow the greater the number of different insects, both good and bad, you are likely to attract to your garden, and the less likelihood of one of them becoming dominant and causing devastation. If eelworm, for example, wipe out your phlox and you have another hundred different plants in the border, the loss will hardly be noticed. On the other hand if the border only consists of phlox then it certainly will be noticed. With a large diversity of plants you will be attracting many beneficial insects such as hoverfly, ladybirds, lacewings, as well as the pests. The former predate the latter and will keep their number under control.

Choice of plants can also be helpful. Many of the older, traditional cottage garden plants have come down to us simply because they have a tough constitution which has allowed them to survive the rigours of the garden. Many of the newer hybrids have been bred for appearance and have lost some, if not all, of their resistance and are therefore much more prone to disease. When visiting gardens, notice those forms which seem more prone to pests and diseases and avoid them.

When selecting plants always reject those that look sickly or are harbouring pests. Only introduce clean, vigorous stock.

Vigorous plants tend to be healthy plants. They are strong enough to overcome mild assaults of pests and diseases, so always grow your plants to the best of your ability. Make certain that they are fed and watered, and are divided when they become congested. Do not overcrowd plants as air circulating between them helps reduce fungal diseases.

By following these simple rules many gardeners find that they do not need to spray their perennial plants from one year's end to another.

If you do have problems do not over-react and spray everything in sight. It is often sufficient to remove the offending pest by hand or cut off the diseased stem. If it looks as though the problem will get out of hand if not controlled then only spray the immediate problem area. There is no point in spraying the whole plant if the pests are only on the shoot tips. If you do you are likely to kill off beneficial insects as well.

If you resort to chemicals, always follow the instructions on the bottle and packet. Never increase the dose, unless instructed to, as it will not help the chemical to solve the problem, in fact the reverse often happens, it inhibits it. Overdosing can also harm the plant. Take all necessary safety precautions and store well out of the reach of children.

The most difficult pests to control are mammals and birds. A deer or even a rabbit in the garden for one night can cause an amazing amount of damage. The only way to keep most of them out is by wiring the boundaries of the garden. This is not so easy with an established garden as there are usually hedges involved. With new gardens put up a wire fence, burying part of it to prevent animals burrowing beneath, and then plant a hedge next to it so the fence is eventually disguised. To keep deer out it must unfortunately be high, 2.5–3m (8–10ft). With older gardens where you cannot put a fence beyond the hedge the only solution is to erect the wire as tight to the hedge as possible and then let the latter grow through it. You can put low fences around individual borders but this looks hideous and should be avoided if possible.

Small mammals such as mice and moles can be trapped either in traps that kill them outright or in a live trap which allows you to remove them to another habitat.

Of all pests with which the perennial-border gardener must contend, slugs and snails must be the worst. There seems to be little that they will not eat, especially in the spring when growth is young and succulent. Undoubtedly bait of some sort is by far the best method. If you dislike using even the 'safe organic' ones then hand picking is the most satisfactory method. Go out at night with a torch and gather up all you can see, but be warned, you will see a lot. Put them in a bucket of water containing a little washing-up liquid or take them to another habitat if you do not want to kill them. After a few nights you will have reduced the population to manageable proportions although regular forays will still be necessary to keep them under control.

The much beloved method of encouraging frogs and hedgehogs to keep control is a delightful idea, but they do not eat enough to make any difference to the populations. Another idea that has severe limitations is putting ashes or grit around the plant on the assumption that the slug will not like to crawl over sharp objects. However slugs do not seem to have the human power of reasoning, as you will see if you go out at night and watch them happily crawling over the grit. It is best saved for other uses.

Pests and diseases are a vast subject, but in many cases the damage caused by the so-called pests is relatively minor. Even the common and disfiguring powdery mildew is rarely fatal and usually takes place after flowering is over, so the plants can be cut back and burnt rather than being given a course of chemical treatment. It should be repeated that in a well-managed garden, perennials do not suffer as much as other plants.

Specialized Areas

Most perennials are grown in borders either consisting entirely of perennials or, more likely, these days, mixed with woody plants and annuals. However, there are one or two areas in which they are grown that need special treatment.

WOODLAND GARDENS

Many perennials that we grow come from a woodland habitat and like nothing better than to grow in a similar environment in our gardens. Some gardeners are lucky and have a garden big enough to accommodate a real wood, while others must make do with a shrub or two. But it is surprising what can be grown even in the latter position.

Most woodland plants like a damp, humusy soil where they can get a cool rootrun and plenty of moisture. These are generally well-drained. Ordinary garden soil can be conditioned with plenty of humus, particularly leafmould. Any other type of humus should be well-rotted as not all woodland plants like conditions too rich. Snowdrops (*Galanthus*) for example, are likely to die out if given a top-dressing of manure. If the soil is on the heavy side then grit will help to make it free draining.

Many woodland plants appear, flower, seed and die back before the trees above them have come into leaf, making use of the moisture and sunshine that is available in late winter and in early spring. Some flower later and require more in the way of light, these are often plants from the margins of woods where the light manages to penetrate under the branches. These can be kept happy by lopping off the lower branches of the trees or thinning them out so that a certain amount of light penetrates. An alternative is to plant them under a north-facing wall where they have plenty of light but no direct sunlight.

An annual top-dressing of leafmould is beneficial and it is preferable not to clear up the trees' or shrubs' leaves. In a natural woodland setting there is rarely need to cut back dying vegetation, just let nature take care of it. In a more formal situation, where woodlanders are grown under a single tree or shrub, then a bit more attention may be required.

One of the worst problems in woodland gardens is blackberry briars sown by birds sitting in the branches above. Remove these as soon as they are seen, otherwise they quickly develop into a major problem.

Peat beds are a specialized form of woodland garden. Originally they were made from a mixture of loam and peat to ensure that there was a moist, slightly acidic soil. Now that it is environmentally undesirable to use peat they are usually made with a mixture of leafmould, bark and pineneedles. The name 'peat bed', however, has still been retained for this type of garden, although the name 'acid bed' is gaining ground.

Whatever it is called a wide range of very desirable plants can be grown in it and it is well-worth constructing if you are interested in woodland plants.

MEADOW AND WILD FLOWER GARDENS

In recent times more and more gardeners have wanted to grow native plants. Some are suitable for the border but the most popular way of growing them has been in a 'meadow'. This grand sounding place may indeed be a field, but more often or not it is the whole or part of a lawn that has been allowed to become overgrown.

Managing this type of garden is not quite as easy as it might seem. The main thing to do is to keep the coarse grasses at bay. If the area is a lawn this should not be too difficult as there are likely to be few present. However, if you are hoping to convert a field then it will need mowing several times a season for two or three years to kill off these coarse grasses.

Once the meadow consists of fine grasses, the flowers can be introduced. You can do this by scattering seed but competition is likely to be so fierce that few will come to anything. A much better approach is to sow and grow on the plants in pots and then plant them out as soon as they are big enough. In this way they quickly establish themselves and then start to self-sow.

Most meadow flowers bloom in spring or early summer. Once they have finished seeding, the sward should be mown, usually in mid to late summer, and again in the autumn. This helps to keep the coarse grasses at bay.

Many native plants are rampant in their own country as conditions are obviously just right for them so be careful about introducing them into formal borders or they might try to take over. Many can be successfully grown in odd corners such as under hedges or in waste areas. This is likely to help to encourage many beneficial insects to the garden.

45

WATER GARDENS

Most gardeners like to have a water feature of some type. This increases the number of habitats and thus the number of different types of plants that can be grown. The plants can be grown in the water or on the muddy margins, or grown in specially constructed bog gardens.

Undoubtedly the best type of habitat is that provided by a natural pond lined with clay, but a lot of plants can be grown in the special lattice pots that have been developed for pond culture. If pots are used be careful about using soilless composts as these can float away. Cover the surface with gravel before submerging. Plants that grow in the water may also float away when first planted in the mud as their roots have yet to develop. Hold down these plants with strips of lead or other weights.

Never plant water plants in water that is too deep for them (guidance is given in the A–Z for different species). Some plants will grow either in water or in the marginal mud but they rarely survive if they dry out, so try and maintain the water levels. Bog gardens should never be allowed to dry out.

Plants grow well around the margins of ponds and in bogs, but so do weeds. It is essential to keep these areas well weeded or they will take over. Many water plants are rampant and are only really suitable for large ponds and lakes. Check what you intend planting just in case it is likely to take over.

Most water plants do not start into growth until the water begins to warm up. There is no point in planting new plants before this happens, which usually means around early summer.

CONTAINERS

Increasingly perennials are being planted in tubs and other containers. Several varieties may be mixed or a single species may be used. There is not much difference between culture in the border and a container. However, there are a few points to bear in mind.

Make certain that the container has fresh compost in it. A large proportion of humus will help to retain moisture. Plants will need lifting and the soil replenishing much more frequently than in the open garden. Never let the soil dry out completely, it may be difficult to re-wet, with the water trickling away down between the side of the pot and the compost. Constant watering is liable to leach away any nutrients, so the plants will need feeding regularly. The best method is to add a liquid feed to the water about once a fortnight. Plants in containers are more liable to cold as the compost in the pot can freeze solid as the sides are open to the air. Either move them inside or insulate the sides of the container with straw.

Cultivation of Individual Plants

INTRODUCTION

Inclusions

The inclusion policy in the following list is very liberal. Gardeners do not think in quite the same precise categories as writers. There cannot be a single one who would only include hardy perennials in a border to the exclusion of sub-shrubs, shrubs or even alpines simply because they fell within those botanical categories. Quite a number of these three categories have found their way into the A–Z simply because they are grown in mixed borders, and if the gardener wishes to have information on them why should he or she be denied it simply because of some rigid categorization?

Similarly there are many plants mentioned that may be thought to be weeds by most gardeners. Even bracken puts in an appearance. But it must be remembered that in recent years there has been a great revival in wildflower and meadow gardens and a lot of the so-called weeds of the herbaceous border have a place here. If you have a large wood at your disposal what can be more tranquil than a large expanse of bracken?

Planting

Unless specified this can be carried out in either the autumn or spring, although many container-grown plants can be planted out at any time unless the weather is too hot or in times of drought. Keep watered until established.

Feeding

Unless otherwise stated feeding is carried out as part of the general application of well-rotted organic material, or a slow-release fertilizer, such as bone-meal, to the whole border.

Top-dressing

Often winter top-dressing is suggested. This should be applied at any time when the weather allows access to the borders, which in some areas may not be before the spring. The reason for suggesting winter is that it is usually possible to dress right up to the plants without covering their foliage, which is still below ground.

Mulching

Winter mulches are sometimes suggested for certain plants. These should be applied early in the winter as they are intended to act as an insulating layer above the crown or over the roots. Later it rots down and helps improve the soil and feed the plant.

Diseases

I have been reluctant to specify particular chemicals in the treatment of diseases as these seem to be constantly changing, and what were once familiar chemicals appear on the banned list. Since I hope this book will last as a work of reference for many years I do not want to include information that future generations may consider dangerous. Where diseases are specified, check with your local garden centre as to what is the most effective, current treatment.

Planting distances

It has been impossible to give the planting distances as these vary within a genus from species to species. It would double the size of the book if these were all listed individually. The reader is referred to the section on planting distances (page 19), and should be reminded that as a rough rule of thumb the distance between plants should be roughly half of the ultimate height of the plant.

1 *Alcea rugosa*
Short-lived perennial treated like its more common relative *A. rosea*.

2 *Cardamine pentaphyllos* (above)
Runs about gently in a woodland-type soil.

3 *Cynara scolymus* (below)
The cardoon likes a deep rich soil and full sun.

4 *Dendranthema* 'Copper' (below)
A relatively hardy rubella chrysanthemum that will grow in any fertile soil.

5 *Diascia* 'Ruby Field'
One of the hardier diascias, with a liking for a soil that does
not dry out too much.

7 *Digitalis lanata*
A biennial, occasionally short-lived
perennial foxglove preferring well-drained
soils.

6 *Dicentra formosa* (above)
An easy group of dicentras that flower
early in the season. They like any fertile
garden soil.

8 *Doronicum* 'Spring Beauty'
An easy perennial that will grow in any
moisture-retentive soil.

9 *Echinacea purpurea*
The purple coneflower is easy to grow, being happy in any fertile garden soil.

**11 *Eupatorium maculatum*
'Atropurpureum'** (below)
Much-loved by butterflies and bees, this plant likes a moisture-retentive soil.

12 *Euphorbia longifolia* (below)
This uncommon spurge will grow in any good garden soil.

10 *Eryngium dichotomum*
The sea hollies like any well-drained soil. They are deep rooted and cannot be moved easily.

15 *Haplopappus glutinosus*
This plant is on the tender side. It needs a well-drained soil and a sunny position.

13 *Fritillaria imperialis*
Crown imperials like an open position in soil that is not too rich.

16 *Helenium* 'Golden Youth'
Very easy to grow, especially if given a moisture-retentive soil and sunny position.

14 *Geranium psilostemon* (pink form)
An unusual colour form of a very easy perennial. It grows in any good garden soil, preferably one that is moisture-retentive.

17 *Hosta fortunei albopicta aurea*
A rich, moisture-retentive soil is needed, preferably in light shade. Watch out for slugs.

18 *Kniphofia* 'Spanish Gold'
A sunny position and a soil that is free-draining but moisture-retentive is ideal.

20 *Lilium canadense*
A stoloniferous lily that dislikes limy and dry soils.

21 *Liriope muscari* (below)
A valuable autumn-flowering perennial that is very accommodating in its requirements.

19 *Lavatera cachemiriana*
A short-lived perennial often treated as a biennial. A free-draining soil is required.

22 *Mimulus lewisii*
A tall mimulus that will grow in drier soils than most of the genus.

24 *Osmunda regalis*
The royal fern must have a moist soil that does not dry out and preferably one that is not limy.

25 *Pennisetum villosum*
The fountain grass needs full sun and will grow in a well-drained soil, although they like a certain amount of moisture.

23 *Nepeta prattii*
Also known as *Dracocephalum prattii*, this uncommon plant from China likes a well-drained soil.

26 *Persicaria capitata*
This plant is on the tender side and will often get cut back in winter, although it usually regenerates.

27 *Potentilla* 'William Rollison'
This herbaceous potentilla will grow in any garden soil, even quite impoverished ones.

28 *Primula* Gold Laced form
These primulas prefer a soil that does not dry out too much and a situation away from the hottest sun.

29 *Primula florindae* (below)
Moisture-retentive soil is essential for this tall primula. A site beside water is best.

30 *Rodgersia aesculifolia* (below)
Rodgersias all like a moisture-retentive soil and a lightly shaded position.

**31 *Sedum telephium maximum*
'Atropurpureum'**
It is essential to place this plant in a sunny
position or the leaves will fade to green.

32 *Stachys macrantha*
This is an easy plant that will grow in any
fertile garden soil as long as it is
reasonably free-draining.

33 *Veratrum nigrum*
This beautiful but uncommon plant needs to have a rich,
moisture-retentive soil and shady position. Watch out for slugs.

34 *Yucca recurvifolia*
A warm, sunny position and a well-
drained soil is essential for this striking
plant.

A–Z

Abutilon (Malvaceae). Really a shrub but often grown in herbaceous and mixed borders. If planted in containers they should be watered regularly, at least once a day in hot weather. Many will need to be supported by a discreet stake or cane. Cut out about a third of the old wood every year to keep the plant vigorous. It is not terribly hardy and may need wintering under glass in a pot. No specific pests or diseases, but they are not the strongest of plants.

Acaena (Rosaceae). Mat-forming, creeping over everything in its path so be careful what you plant next to it, or make certain it is regularly cut back to check its spread. The seeds are held in burs which can be painful if trodden on with bare feet, so be careful if it is planted on the edge of terraces, patios or laws, near where people are likely to be unshod. They have the advantage that they will grow in virtually any soil, even the poorest. Waterlogged soils, however, should be avoided. They like a sunny position, require little attention, and do not seem to suffer from any specific pests or diseases.

Acanthus (Acanthaceae). Bear's Breeches. Acanthus like a deeply-cultivated, rich, but well-drained soil but will grow on poor soil, even on chalk. They are reasonably drought-resistant. Most plants take a couple of seasons to settle down. They are likely to spread, both by running rootstock and by self-sown seedlings. Dig around the plant each year to keep it in check, but be certain to remove every scrap of root otherwise new plants will erupt. Remove any seedlings straight away otherwise they are difficult to get out, also, any piece of root left will create a new plant. Seeding can be reduced by cutting off the flower spikes soon after blooming, but this is a shame as the spikes are attractive even while in seed. They should be grown in sun; they will grow in shade, but will not flower so well. Although large they can be grown in tubs. *A. spinosus* may need individual flower spikes to be supported, this is particularly important as they are in flower for such a long time. In exposed areas there may be the need to support the whole plant with pea-sticks to about 60–75cm (24–30in) high. The shorter species, *A. mollis*, for example, should be self-supporting except in areas of excessive wind. Acanthus are evergreen but can become tatty, in which case the foliage can be cut back during the winter tidy-up. Wear gloves when removing old flower stems as they can be very prickly. They can suffer from mildew after a dry spell, especially if they are in a sheltered spot. Spray with a fungicide before the disease really takes hold. Slugs and snails can be a problem for young growth. Trap or bait them. Top-dress the soil around the plants with organic material to revitalize it. They are hardy but dislike wet winters. In really cold areas they may need a mulch of bracken to help them through prolonged frosts.

Acerphyllum (Saxifragaceae). See *Mukdenia*

Achillea (Compositae). Yarrow. Achilleas like a light, free-draining soil in full sun. The soil should be fertile but not too rich, otherwise the plants become overgrown and floppy. Some of the taller achilleas need support, especially if they are planted in a windy spot. Some such as *A.* 'Salmon Beauty' need the support because they are floppy, others, *A. grandiflora* for example, because they are rather large and need the supports to prevent them taking up too much space and crowding their neighbours.

Shorter forms, such as *A.* 'Coronation Gold', should be able to support themselves except in really windy areas. A cat's cradle of pea-sticks or crossed wires about half-way up the plant is sufficient. They withstand drought reasonably well. They may show signs of distress but usually recover. Cut back all stems to the ground after they have finished flowering this sometimes promotes further flushes of flowers. They should all be removed in autumn or during the winter tidy-up. Clumps can die out in the centre and impoverish the soil. Dig up every three or four years, rejuvenate the soil and replant the young, more vigorous pieces from the edge of the clump. Most spread slowly, enlarging the clump, but *A. ptarmica* and its cultivars tend to spread like greased lightning and should be kept in check by digging round the colony each year to remove questing roots. Do not plant in borders where they can become a nuisance, as they have a habit of coming up through other plants, necessitating wholesale removal of the border to eradicate it. The same applies to the British native *A. millefolium*. Some, such as *A. taygetea*, *A. ptarmica* and their various forms, suffer from mildew, especially if grown in an enclosed area. Spray with an appropriate fungicide. This and other woody, silver-leaved forms can become tired and leggy and will often die after only one or two seasons. Replace every two or three years with new plants to ensure that they are vigorous and tidy. Otherwise they do not generally suffer from any particular pests or diseases.

Achlys (Berberidaceae). Deerfoot, Sweet-after-death, Vanilla Leaf. This is a single-species genus (or possibly three, depending which taxonomist you follow). Being a woodlander it likes a cool, moist position in light shade. The soil should be deep and leafy, and moisture retentive. This is a spreading plant but there is no need for regular division except for propagation purposes. If grown in woodland conditions there is no need to tidy-up; otherwise remove foliage as it dies back in autumn. It is hardy and needs no protection.

Acidanthera (Iridaceae). Abyssian Gladiolus. Bulbs that like a free-draining soil in full sun. They can be left in the ground over winter in warmer areas but need to be lifted in colder districts and stored in a frost-free place as one would with gladiolus. Dust with a fungicide before storing in dry sand. Replant in spring. Growth is usually late to appear, so mark the ground carefully to avoid disturbing or over-planting them. They come into flower very late in the season, sometimes too late to avoid frosts, so start the corms into growth by planting them earlier into pots which are kept in a greenhouse.

Aciphylla (Umbelliferae). Speargrass. These can be vicious plants as the leaves are spear-like, as their name suggests, and very sharp. This makes weeding very painful so try and mulch around them if possible. This is best done with grit as they should not stay wet around the neck as they can rot off at this point. They like a free-draining, moisture-retentive soil with humus added to it. They require a lime-free soil. They will grow in either full sun or light shade.

Aconitum (Ranunculaceae). Monkshood, Wolf's Bane. A large genus with many garden-worthy plants. The majority like rich, cool soils, in a light shade, but they will tolerate a sunny position if the soil retains enough moisture. If the conditions are right they make better flowering plants in the sun. They take a time to settle down after disturbance so should be left alone for as long as possible before breaking up the clump, which may have to be done every five years or so to revitalize it. If the clumps become congested the plants become smaller and flowering diminishes. Transplant in autumn as they break into growth early, before the winter is over. Lift, rejuvenate the soil, and replant the largest tubers. The taller species, particularly those with branching stems, require staking, preferably with pea-sticks that become hidden in the foliage. The climbing species, such as *A. volubile*, will need some support; a shrub being an obvious choice as this would be its host in the wild. A good mulch should be provided both to feed the soil and keep the roots cool and moist. The roots are poisonous and under no circumstances should be eaten and it is a good policy to wash hands thoroughly after planting or replanting. Deadhead after flowering and then cut down when the leaves turn brown or, if necessary, cut the stems down to the ground after flowering. If left to late winter the stems pull away very easily. Not many problems with specific pests or diseases, except that the popular *A. carmichaelii* var. *arendsii* can suffer from sclerotinia stem rot if damaged or bruised. Spray with a fungicide. Most of the aconitums can suffer from powdery mildew, especially late in the season. Cut back and burn affected parts. Also burn any plants suffering from smut which shows up as black spots on the leaves.

Acorus (Araceae). Sweet Flag. A waterside plant that is best grown on the margins of ponds or streams. It can be grown in the water or in boggy ground. It can be grown in an ordinary border if is moisture-retentive enough and if it is kept watered. Plants in a dry atmosphere tend to get mildew which need treating with a fungicide, although it would be better to either abandon the plant or put it nearer water. It is a creeping plant and benefits from being split up every four years or so to keep it tidy and fresh-looking.

Actaea (Ranunculaceae). Baneberries. These are woodland plants and prefer the kind of conditions that they would meet in these circumstances, namely a moist, humus-rich soil and light shade. Tidy-up the dying foliage and stems in winter, tidy-up, but under woodland or wilder conditions they can be left to decay naturally. A mulch of leafmould or composted bark will help maintain the soil. The berries are poisonous. They are perfectly hardy.

Actinotus (Umbelliferae). These are tender annuals and perennials that are usually treated as annuals in colder areas. Plant out after risk of frost has receded in a sunny position in rich but well-drained soil. Discard in the autumn.

Adenophora (Campanulaceae). Ladybells. These are closely related to the *Campanula* and should be treated in the same way. Provide a deep, rich, moisture-retentive, but well-drained soil. They possibly have a preference for alkaline soils but will grow in most garden conditions. Either sun or light shade is acceptable, although they do best in a warm spot. Their deep fleshy roots dislike being disturbed so leave them *in situ* for as long as possible. They do not clump up so there is no need to divide. They do not seem to suffer from any specific pests or diseases.

Adiantum (Adiantaceae). Maidenhair Ferns. These ferns like an acid, humus-rich soil through which they can gently run. They like a cool position out of the sun and will scorch if in direct sunlight. If these need moving or splitting do so before growth commences in the spring. *A. pedatum* loses its foliage in autumn and it needs to be pulled away at any time between turning brown and the early spring. *A. venustum* is evergreen and needs to have its foliage cut off in late winter or early spring, so that the new growth can be seen to advantage. No particular diseases or pests seem to be specific to them.

Adonis (Ranunculaceae). Pheasant's Eye. These like the classic well-drained, moisture-retentive soil. They should be planted where they can flower in the sun but they like a cool, lightly-shaded position during the summer, so under or near deciduous trees is a possibility. They can be divided or transplanted if necessary, but they can take a long time to settle down, several years in some cases. Do not cut back until they have died down. Lightly top-dress the soil with organic material in autumn. Adonis do not have any specific pests or diseases to worry about except in early spring when slugs and snails can eat off the emerging shoots. Use your preferred method of attack to deter them. They are hardy and should need no winter protection.

Aethionema (Cruciferae). These are plants of well-drained soils and hot sunny positions. They will do best on a rock garden but will happily grow in crevices in walls. If starved or too dry the plants will be small, but do not over-feed or over-water. Alkaline soils are preferred but they will grow well on neutral or even mildly acid ones. They are not long-lived but self-sow, providing ample replacements.

Agapanthus (Alliaceae/Liliaceae). African Lilies. The beautiful agapanthus is not difficult to grow. They like a rich, moisture-retentive soil, but will also grow in quite dry conditions. It should be in a warm, sunny position, but I have seen it growing in light shade although this has not much to recommend it. The most commonly sold forms are now hardy and need not be moved inside for winter, unless they are in tubs which may freeze solid. They do, however, object to too much moisture round the roots during the winter. A well-drained, moisture-retentive soil is the answer. Plant with their growing points just below the surface. Avoid digging near them as the roots are very brittle and resent disturbance; instead mulch round them in the autumn with chipped bark, chopped bracken (wear a mask while chopping it) or even bonfire ash. For the same reason do not move or transplant them unnecessarily or they may take a while to settle down. If they must be moved do this while in full growth as new roots are more likely to form. These thirsty plants should be well watered in the growing season. They have a tendency to grow towards the light and are therefore best grown in south-facing borders, otherwise they are inclined to lean away from their viewer. If grown in tubs they should be rotated regularly so that the clumps develop evenly. Water during the growing season if the rains fail. Remove the flowering stems and yellowing leaves from the deciduous varieties as they die back in autumn. The flowering stems can be cut off immediately after flowering if you do not want the seed. This saves the plant's energy, but the developing seed heads can be attractive in their own right. The evergreen types are not so hardy and should be grown in tubs that can be moved inside for winter protection. Remove any tatty or dying leaves as well as spent flower stems. Keep the tubs moist and give a regular liquid feed in the growing season.

Agastache (Labiatae). Mexican Bergamot. The agastaches are a small genus of short-lived and annual plants that will thrive in any fertile garden soil, and often tolerate quite dry conditions. A sunny position will be welcome. They are not particularly hardy but most will self-sow providing ample seedlings to replace the lost plants. For special forms it would be advisable to take basal cuttings to ensure that there are replacements in case of a severe winter.

Agave (Amaryllaceae). Century Plant. These plants generally need glasshouse protection but *A. americana* will grow outside in a warm, sunny spot in milder areas. It likes a well-drained, lean soil. The older the plant the more likely it will survive frosts. Winter protection to keep it dry will be appreciated. In colder areas grow in a container and move inside during winter.

Agropyron (Gramineae). See *Elymus*

Ajuga (Labiatae). Bugle. While the bugles will grow in quite dry soil they are happiest in moist ones. They will grow in full sun, especially if the ground is moist, or light shade. In the latter position they will not flower so well and bronze-leaved forms are likely to turn green. If the soil is too dry they will quickly show signs of distress and will need watering or moving. They are useful for growing on heavy soils. Ajugas are thick carpeters and can be invasive if not kept in check. The best time to lift and split congested plantings is in autumn, so that they are ready to perform again the following spring. In areas where the plants will not have time to re-establish themselves before winter sets in it will be necessary to leave division until the spring, which means that a year's flowering is likely to be lost. They are evergreen, so tidy up in autumn by removing any dead leaves and flowering spikes. Check their spread once a year if there is any danger of them getting out of control.

Alcea (Malvaceae). Hollyhocks. (*A. ficifolia* and *rosea* have been moved back here from *Althea*). Although perennial they are best treated as biennial. Fortunately they come easily from seed so it is not difficult to replace them; indeed they often self-sow. They can be planted in any good soil as long as it is reasonably free-draining. They prefer to be in a sunny situation. When young they are able to stand without staking, except in windy areas, when older the stems split off from the woody base of the plant and may need staking. When planting out, do not allow the plants to become pot-bound as the straighter the tap roots are the better. These should be planted vertically as they will give better anchorage if encouraged to delve deeply. The plants can be planted with their crowns below the soil level also to help prevent wind rock. They suffer badly from rust, this can be treated with a fungicide. Since it is such a common disease it is safe to assume that your plants will get it and they should be sprayed before it is seen as a preventative measure. Another way to avoid it, or at least lessen its impact is to replace the plants each year from seed. If the disease becomes bad, give up growing them for a few years. *A. rugosa* is supposed to be immune to rust but unfortunately it is not, although it is not so crippling as with *A. rosea*.

Alchemilla (Rosaceae). Lady's Mantle. This is quite a large genus of which *A. mollis* is of most interest to gardeners. They all will grow in a wide range of soils, even quite poor ones. They do best in the open but will grow in light shade. *A. mollis* looks particularly good near water. It is an inveterate self-sower. This would not matter except that it is not the easiest of plants to extract, especially if it has planted itself in the middle of another plant, or in a crack in the paving. However, it is a plant that few gardeners would want to be without so it is worth putting up with this either by assiduously weeding them out or by sheering over the plant before the seed is set. The latter is the preferable course as the plant puts up a second crop of fresher leaves, which are well worth having. *A. conjuncta* needs to have the dead wiry stems removed before spring, but there is no need to cut to the ground as with *A. mollis*.

Alisma (Alismataceae). Water Plantain. These plants grow in shallow water on the margins of pond and pools. They can become a nuisance as they are self-sowers, so cut back stems as soon as they have finished flowering. These are good for dried flower decorations.

Alliaria (Cruciferae). *A. petiolata*, Garlic Mustard, is a British native that gardeners may be tempted to grow in the garden. Desist. It is a terrible weed with tap roots that are difficult to extract, especially from the middle of other plants where it inevitably manages to put itself. It seeds copiously and once introduced to a garden it is very difficult to eradicate.

Allium (Alliaceae). Onions. Most alliums prefer a sunny position but the invasive *A. triquetrum* and *ursinum* prefer shade. *A. pulchellum*, which one tends to think of as sun-loving, will also grow in shade as will *A. moly*. They are happy on a wide range of soils, but most prefer gritty, free-draining ones. Plant at about three-times the diameter of the bulb. The foliage of many alliums is beginning to die and look tatty at the time that it is in flower. They can either be pulled off or, better still, hide the base (and leaves) of the taller alliums amongst other plants so that only the flower heads are visible. Most alliums seed themselves around, some far worse than others. One of the worse is *A. pulchellum* so remove flower heads before it drops it seeds. Unfortunately the problem is compounded because the flower-head often produces and drops bulbils as well. *A. triquetrum* is another spreading terror but this time it should be avoided as it has none of the charm of *A. pulchellum*. Similarly be careful of *A. neapolitanum*. Some onion heads, *A. christophii* for example, are eagerly sought after by flower arrangers. These are worth harvesting carefully. Many onions bulk up quickly, forcing bulbs to the surface as they become congested. Lift and split in autumn, every other year if necessary. All are hardy although precocious foliage of some, *A. giganteum* for example, may be hit by late frosts. Ornamental onions are generally free from disease although they could be attacked by onion fly.

Alonsoa (Scrophulariaceae). Although these are perennial plants they are best treated as annuals in areas where there are likely to be frosts. Plant out in any fertile soil as long as it is free-draining. They will grow best in a warm, sunny position. Taller species may need support, meshed pea-sticks being ideal. Discard after flowering.

Alpinia (Zingiberaceae). Ginger Lily. Tender plants that will be cut to the ground by frosts but should shoot again if the temperatures are not too extreme. Plant in a rich, moisture-retentive soil. Keep well watered during the growing season. In autumn enrich the soil with a top-dressing of organic material, which also acts as a thermal mulch. Cut back stems as they flower.

Alstroemeria (Alstroemeriaceae). Peruvian Lilies. Although once considered tender, increasing numbers are being grown outside in colder areas. Planting deeply seems to help them through cold spells, although if they are planted just below the surface they will find their own depth, though this may make them vulnerable during the first winter. Help by mulching or protecting them. However, I once rather stupidly left some plants I had been given lying in a polythene carrier bag in the garden for a whole winter and they all survived, coming through a number of frosts. The young shoots emerge early and can be cut back by frosts. The soil should be a rich, fertile, free-draining one. In theory they do not like heavy ones, although I grow *A. aurantiaca* very successfully in quite sticky conditions. This plant can become invasive and as it will tolerate light shade, it might be best to relegate it to a wilder part of the garden, or at least contain it in some way. The other species and forms are more limited in their territorial ambitions. The roots are very brittle and resent disturbance. It is often easier to start from scratch rather than move existing colonies. They will need support from pea-sticks. *A. aurantiaca* can be supported by growing through low bushes. The seedheads are attractive and can be left after flowering until the autumn tidy-up; top-dress with organic material in autumn or early winter.

Althaea (Malvaceae). Marsh Mallow. The same principles apply as to *Alcea* to which the main members of this genus have been moved. *A. officinale*, however, will grow in much moister soil.

Alyssoides (Cruciferae). Similar to the wallflower, *Erysimum*, and is cultivated in the same way.

Alyssum (Cruciferae). These like a dry soil and will often grow in very poor conditions, including crevices of walls. A sunny position is to be preferred. Shear over after flowering; the plants may look mutilated but they will soon leaf over again, making better, compact plants, than if left. They are prone to downy mildew, which appears as white powdery spots; and which should be treated with a fungicide. They can be attacked by club root, in which case dig up and burn.

Amaryllis (Amaryllidaceae). The bulbs should be deeply planted, the top 12.5–15cm (5–6in) below the surface. This will protect them from cold. A sun-baked spot against a southern wall is the best type of situation. Avoid planting other plants that are liable to overshadow them. They can take several years (possibly as many as five, and are likely to take seven from seed) to settle down and grow to flowering size, so prepare the ground well with plenty of well-rotted humus and also gravel or sharp sand to improve the drainage, if necessary. Planting time can be in the spring although some recommend late summer and early autumn. Although it has been traditional to lift the bulbs during winter they seem to be much better if left in the ground, unless it is a very cold or wet area. They will need lifting every few years when they have become congested. This is best carried out in mid-summer after the leaves begin to die back. Protect from slugs.

Amsonia (Apocynaceae). Blue Star. A small genus of hardy plants that like a fertile, well-drained, moisture-retentive soil. They will grow in full sun, as long as the soil is moist, but are normally grown in light, dappled shade. Cut back after flowering and again once the frosts have killed off the foliage. If used as cut flowers staunch the flow of sap with sand or a flame. No specific pests or diseases.

Anacyclus (Compositae). A small genus of low-growing annuals and perennials that like a well-drained soil in full sun. They are hardy, but can suffer from winter wet, for which covering with a glass or a light will help. Cut back during the autumn tidy-up. No need to over-feed. They are short lived.

Anaphalis (Compositae). Pearl Everlasting. These will grow in soil that is quite moist, much moister than other silver-leaved plants will tolerate. Dry soils are also tolerated but they should be watered if they show signs of drooping, and they should be kept well watered in dry spells. Dry soils can also induce mildew. They prefer a sunny site but will take a certain amount of light shade, provided, again, that it is not too dry. Some species are rhizomatous and can become invasive (such as *A. cinnamonea* and *A. yedoensis*), so should be planted where this is not a problem, or they can be kept in check by removal of excess growth each autumn or spring, although spring may be preferable. Plant out in either autumn or spring. Cut back old stems in the autumn to avoid spoiling the new spring shoots. They will tolerate poor soils but do better if the soil is top-dressed each spring.

Anarrhinum (Scrophularaceae). A mixture of annuals and perennials, some shrubby. They prefer an ordinary, well-drained soil in full sun. They will need winter protection in colder areas.

Anchusa (Boraginaceae). They prefer full sun and a deep, well-drained soil which contains a quantity of rich humus. Top-dress in the spring and do not allow them to get too dry, although they will not tolerate wet conditions. Most of the taller species need staking, particularly in windy areas. They are short-lived and new plants should be produced every year, or at most every other year, to ensure continuance. Cut back after flowering.

Andropogon (Gramineae). A grass for a well-drained, fertile soil in full sun. Any transplanting should be carried out in spring. Cut back to ground level during the autumn tidy-up.

Anemone (Ranunculaceae). These must be treated in several distinct groups. With the wood anemone group (including *AA. nemorosa, blanda, ranunuculoides* and *apennina*) do not purchase dried-out roots of these plants which are so often offered by mail order firms or garden centres. If you do acquire some, soak overnight in water before planting out. Although anemone are not happy growing in pots they are best purchased in growth in pots so that you see that you get not only live but also the correct plants. They are happiest in a leafy soil that does not dry out, although they do not like it to be too wet. The soil can be either acid or alkaline. They prefer a shady, cool position under deciduous trees or shrubs for example, but will grow in full sun if the soil is not too dry. They spread to form large colonies but do not need dividing up except for propagation purposes. They retire below ground in late spring or early summer and need little if any attention. Label to avoid overplanting during the long dormant season when nothing is visible above ground. The *A. nemorosa* group can suffer from anemone rust which shows up as rich-brown spots on the undersides of the leaves. It also forms black rot which attacks the rhizome and is rarely seen until the plant is dead. The best way of coping with both these cases is to burn them. Pheasants seem to relish the young growth of some *A. nemorosa* and can sometimes destroy a whole colony. The Japanese anemones *AA.* x *hybrida, hupehensis, japonica* and the like resent disturbance and can take a long time to settle down again, if indeed they do. It is better to take root cuttings in the late autumn and start again with fresh plants if you wish to start a new bed or revitalize an old one. If you do clear a bed, make certain that you get every bit out otherwise any piece of broken root will form its own root cutting and before long there will be a new plant. *A. vitifolia* can be difficult to get going outside. Plant out a healthy, pot-grown plant in spring, so that it has a chance to establish itself before the following winter. Cover during the first winter with a cloche if severe weather is imminent. The Japanese anemones can become invasive once they are happy. Dig round the colony every year to keep them in check. They like a free-draining but rich, fertile soil to produce of their best. Poor soils will stunt their growth, but they will grow on chalky or alkaline soils. They will happily grow in light shade provided there is not too much competition from tree or shrub roots. They will also grow in full sun, although this can bleach the colour of their flowers. This group seems to be generally free of pests and diseases although occasionally they are affected by eelworms noticeable by the brown, angular patches that they cause on the leaves. *A. magellanica* will grow in any well-drained soil and is reliably hardy. *A. canadensis* can travel like the wind so be careful if you introduce it. It likes moist woodland-type soil and will grow in either sun or shade. *A. virginiana* prefers woodland conditions as does *A. sylvestris*, although it will also grow in sun. The latter can become a little invasive but it is not too difficult to cope with. The *A. narcissiflora* group, which includes *A. polyanthes* and *A. rivularis*, like a moisture-retentive soil. They will grow in either light shade or full sun, although they do best with a cool rootrun. The final group are the bulbous members of the *AA. coronaria* and *pavonina* group. These plants require a warm sunny position in a well-drained soil. Plant out in early autumn. The former are often best treated as annuals with new stock being raised from seed planted each year, although existing bulbs can be dug up after flowering and replanted in the autumn. The latter are left in the soil if they are in a well-drained position and will continue year after year. They will mildly self-sow if the fluffy seed heads are not removed.

Anemonopsis (Ranuculaceae). False Anemone. This single-species genus likes a cool, lightly-shaded position in a moisture-retentive soil, sheltered from the wind. Plant out in autumn or spring.

Angelica (Umbelliferae). Grown mainly as a herb although it has got decorative qualities. It will grow in any fertile garden soil that is not too dry, particularly if grown in the sun when the soil should be kept moist. Cut back after flowering to prevent it seeding around. Being tap-rooted, any transplanting should be carried out while the plant is still very young. Short lived.

Anomatheca (Iridaceae). Species from *Lapeirousia* have been moved into this genus. *A. laxa* is the only hardy species. Plant in the spring in a well-drained, sunny position about 5cm (2in) deep. A light top-dressing of a potash-rich fertilizer helps keep them vigorous. They will self-sow around, but rarely become a nuisance.

Anthemis (Compositae). Anthemis like a well-drained, but not too-dry, soil and an open, sunny position. *A. punctata cupaniana* is one of the most amenable. Remove blooms after flowering, cutting back to a new shoot which will keep the plant flowering throughout the summer. Cut back hard in autumn to prevent it becoming too leggy. It is not too long-lived but easy to propagate (just push pieces into the soil and they will usually root). It grows quickly from cuttings, and better displays are achieved by regular replanting. All dislike wet winters. Cutting back or renewing plants will allow the air to circulate around the plants, helping prevent the leaves from becoming a mushy mess and then plant rotting. *A. santi-johannis* is only a short-lived perennial. It will suddenly give up in mid-season for seemingly no apparent reason. For certain results it should be treated as a biennial and sown every year. It does self-sow, producing enough seedlings to perpetuate itself, but they are difficult to transplant unless you take a good lump of soil with them. *A. tinctoria* also produces better plants if regularly renewed from cuttings in the spring. The younger plants are less susceptible to mildew. Another way of avoiding mildew and colonies dying out is by dividing them every year in the autumn. Either way the younger plants are likely to be shorter and less susceptible to the wind, although they will still appreciate some support. They will also be more floriferous. Deadhead down to new buds in mid summer to induce continuing flowering until the frosts.

Anthericum (Anthericaceae/Liliaceae). Bulbous, clump-forming plants. They will grow in any fertile, well-drained garden soil in full sun. Any tidying-up should be done in the autumn as they start into growth in early spring.

Antirrhinum (Scrophulariaceae). Snapdragons. The bedding antirrhinum usually used as an annual is in fact a short lived perennial and will flower in its second and possibly subsequent years. However, the plants will get leggy unless cut back. Do this in the autumn or after flowering. Cut back leaving a section of green on each stem instead of going right back into the old brown wood. The bedding varieties will self-sow but will not necessarily come true. Their lifespan can be curtailed by rust. Some varieties are supposedly more resistant than others, but treatment with a fungicide may still be needed to hold back the disease. They probably need spraying every fortnight or so if you have time and do not mind such a regime.

Aponogeton (Aponogetonaceae). Water Hawthorn. Although *A. distachyos* is South African it is totally hardy. In warmer areas it is evergreen but in colder ones it is cut back each winter. It grows in the deeper parts of ponds, down to 90cm (3ft), so the roots are generally well protected and will shoot again. Other species are not so hardy.

Aquilegia (Ranunculaceae). Columbine. They are short-lived perennials and stock should be regularly replaced. With the tendency to self-sow there are usually enough seedlings around for their continuance, although they may not come true from seed. Rogue out any that are not required before they seed. Resenting disturbance they should be transplanted as young as possible. They generally like a well-drained, but moisture-retentive soil, reasonably well endowed with organic material. Full sun or partial shade will be suitable. The lower-growing alpine forms need full sun and a sharp-draining soil. Deadhead after flowering, but only remove the flowering stems and leave the basal leaves until autumn. Many of the long-spurred forms are best treated as biennials and grow afresh from seed each year. If treated in this way dig out as soon as they have finished flowering and replant the area with summer bedding. Aquilegias can suffer from several fungal diseases including mildew and rust. Either treat with a fungicide or cut back and burn if the flowering period is over. Leaf miners can make silvery channels in the leaves. Spray with the appropriate chemical.

Arabis (Cruciferae). Rock Cress. These low-growing plants will grow in most well-drained, including chalky soils and should be given an open position. They are mat-formers that should be trimmed over after flowering to remove any straggling stems. Being members of the cabbage family they are prone to the same diseases and are martyrs to downy mildew. They can also suffer from arabis midges which create galls that cause deformed flowers and reduce flowering. Treatment with a systemic insecticide at intervals from spring onwards should cure the problem. There are several generations of midges in a year so make certain that there are no red eggs in the leaf buds after the insect has been controlled. The plants are not long lived but are easy enough to perpetuate by simply pushing pieces into the soil.

Aralia (Araliaceae). These will grow in any fertile soil that is reasonably moisture-retentive. They prefer a slightly-shaded position. They all tend to be rather large and need plenty of space to spread, and will become naturalized if left undisturbed.

Arctotis (Compositae). African Daisy. These are near tender plants that will only tolerate a degree or so of frost. Take cuttings in autumn so that they can be overwintered under glass. They like a rich, well-drained soil. Once established they will tolerate dry conditions, although they do appreciate plenty of moisture during the spring. Plant out in full sun. Cut hard back after flowering.

Argemone (Papaveraceae). These are either annuals or short-lived perennials. Several will self-sow giving them a perennial status. They like a free-draining soil that can even be quite poor although they obviously do much better in fertile conditions. Do not cut back or remove until they have finished seeding to ensure subsequent generations. Wear gloves when tending or removing the plants as they are particularly prickly.

Argyranthemum (Compositae). These are some of the refugees from what was called *Chrysanthemum*. They are on the tender side although they will come through mild winters. To ensure their survival take cuttings in autumn and overwinter under glass. They like a rich, well-drained soil in a sunny position. Deadheading will help to keep them flowering. Cut to within a few inches of the ground in the autumn.

Arisaema (Araceae). A genus of plants that have become popular in recent times. The majority prefer cool, partially shaded conditions although *AA. candidissimum* and *flavum* will grow in a more open position as long as they have a moisture-retentive soil. They all like a leafy soil that is both moisture-retentive and free-draining. Avoid wet and waterlogged conditions. They are relatively hungry plants that appreciate an enriched soil. Most are hardy and need no winter protection although some of the earlier-appearing plants can be effected by late frosts. Most are very late appearing above ground, some not until summer, so mark their positions to avoid over-planting or accidental disturbance. If plants have to be moved do not allow them to dry out. No staking is required and they will naturally die back at the end of the season. They will eventually form large clumps, but division is rarely required except for propagation purposes. Clear away the old foliage as it dies back in the autumn or during the winter clear-up.

Arisarum (Araceae). Mouse Plant. These curious plants like a cool, shady position in a moisture-retentive soil. They are not totally hardy and can suffer in severe winters. Tidy-up in the autumn.

Aristolochia (Aristolochiaceae). Curiously-flowered plants that will grow in most soils. They prefer a sunny position. The main species grown, *A. clematitis*, is rather invasive and should be kept in check. Tidy-up in the autumn.

Armeria (Plumbaginaceae). Thrift, Sea Pink. Plants for the front of the border or rock garden where they can be in full sun and, preferably, have a free-draining soil. Cut off the flowering stems when the blooms fade. The plants will become rather loose and straggly and should be replaced. This can be simply done by poking pieces of stem into the soil where they will readily root. They can suffer from rust. Spray with a fungicide.

Armoracia (Cruciferae). Horse-radish. *A. rusticana* is occasionally grown as an ornamental plant, especially in its variegated form. It likes a deep, rich soil. Transplant when young as it resents being moved but be certain to remove all pieces of root if you wish to get rid of the plant as it regenerates from even the smallest piece. It prefers a sunny position. Cut to the ground in autumn. It can be attacked by slugs and snails.

Arnebia (Boraginaceae). Prophet Flower. *A. pulchra (echioides)* needs a well-drained soil and a sunny position. Cut back vegetation in the autumn. It is hardy but not long lived.

Arnica (Compositae). Well-drained soils (preferably lime-free) are needed for these plants. They should not be too rich otherwise the plants become over-large; avoid applying fertilizers. Remove flower stems after flowering.

Artemisia (Compositae). Wormwoods. With the exception of *A. lactiflora*, which prefers a heavier, moisture-retentive soil, the artemisias like light, well-drained soils, preferably in full sun. The shrubby types should be cut back almost to ground level in the spring and the dwarfer forms just given a trim to keep them tidy. *A.* 'Powis Castle' might succumb to drastic treatment unless there are already signs of new growth appearing at the base, so wait until you see it before cutting back. This plant can also badly suffer in late spring/early summer from blackfly on the young shoots. They are so numerous that spraying is generally the only way of coping with the outbreak. The herbaceous plants should have dead and dying material removed in autumn otherwise the flopping, decaying foliage can become home to many slugs and other pests. Several of the species are badly damaged in spring by sparrows stripping off the young leaves. *A. dracunculoides* should be frequently divided in early spring when its old growth is also cut back. *A. lactiflora* is a tall herbaceous plant that is strong enough to manage without support except in very windy areas. It prefers a moisture-retentive soil and is reluctant to deal with a drought. *A. arborescens* deteriorates after its third or fourth year without actually dying. Replace it every three years.

Arum (Araceae). Most arum seem to like woodland conditions of a leafy soil and light shade. Their preferred position seems to be in hedgerow bottoms. The pretty *A. creticum*, however, prefers a sunny position with a sharp, free-draining soil. Watch out for the native British arum, *A. maculatum*. This can become a pest if it gets into borders. The fleshy roots are often deeply buried and seem to defy attempts to extract them. Try and get them at the seedling stage. It is surprising how widely birds manage to distribute their red berries.

Aruncus (Rosaceae). Tough plants that rarely have any problems. They like a moist soil with plenty of organic material added to it. Plant in a sunny position or in light shade. They can self-sow prodigiously so cut off seeding heads, attractive as they are, if you wish to prevent this. Cut back to the ground in the autumn tidy-up.

Arundinaria (Gramineae). See *Drepanostachyum, Pleioblastus* and *Sinarundinaria*

Arundo (Gramineae). Giant Reed. This tall plant will grow in any fertile soil, but it must have a sheltered, warm, sunny position. Cut back the tall stems in early spring before the new shoots start into growth. If this operation is left too late the young shoots emerge and, being brittle, can be easily broken off. In a mild winter the stems may come through undamaged but they are still worth cutting back as they will not have the quality in their second year of new shoots. The variegated form, *A. donax* 'Variegata', is on the tender side and should be given winter protection of bracken or ferns. In colder areas it can, with care, be lifted and overwintered inside in a pot. If it needs dividing do so in mid-spring. It needs a really hot summer to bloom.

Asarina (Scrophulariaceae). These accommodating plants will grow in shade, and quite dry shade at that. They are not long-lived but usually self-sow around. They are evergreen and need no tidying.

Asclepias (Asclepiadaceae). Milkweed. This is not a particularly hardy genus but some will survive in warmer areas, *AA. speciosa* and *tuberosa* seem the hardiest. They need a good, moisture-retentive soil and a warm, sunny position. They are late, appearing into growth (May) so do not plant on top of them or throw them away thinking they have succumbed to the winter. Clearly labelling them will help to remind you that they are there. They object to being transplanted so propagate in pots and do not move once in their permanent position unless replacement plants are available. Plant out in spring. *A. tuberosa* is surprisingly drought resistant. Cut back as the flowers go over and before they seed. Most exude a poisonous milky sap when the stems are cut so be careful. Avoid *A. syriaca* as it can become an invasive pest.

Asparagus (Ashodelaceae/Liliaceae). Sometimes grown as foliage plants these are cultivated in the same way as if they were in the vegetable garden. A light, well-drained, but humusy soil is required. They should have a sunny position. Top-dress with well-rotted manure in early spring. Once planted avoid transplanting as they resent disturbance. Since they self-sow cut back before they seed.

Asperula (Rubiaceae). Woodruffs. Spreading plants that can colonize whole areas but they are reasonably easy to control. They like a moist, woodland-type soil and a cool, lightly-shaded position. Tidy-up the dying foliage in autumn. The alpine forms need a hot, sunny position in a well-drained soil.

Asphodeline (Asphodelaceae/Liliaceae). A well-drained soil and a sunny position are required. Leave the stems after the flowers have died back as the globular seed pods are attractive in their own right. Cut down when they begin to look scruffy. They will self-sow but the seedlings are easy to remove if you do not want them.

Asphodelus (Asphodelaceae/Liliaceae). There are not many that can be grown in the open garden although *AA. albus* and *cerasiferus* will grow if they have a free-draining soil, that should be dry in summer and a sunny position. They do not like a soil that is too rich. Cut off flowering stems after flowering or seeding.

Asplenium (Aspleniaceae). Spleenworts. These ferns like a humus-rich, moisture-retentive soil but it should be well drained. They like chalky conditions and seem to appreciate old lime mortar in the soil. They will often grow in old walls and do very well when planted in vertical positions. A shady position is preferred. They tend to sow themselves around the garden indicating the type of site they prefer.

Remove old foliage in the spring, so that the new, emerging fronds can be seen at their best.

Astelia (Asteliaceae/Liliaceae). Any moist, fertile garden soil in either sun or light shade is suitable for these plants. Remove flowering stems after flowering and tidy-up the foliage in autumn and spring.

Aster (Compositae). Asters, Michaelmas Daisies. Plant in any fertile garden soil, but they do best in soils that do not become too dry. A sunny position with plenty of circulation of air is required. Most of the asters need replanting every three or four years; using divisions from outside of the old plants and discarding the old, woody central portions. Michaelmas daisy types (*AA. novae-angliae* and *novi-belgii*) can be dealt with at anytime after they have finished flowering, but the clump-forming types, such as *A.* x *frikartii*, should be left to the spring. These do not split very well, so it is best to start new plants from cuttings. The late-flowering varieties, especially the michaelmas daisies which have fibrous roots, can easily be transplanted while in flower which makes them valuable for filling gaps in the autumn border in order to maintain a sequence of flowering plants. The plants can be kept in rows in a reserve bed, possibly in the vegetable garden. Water them well several hours before moving, dig up much of the soil round the rootball as possible, and then transplant to their flowering position. Water again once they are bedded in. They should not notice the move. The stiffer-stemmed forms will not require staking, nor will most others if they are in a sheltered spot. Some, *A. sedifolius*, in particular, need to be supported, preferably with hidden pea-sticks. Michaelmas daisies, *A. novi-belgii*, suffer badly from mildew, wilt and tarsonemid mites which inhibits the flowering. An open position sometimes helps with the mildew problem, as can regular drenching with a fungicide if you do not mind spraying. Not much can be done about the wilt except burning affected plants. The mites are more of a problem during hot summers but like the wilt there is little that can be done to control them, short of burning the plants. Unless you are wedded to this group it is better to use some of the other asters including *A. novae-angliae* which are coarser versions of the Michaelmas daisy. Slugs can be a problem with emerging shoots, especially on the clump-forming varieties. Most of the true species are sufficiently disease resistant to cause little problem. Cut down old flowering stems at any time after flowering. The later it is left the more difficult it is to extract them without damaging the new basal growth.

Astilbe (Saxifragaceae). False Goat's Beard. Astilbes are lovers of moist, humus-rich soil. If it dries out the astilbe's leaves turn brown and sear. Drooping leaves indicate that it is time to water the whole border. They will grow in full sun if the soil is moist enough, but they will also grow in light shade. Their rusty seed heads can be left on for winter decoration and removed in the spring before growth recommences, or removed any time after flowering. They can become congested, diminishing their size, so dig out every few years to revitalize the soil and replant. Never dig or cultivate around these plants as their roots are near the surface. Handweed and mulch with organic material to suppress weeds, feed and retain moisture. No need to stake. Completely hardy.

Astilboides (Saxifragaceae). A one-species genus that requires a moist, humus-rich soil that does not dry out. Does well in light shade but will grow in sun if soil moist enough. Cut down in the autumn tidy-up. A mulch or organic material will be appreciated.

Astragalus (Leguminosae). These plants will grow in most well-drained garden soils, including dryish ones. There is no need to feed to any extent. They like a sunny position. Cut back after they have finished flowering and again during the autumn tidy-up. They resent root disturbance.

Astrantia (Umbelliferae). Masterwort. These all like a moisture-retentive soil, preferably in light shade although they will grow in the open as long as the soil is not too dry. They will seed around so remove the flower heads before they have the opportunity. They also spread underground but rarely at a pace that causes a nuisance. Cut back the rest of the foliage in the autumn. Do not usually require support.

Asyneuma (Campanulaceae). Any well-drained garden soil can be used for these plants, a rock garden being especially suitable. They like a sunny position. Cut off flower heads after flowering or seeding, and tidy plants in the autumn.

Athyrium (Athyriaceae). Lady Fern. Like so many ferns this likes a moist, woodland-type soil with plenty of leafmould in it. It prefers to grow in light shade. Mulch, preferably in both autumn and spring, and divide up the colony if it becomes too congested. Do this in spring before growth begins. Cut back the dead foliage in early spring, again, before growth begins.

Atriplex (Chenopodiaceae). *A. hortensis* is strictly an annual but it self-sows around making it an honorary perennial. Thin seedlings to about 30cm (12in) apart to let the remaining ones develop to their full potential. It will grow on most soils but will become more lush on well-fed ones. Remove before too many have cast their seed.

Aubrieta (Cruciferae). Plants that will grow in most soils including very dry ones. They will grow in crevices in walls. They like a sunny position otherwise they become leggy and do not flower very well. Cut back after flowering to keep the plants compact; they will quickly reshoot.

Aurinia (Cruciferae). See *Alyssum*

Baldellia (Alismataceae). A water plant that will grow in shallow water or in a bog garden. It is only a low plant but does travel rapidly forming a large colony, so only plant where it can spread. Cut back in late autumn.

Ballotta (Labiatae). *B. pseudodictamnus* and the similar *B. acetabulosa* are the species most commonly grown. They like a well-drained soil in full sun. Being felted they dislike wet winters and benefit from being protected by a sheet of glass, or by being replaced each year. Best planted in spring. Cut back during autumn or winter tidy-up, certainly before growth restarts in the spring. Avoid planting the British native *B. nigra* as it is rather foetid and has little to recommend it.

Balsamita (Compositae). See *Tanacetum*

Balsamorhiza (Compositae). Balsamroot. This small North American genus likes a well-drained soil in a sunny position. They have long tap roots and resent disturbance so plant out while young. Balsamroot dislike winter wet and should be protected with a sheet of glass or a light if necessary. Cut off flower stems after flowering.

Baptisia (Leguminosae). These like a deeply-cultivated soil that is free-draining. It should not be too rich and nor be alkaline. They will grow on quite poor soils and are reasonably drought resistant. A sunny position is to be preferred but they will also grow in light shade. Being tap-rooted the baptisias dislike being disturbed, so grow new plants rather than trying to transplant. In rich soil where they are likely to grow lush, and in exposed areas they may well need some support. Unless they are in very well protected positions they will need staking to about 75cm (30in). Remove flower heads after flowering (or after seeding if you want the seed) and cut down remaining foliage during the autumn clear-up.

Barbarea (Cruciferae). American Land Cress, Winter Cress. The double and variegated forms of *B. vulgaris* are those mainly seen in gardens. These and the less garden-worthy species like a humus-rich, moist soil to give of their best. Deadhead or discard after flowering unless seed is required. They are either annual or short-lived perennials and need regular replacement.

Begonia (Begoniaceae). Most are tender but *B. grandis* is hardy in warmer districts. It will need a warm, sheltered position, preferably in partial shade. The soil should be rich and humusy so that it remains moist. Plants are not long-lived and older ones may die over winter but are likely to bequeath some young plants that are growing from surrounding bulblets. Cut back foliage in autumn and apply a bracken or straw mulch to help it through the winter.

Belamcanda (Iridaceae). Blackberry Lily. These rhizomatous plants like a well-drained soil in full sun, but will also grow in a light shade. They spread but in cooler areas are short-lived so they rarely become a nuisance. Replace frequently with new plants, planting in the spring. Cut back flower stems after flowering and the leaves in the autumn. In colder areas they will benefit from a winter mulch or even being lifted and stored in a frost-free place in dry sand, but they seem to do best if they are left undisturbed for about four years or so.

Bellis (Compositae). Daisy. Edging or bedding plants that will grow in any good garden soil, preferably in full sun, but they do not like hot, dry conditions. They self-sow but the resulting plants are often a disappointment so cut off fading flower heads before they seed or remove all seedlings.

Bergenia (Saxifragaceae). Bergenia will grow in either sun or shade but they will flower more freely in the former. Likewise they will grow in either dry or moist soil but again doing better in the latter. Some people like to feed bergenias by top-dressing with well-rotted manure after flowering. As well as feeding the plants this has a tendency to produce good colour in the leaf of those that have purple foliage during the winter. A sunny position also helps with winter colour. However, others prefer not to feed as this tends to produce softer growth which can be knocked off during a hard winter. I think there is scope here for experiment within your own situation. They can be left indefinitely but they can become rather woody with the older, central part of the colony becoming very tired with hardly any flowers. They are much healthier if they are dug up from time to time and the soil rejuvenated before replanting. It is best to do this in spring after flowering, although it can be left until the autumn but this gives the plants less chance of recovering before their next flowering season. Replant good sections of rhizome with the associated foliage. There should be plenty of material. If not cut some rhizomes into 2.5cm (1in) lengths and plant below the soil. These will put down roots and form new plants. Bergenias are evergreen but obviously the leaves die, sometimes many in the autumn. Cut them off whatever the season. *B. ciliata* prefers a shady position and does best in woodland-type soils with plenty of leafmould to retain moisture. It will grow in sun but then it must have a moist soil.

Berkheya (Compositae). A large genus of which one or two are in cultivation. They like a well-drained, reasonably fertile soil in full sun. They are not completely hardy as they are susceptible to both cold and winter wet. Covering with a sheet of glass or a light will help them through in colder areas. Plant out in spring. Remove flower heads after flowering, and foliage in autumn tidy-up. They can be a bit prickly.

Beschorneria (Agavaceae). Yucca-like plants that like dry, hot conditions as long as they are reasonably fertile. Not completely hardy, best grown in the warmer areas unless protection can be given. Remove flowering stem after flowering and tidy the basal leaves whenever necessary.

Besseya (Scrophulariaceae). Kitten-tails. A small genus related to the *Synthyris*. The easiest are the woodlanders (e.g. *S. arizonica*) and should be planted in a moist, humus-rich soil in light shade, on a peat garden perhaps. Others are high alpines and require sharp-drainage and full sun on a rock garden or similar situation.

Bidens (Compositae). A moderately-sized genus of annuals and perennials, a few of which are grown in gardens, in particular *B. ferulifolia*. It requires a reasonably well-drained soil in full sun. Plant out in spring. Deadhead after flowering and cut back to the ground in the winter tidy-up.

Betonica (Labiatae). See *Stachys*

Biscutella (Cruciferae). These are plants of well-drained soils and full sun, being small, a rock garden makes an ideal position. Do not provide too rich a soil. They are either annuals or short-lived perennials and need regular replacement, but being crucifers it is wise to change their position when replanting.

Bistorta (Polygonaceae). See *Persicaria*

Blandfordia (Liliaceae). Christmas Bells. A small genus that is not very hardy and should only be grown in warmer areas. Plant in a well-drained soil that should be moisture-retentive. The pH should be either acid or neutral. They need a warm, sunny position but light shade in hotter regions.

Blechnum (Blechnaceae). Hard Fern. As with so many ferns these like a humus-rich, moisture-retentive soil in partial shade or even full sun, if it is not too hot. Some will take quite dry conditions (avoid drought conditions though). The soil should be lime-free. These are evergreen ferns (sometimes semi-evergreen) so there is no one time in which they should be cut back, but remove old leaves as and when they begin to die back. Often, however, the leaves are blackened by frosts and it is necessary to cut them off at the end of winter. Most are reasonably well behaved, although *B.*

penna-marina travels quite extensively and may need to be kept in check. It is a large genus only a few of which are hardy.

Bletilla (Orchidaceae). A small genus of which *B. striata* is the one most frequently found in cultivation. They all like a cool, humus-rich, moisture-retentive soil and will grow in either partial shade or full sun, an ideal position being where it gets sun except during the hottest part of the day. Do not plant too deeply, a maximum of 5cm (2in) is sufficient. The bulbs are hardy but the emerging shoots (it is one of the earliest to flower) can get caught by late frosts and so may need protection. Leave undisturbed and it will eventually make large drifts.

Bocconia (Papaveraceae). See *Macleaya*

Boltonia (Compositae). This small genus is closely related to the asters and as such should be treated in a similar manner. They will grow in most fertile garden soils. Full sun is the preferred position although they will take a small amount of light shade. The taller ones will need staking although one of the most popular, *B. asteroides*, has a form 'Snowbank' which is shorter and less likely to flop, except in shady or exposed positions. *B. latisquama* will grow to about 2.4m (8ft) and needs staking at about 1.5–1.8m (5–6ft). Do not leave it too long (about three or four years) between dividing as it can get congested and tired. Cut back the dead stems at any time during autumn or winter. Do not leave it too late in the spring otherwise the new growth may be damaged.

Bomarea (Alstroemericeae/Liliaceae). A South American genus of twining plants that will survive in warmer areas, especially if planted in a sunny, sheltered position against a wall. A mulch during winter may also help. Grow the twining species up through low shrubs or pea sticks. They need a reasonably fertile soil, but it must be free-draining.

Bongardia (Podophyllaceae/Berberidaceae). The single species, *B. chrysogonum*, is a tuberous plant that is hardy but needs to be kept dry during the summer which really makes it a plant for the bulb frame rather than the open ground, although it will survive there if the summer drought can be provided and the position is free-draining and hot. The plants are summer-dormant and need little attention beyond removing the dead foliage once the plant dies down. It does not increase vegetatively so there is no need to disturb the plants. Being summer-dormant label clearly to avoid overplanting or accidental disturbance. They do well on calcareous soils.

Borago (Boraginaceae). The annual *B. officinalis* is a self-sower and counts almost as a perennial. Cut it back as soon as it finishes flowering to prevent it from seeding too prolifically. Because the plant suffers from powdery mildew get rid of it as soon as possible. *B. laxiflora* is a perennial that also self-sows. Any transplanting should be carried out while the plants are still young as they produce a deep tap root which means they resent disturbance. The rosettes remain green over winter, but the top foliage dies back to a black mass which should be removed as soon as possible to prevent the crown rotting. They will both thrive in most fertile or even infertile soils, and although they undoubtedly grow best in sun they will tolerate just a little light shade. They are both a bit floppy but this is part of their character and it is not usual to stake them. *B. laxiflora* is not completely hardy (it comes from Corsica) but will survive most winters.

Bouteloua (Gramineae). Grama Grass, Mosquito Grass, Signal Arm Grass. These are prairie grasses and like nothing better than a hot sunny position and a well-drained soil. The best time for planting is in the spring, which is also the time for any dividing. They can form large clumps but are not invasive. Shear over in late winter.

Boykinia (Saxifragaceae). The genus once again includes *B. jamesii*, which was previously in *Telesonix*. These like a woodland-type soil, that is humus rich and moisture-retentive. They tend to be unhappy in calcareous soils. They also like a light shade. Tidy up in the autumn, top-dressing with leafmould or bark. They are hardy.

Briza (Gramineae). Quaking Grass, Trembling Grass. A genus of mainly annuals. They will grow in most fertile soils and prefer a sunny position. Plant out in spring. The majority are tender and will need protection if grown. Cut back in spring to let the old foliage give some winter protection. If a winter mulch is applied, cut back in autumn.

Brodiaea (Alliaceae/Liliaceae). (See also *Triteleia*). This genus is very closely allied to the *Allium* and is treated in a similar manner. They like a well-drained (particularly a mildly calcareous) soil in a warm sunny position, against a wall perhaps. Plant out in the autumn. The clumps can become congested and will need breaking up from time to time, preferably in the autumn.

Brunnera (Boraginaceae). *B. macrophylla* is the only species of this small genus in general cultivation. It likes a cool, shady position in any fertile soil, preferably moisture-retentive. It will grow in full sun in cooler climates, but in warmer ones it will only do so if there is plenty of moisture in the soil. It tends to spread but not in an offensive way and is usually controllable. They also self-sow which may be a problem if you grow named-cultivars as these may not come true, and needs regular roguing out. Tidy-up in autumn.

Buglossoides (Boraginaceae). The main species here is *B. purpurocaerulea* (previously known as *Lithospermum purpureo-caeruleum*). This is a sprawling plant with erect stems, with a tendency to run, rooting. Little can be done to neaten it. As the running stems root at the tips it needs to be cut back at least once a year, and any rooted pieces removed if it is to be kept in check. It has the advantage that it likes to grow in light shade and that it seems reasonably pest- and disease-free. The shiny seeds are attractive and it can be left for winter decoration, cutting back in spring before new growth starts.

Bulbine (Asphodelaceae/Liliaceae). These are Australian or South African plants and one would expect, they are not completely hardy. Plant out in a warm sunny spot, say against a wall for example. They like a well-drained soil and will cope with dry conditions. They have a habit of self-sowing rather prodigiously, so deadhead after flowering. Plant in autumn.

Bulbinella (Asphodelaceae/Liliaceae). These prefer a lime-free, humus-rich soil that is moisture-retentive. These like to be moist during the growing season but should not sit in stagnant water, especially in winter. The position can be either in sun or light shade. *B. rossii* is dioecious, and so you will need both male and female plants if you want to get seed. Tidy-up as the foliage dies back. *B. floribunda* is dormant in late spring and summer so be careful not to disturb or overplant it. Divide plants when they become congested.

Buphthalmum (Compositae). A humus-rich, moisture-retentive soil is best for these plants although they will grow in any fertile garden soil. Some are quite tall but generally do not require staking. Deadhead after flowering and tidy away in the autumn. For *B. speciosum*, see *Telekia speciosum*.

Bupleurum (Umbelliferae). As well as shrubs there are some perennials in this genus of which *B. falcatum* is the most commonly grown. It will grow in any fertile garden soil, and seems to like well-drained ones. Although preferring sun it will happily grow in a little light shade. It is a vigorous self-sower so it should be cut back as soon as it has finished flowering to reduce the number of seedlings with which to contend. Cut down to the basal rosette. If left until the winter tidy-up, the base of the stems will still be green and in leaf. Don't worry about this and cut them off at the base. Being green, cut rather than tug at the stems otherwise the plants are likely to uproot or snap off at the root. *B. falcatum* is not long-lived but there are always plenty of self-sown seedlings to continue its presence. *B. petraeum* seems to prefer a calcareous soil.

Butomus (Butomaceae). Flowering Rush. *B. umbellatus* is the only member of this genus. It is a pond plant that will grow in still water up to about 50cm (18in) deep. It will also grow in the muddy margins as long as they are kept moist. If planted in containers it must be in lattice pots from which it can spread as it does not like to be restricted, with flowering reduced. If it is grown in a normal pot it will need splitting and repotting each year. It tends to spread both by its rhizomes and also by small bulbils. It is hardy.

Caccinia (Boraginaceae). Plant in a well-drained soil that need not be particularly rich. They do like a position in full sun. Cut back the fading foliage in the autumn. Caccinia are deep-rooted and do not like disturbance so plant out while still young, and start again with new plants rather than try and move existing ones. They are perfectly hardy.

Calamagrostis (Gramineae). Unlike many grasses several of this genus come from slightly-shaded woods and so can be used for growing in the shade. They also often grow in very damp situations, so can be used for similar garden conditions although they will also grow in ordinary garden soil. Some have creeping rhizomes and either need control or lots of space. *C. x acutiflora* 'Foerster' is one of the best forms and is not invasive. Shear over the plant during the winter to remove all the old foliage. Set out new plants or move during mid spring. They are hardy.

Calamintha (Labiatae). (Now often classified as *Clinopodium*.) The Calamints will grow in any reasonable garden soils. They prefer a sunny position, although *C. grandiflora* will grow in light shade (it grows in beech woods in its native habitat). Set out young plants in either autumn or spring. This species also prefers a moister soil than the others, again reminiscent of its woodland habitat. They are best planted towards the front of a border, preferably beside a path where their aromatic leaves can be appreciated. *C. nepeta* and its various forms are short-lived and will often die out during a wet winter, especially if they are in a heavy soil. Shear over after flowering or in the autumn (which usually coincide).

Calanthe (Orchidaceae). This is a very large genus of terrestrial orchids, many of which come from tropical regions. The hardy species grow in woodland conditions of light shade and a leafy, humus-rich soil. Most are evergreen and need little attention except to remove old flower stems and any dying leaves. The leaves can become tattered by the end of the growing season so that it may be necessary also to remove any unsightly foliage. If they need moving, do so soon after the flowers fade.

Calla (Araceae). Bog Arum, Water Arum. The single representative, *C. palustris*, is a plant from bogs and other wet areas, as its name implies. It will happily grow on the edge of ponds or streams in shallow water (up to about 15cm (6in) deep), or in wet soil. Sun is preferred but it will also grow in a light shade. It is a creeping plant and may need a bit of control in smaller ponds. Young plants are unlikely to flower until their second year. They are hardy.

Callirhoe (Malvaceae). Poppy Mallow. A small genus of mainly perennial plants. They all like a well-drained, light soil that does not become too wet during the winter (they may need protection with a sheet of glass in wet areas). A sunny position is also required. Being tap-rooted they are not too happy with being disturbed, so either use new plants if you need them elsewhere or dig up with the maximum of earth around the roots.

Caltha (Ranunculaceae). Kingcups, Marsh Marigolds. This is a genus of waterside plants and although they will grow in ordinary soil if kept moist, they do best either beside or just in the water. They will also grow well in bog gardens. CC. *palustris* and *polypetala* are particularly good for growing in shallow water. Whatever the soil it should be rich in humus. There is a preference for sun but they will also grow well in light shade, especially if it is provided by deciduous trees or shrubs. Planting and transplanting is best carried out after flowering, through to the autumn. The white form of *C. palustris*, *C.p.* 'Alba', can suffer from mildew. This can be sprayed with a fungicide, but a better alternative is to grow the white *C. leptosepala*.

Camassia (Hyacinthaceae/Liliaceae). These are bulbous plants of damp areas and should therefore have a moisture-retentive soil that is rich in organic matter. They like a sunny position. Plant about 7.5cm (3in) below the surface of the soil. The stems look scruffy as they go over in mid-summer and can be cut back to the ground. Some gardeners like to leave them as they become attractive once the seed pods have plumped out. Camassias can become very congested and need to be lifted and divided every few years. Do this in the dormant period after they have died back. They recover from this operation very quickly.

Campanula (Campanulaceae). Bellflowers. This is a very large genus with many species and cultivars in cultivation, many (especially the alpine forms) requiring slightly different conditions in which to succeed. Generally they will grow in any fertile garden soil as long as it is free-draining, and most will grow in alkaline conditions; indeed some (*C. glomerata* for example) seem to prefer them in the wild. Performance is best in richer soils but they will grow under quite spartan conditions, *C. poscharskyana* for example will grow in dry walls. Most species grow best in full sun but many such as *C. persicifolia* will also grow quite well in light shade. Some, such as *C. trachelium* while growing in sun prefer light shade. Not all are well behaved and it is best either to avoid or keep an eye on invasive plants such as *C. punctata* and *C. rapunculoides* (only plant them where they can run wild if you want to grow them.) *C. persicifolia* and *C. takesimana* can also be a bit of a nuisance in the wrong place as they also spread underground. The former also sows itself liberally, but it is a beautiful plant so the extra attention to keep it under control is worth while. Tall species such as *C. pyramidalis* and *C. lactiflora* need staking with branching sticks at an early stage. Even some of the lower-growing members of the genus, such as *C. glomerata*, may need similar support. Several, including *C. lactiflora*, can be dead-headed (just remove the top of the plant) to encourage a second flush of flowers. White forms look terrible as the flowers go over and turn brown; and these likewise should be deadheaded. Cut back flowering stems to the ground in the autumn or after flowering if so wished. Some plants, such as *C. persicifolia* can become congested and seem to prefer being lifted and replanted every two or three years. This is particularly so of some of the double varieties. There are no real problems with diseases but watch out for slugs, especially on some of the smaller species. Occasionally leaf spot (brown or white spots) can be a problem. Spray with a fungicide.

Canna (Cannaceae). Canna like a fertile, organic-rich soil as they are hungry feeders. They like a warm, sunny site. Never let either of these dry out during the winter, nor make them too wet or the rhizomes may die, the soil should be the classic combination of moisture-retentive but free-draining. There must not be any surplus moisture hanging around their roots. A liquid feed in early autumn is likely to be beneficial in keeping them flowering and a top-dressing of rich compost or manure applied in the winter will help them the following year. Deadhead as necessary. In milder areas they can be left in the ground although they should be given a protective winter mulch of bracken or straw. In colder areas lift at the first frosts and store the rhizomes, after washing, in a frost-free place in either soil or peat. To get plants off to a good start the following year they can be planted in pots about a month before they are due to be planted out (not until the frosts have passed). Snails can be a bit of a problem so take counter-measures.

Cardamine (Cruciferae). Bittercress, Cuckoo Flower, Lady's Smock. This genus has been increased to take on board many of the species that were once known as *Dentaria*. These are all plants that come from a woodland situation and they appreciate a leafy soil, with plenty of light humus that keeps moist, and a light, dappled shade. Some, *C. pratensis* for example, will happily grow in a bog garden. It is quite a good idea to top-dress with bark or leafmould. If the soil is not too dry most will also grow in full sun. Most spread by underground means and can be a bit invasive but if given enough space, in a woodland garden for example, they should be little trouble. Cut back as the foliage begins to fade as most are summer dormant. Label clearly so that they are not accidentally dug up or overplanted while they are resting below ground.

Cardiocrinum (Liliaceae). These are hungry feeders and the soil should be deeply cultivated with as much organic material as possible dug into it to allow for this. In fact it is a good idea to dig a large hole (at least 60cm (2ft) deep) and fill it with well-rotted manure before planting. In spite of their huge size cardiocrinums need only be planted with about 4cm (1.5in) soil above them. They like a position in dappled shade. Between shrubs is an ideal situation. Plant out in the autumn using freshly dug bulbs, do not use dried out specimens as these may well not survive. Top-dress every year with manure or rich compost. These take a long time, up to eight years, between germination and coming into flower. Unfortunately they are monocarpic and immediately die after flowering and seeding, but the waiting time for the next generation is less as they usually produce offsets that flower in a shorter period, about three years. Replant in a freshly prepared site, again with plenty of organic material. Do not cut down after flowering as the seed pods are spectacular, and are much in demand for dried arrangements.

Carduncellus (Compositae). These thistles like a well-drained soil in full sun. Any shade will draw them and make them out of character. They will tolerate relatively poor conditions, indeed if the soil is too rich they become over-drawn and rather weedy looking. They are hardy but dislike winter wet so protect with sheets of glass or polythene lights if there is likely to be a problem. Remove the heads before seed is produced to reduce the chance of them taking over.

Carex (Cyperaceae). Sedge. This is an enormous genus of over 2,000 species, most of which are of little use in the garden. As one would expect they vary in their requirements. Most will grow in ordinary garden soil but some such as *C. pendula* prefer a moister situation. This plant also likes a shady position while others may prefer more sun. The New Zealander *C. buchananii* will grow in garden soil but does better in moist conditions but unlike the pendulous sedge prefers an open position. Several carexes will grow in quite wet conditions. *C. elata* 'Aurea' (syn. *C. stricta* 'Bowles' Golden') can be grown in several inches of water as well as in normal borders. Its bright golden colour is subdued if it is planted in shade. It is not too happy about being divided and may take a while to settle down again after such an operation. This applies to quite a few of the genus. Some, *C. riparia* in particular, can be invasive, although its variegated form, *C.r* 'Variegata', is much better behaved. They are mainly evergreen and dead foliage can best be removed by passing gloved fingers through the clump.

Carlina (Compositae). Everlasting Thistles. Most gardeners will probably feel that they need little instruction on how to grow thistles, but it is an interesting group of plants of which there are many yet to come into cultivation. It should be said that not all of them are thugs. The main two that are in cultivation are both stemless, *C. acaulis* and *C. acanthifolia*. Both like a well-drained soil that should not be too rich. A chalky soil is perfectly acceptable, indeed they often grow on such in the wild. They should have a position in the open in full sun, otherwise they become drawn and out of character. Both have tap roots and so resent disturbance. Plant out as young as possible and leave them where they are. If you need to move them start again with new plants. They are not blameless as they can self-sow, but they do not run, in fact *C. acanthifolia* is monocarpic and dies after flowering and seeding. Leave on the old flower heads, as they make an attractive dried feature.

Catananche (Compositae). Blue Cupidone, Cupid's Dart. This is a small genus of which *C. caerulea* is the only one grown, and this mainly in the form 'Major'. They will grow in any garden soil as long as it is well-drained. Chalky soils are no problem. They prefer an open, sunny site. Cut to the ground during the autumn or winter clear-up. They have tap roots and so are quite difficult to move once they have matured, although it is possible with care. However, they are relatively short-lived so it is often a good thing to start with new plants rather than re-establishing old ones. Some gardeners advocate keeping the plants for only three years and then renewing them. In this way the plants are always in their prime and most floriferous. Although it may be unexpected, slugs and snails dine well on this plant and need controlling if it is to flower.

Catharanthus (Apocynaceae). Madagascar Periwinkle. Rose Periwinkle. This genus is only hardy in the warmest areas and elsewhere should be treated as an annual. A moist, humus-rich soil is required and, unlike the periwinkle namesakes, it should have a position in full sun. The warmer the position the better chance it has of overwintering. It will stand very hot conditions in summer provided the soil does not dry out.

Caulophyllum (Berberidaceae). Blue Cohosh, Papose Root. This is a two-species genus with *C. thalictroides* being the main representative in gardens. It is a woodlander and likes a cool, semi-shaded even quite deeply-shaded position with a leafy, moisture-retentive soil. It does not like alkaline soils. It spreads slowly and can eventually form large colonies but generally does not need to be disturbed except for propagational purposes. Remove old foliage and stems when the plant dies down. They are perfectly hardy.

Cautleya (Zingiberaceae). This is a genus for warmer regions but as with several of the gingers they are possibly hardier than they have been given credit for. They obviously prefer a warm position in the garden, against walls perhaps, but they should not be too hot in summer. The soil should be moisture-retentive but well-drained at the same time. They will grow in full sun or light shade as long as the latter does not become too cold. Planting or transplanting should be undertaken in spring as the soil is warming up and growth is starting. In colder areas they can be lifted and stored overwinter, but be careful not to damage the roots as any wound may allow in rot. Dust with flowers of sulphur before storing.

Cedronella (Labiatae). Most of these have moved to *Agastache* but *C. triphylla* (*C. canariensis*), Balm of Gilead, remains. This is a herb that likes a well-drained, reasonabe soil in full sun. Cut back stems in autumn.

Celmisia (Compositae). These are New Zealand plants, most of which come from areas that are constantly moist and often wrapped in clouds. Thus a moist, humid climate suits them best in cultivation, they are not so easy to accommodate in drier parts. Although they like a moist soil it should be well-drained so that there is no stagnant water around the roots and possibly more importantly, the collar. This is particularly true during the winter when they may need protecting with sheets of glass or polythene lights to keep them reasonably dry. The soil should not be too rich but remember that well-drained soils that are kept moist tend to have most of the goodness leached out of them, so make certain they do not starve by top-dressing in spring and occasionally during the growing season. The soil should be lime-free. Remove any dead, dying or rotting foliage on sight. Celmisias can be grown in the open if the soil if moist enough, but a very light shade should be given in hotter climates.

Centaurea (Compositae). Cornflowers, Hardheads, Knapweeds. This is a large genus of which, perhaps surprisingly, some are shrubs. However, the majority are perennials of which several are in cultivation. They will grow in most garden soils as long as they do not dry out too much but on the other hand they should be well drained. Many grow on chalk in the wild and so will also do so in gardens. They are plants of open spaces and so like a sunny position. Most should be cut back to the ground after flowering or left until the autumn clear-up. The early-flowering *C. montana* should be cut back after flowering, partly because it can suffer from mildew if left standing and partly because doing so encourages a second flush of flowers, if you are lucky. This plant can be a nuisance as it self sows and if a piece of root is left in the ground while moving it it will shoot up again. It is a floppy plant but there is no satisfactory way of staking it, although short pea-sticks help. Many of the centaureas will stand up without extra support unless they are in exposed positions. *C. dealbata* will nearly always need support. They need dividing if they become too congested, but most can go about five years before this is necessary. *C. montana* may need splitting a bit more frequently to keep it vigorous and to prevent it spreading too far. *C. dealbata* can also become a bit too invasive and may need to be kept in check. Most in cultivation are perfectly hardy. *C. gymnocarpa* is grown mainly for its grey leaves. Many gardeners prefer to remove the flower stems as they appear in order to keep it purely as a foliage plant. It is not altogether hardy and cuttings should be taken in autumn and overwinter under glass as insurance.

Centranthus (Valerianaceae). Red Valerian. They will grow on most soils as long as they are not wet. However it does best in well-drained soils. Flowering is best if the plants are not over-fed. Self-sown plants often appear in shingle or on walls indicating the kind of spartan conditions that they are happy in. They will do best in a sunny position but will tolerate a little light shade. They are tap-rooted which makes them difficult to move; it is easier to start again with new plants rather than try and transplant them. After the first flush of flowers cut back to near the ground. This will not only prevent the plant self-sowing and also encourage a second flush of flowers. Cut back after these as well to prevent too much self-sowing.

Cephalaria (Dipsacaceae). Any good garden soil will do, preferably well-fed with organic material, a sunny position is important. The main garden species is *C. gigantea*. This is deep-rooted so plant out while the plants are still young. Start again with new ones rather than trying to transplant if you wish to move mature plants. Can self-sow rather vigorously so it is preferable to deadhead as soon as the flowers are over. If they do self-sow remove the seedlings before their roots delve too deep otherwise you may have problems getting them out of other plants. There is a clone which is reputed to be sterile. Get this one if you can. *C. gigantea* is very tall and needs staking in exposed positions but manages to keep upright in more protected places. If the growing tips are taken out early it can become bushier at the expense of height. Top-dress with manure during the winter. Carefully divide or start again after about five years if the vigour declines.

Cerastium (Caryophyllaceae). Snow-in-Summer. These are easily grown plants that will grow on a range of soils as long as they are reasonably well drained. They are quite happy growing in spartan conditions such as on a wall. They will grow in light shade but look thin and miserable. A sunny position is a better bet. Shear over after flowering to keep the plant neat and compact. Getting weeds out of a patch of *C. tomentosa* can be very difficult; pieces are always left behind to start again, so remove the whole lot and replant with fresh cerastium, it will not take long to establish. Clumbs can get a bit straggly and benefit, anyway, from being replaced every so often. Can become a nuisance when it is happy and may need controlling or planting where it can ramp to its heart's content.

Ceratostigma (Plumbaginaceae). Most of these are shrubs but some are herbaceous in habit. Plant out in a well-drained soil that is well-endowed with compost or manure. Although they will tolerate shade a sunny position is perhaps best. If possible arrange for them to have a cool rootrun and the top-growth in sun. Cut back the woody stems of *C. plumbaginoides* almost to the base in the spring before the new growth starts. *C. willmottianum* may be cut back by frosts (or can be cut back by the gardener if necessary to keep it tidy). This will mean that it will be late into flower during the coming year.

Cestrum (Solanaceae). These are strictly speaking shrubs, but in a normal winter behave like herbaceous plants. *C. parqui* is the only reliable hardy species and that can get cut back by a cold winter. It requires a sunny position to flower well. Plants that come through the winter unscathed flower earlier and longer so there might be a case for giving it some protection. If they come through a series of mild winters then cut out a third of the old wood to the base every year. Do this after flowering. Remove any wood to the ground, that is lost through winter weather. One or two others, *C. fasciculatum*, for example, may be hardy enough if planted in a warm spot. They will grow in any fertile soil that is not too dry. Added organic material will help provide moisture and nourishment.

Chaerophyllum (Umbelliferae). The one grown in gardens is *C. hirsutum*, usually in its *roseum* form. It will grow in any ordinary garden soil and likes either a sunny or lightly shaded position. It flowers in the spring and if cut back after flowering will produce another flush. Being deep-rooted it does not like being disturbed; so plant out when young and start again with new plants rather than trying to transplant.

Chamaelirium (Liliaceae). Blazing Star, Rattlesnake, Wand Lily. This monospecific genus (*C. luteum*) is closely related to *Veratrum* and likes similar conditions to *V. nigrum*. That is to say, moist, woodland-type soil, with plenty of humus, and light, dappled shade. The plant is dioecious so both plants are required if seed is needed. The male has the better flowers.

Chasmanthe (Iridaceae). These bulbous plants (corms) are on the tender side and can only be grown in warmer areas. Even here they are best planted in a warm, sheltered position. They like well-drained soil, but make certain they do not dry out too much during spring when they come into growth. They can be planted quite deep (15cm (6in) or more) to avoid frosts; alternatively lifted in autumn and stored in a frost-free place over winter. Cut back flowering stems and leaves as they die back after flowering.

Cheiranthus (Cruciferae). Wallflowers. Most of the species that were once gathered here are now under *Erysimum*, but the treatment is the same. They like a well-drained soil, they will even grow on walls (hence the name). They dislike winter-wet and can suffer from wind-rock in exposed positions, with conical holes produced in the soil around the stems which fill with water. A sunny position is required. They can suffer from cabbage-related diseases, such as clubroot, so do not plant biennial forms on the same ground two years running. Remove biennial forms as soon as they have finished flowering. The perennial forms are short-lived and it is sensible to take cuttings every year so that there are plants in reserve.

Chelidonium (Papaveraceae). Greater Celandine. *C. majus* is an old cottage garden plant and was often found growing under hedges. It prefers a shady position with a moist, humus-rich soil, but it will grow in a wide range of positions and soils. Tidy-up the plant by cutting to the ground in autumn. It oozes a harmless orange sap if the stems are broken but it should not cause problems if it gets on the skin. (It was used, and still is, used for curing warts). Cut down after flowering to prevent it seeding too much.

Chelone (Scrophulariaceae). Turtlehead. These valuable autumn-flowering plants like a moisture-retentive soil that is rich in organic matter. They will take full sun or light shade. Cut to the ground during the autumn clear-up. They are susceptible to mildew, especially in dry weather. Keep the soil moist and spray with a fungicide if necessary. The clumps are spreading but not invasive. If the clumps become congested and vigour begins to flag, divide them up. They are usually strong enough not to need staking. Cut to the ground during the winter tidy-up.

Chionochoa (Gramineae). Tussock Grass. These need a well-drained soil, preferably in a sheltered position from cold winds, but open to the sun. Cut down during the winter tidy-up. This grass is tussock-forming and does not run.

Chrysanthemum (Compositae). See *Argyranthemum, Dendranthema, Leucanthemella, Leucamthemopsis, Leucamthemum, Nipponanthemum,* and *Tanacetum.*

Chrysogonum (Compositae). Golden-knee, Golden Star. *C. virginianum* is the species mainly grown. Plant in a moisture-retentive but free-draining soil, a woodland-type would be ideal. It will grow in full sun if the soil is kept moist but does best in part shade, especially in hotter regions. Plant out in spring.

Chrysopsis (Compositae). Golden Aster. These will grow in any good garden soil but have the advantage of tolerating quite dry conditions and are therefore good for growing in sandy soils. They prefer a sunny position. They will survive most winter frosts although they will be cut to the ground by the first ones. Tidy-up the plants in early winter. Plant out in spring.

Cichorium (Compositae). Chicory. These are mainly grown in the vegetable garden, although *C. intybus* is sometimes grown for its blue flowers. They like a well-drained soil, preferably on the alkaline side. Plant in full sun to get the best results as the flowers shut in dull conditions. Sow where they are to flower or move at a young age.

Cimifuga (Ranunculaceae). Bugbane. A well-drained, woodland-type soil is ideal for these plants. A certain amount of moisture is preferable. They will grow in sun or partial shade, the latter being preferable as it gives them a cool rootrun. These can be left undisturbed in the ground indefinitely. Although most species are tall they do not need staking unless they are in an exposed position.

Cirsium (Compositae). They grow in any good garden soil but do best in those that are moisture-retentive. A place in the sun is preferred. It is best to remember that these are thistles and some species can become invasive. They are hardy and disease-resistant. *C. rivulare*, the most commonly grown, is quite tall and often requires some form of support to prevent it flopping.

Claytonia (Portulacaceae). Spring Beauty. These are essentially woodland plants and are best grown in a moist, woodland-type soil in light shade. They can seed around and become a little invasive but are not too difficult to keep under control. They are best kept for the wild garden.

Clematis (Ranunculaceae). There are several herbaceous clematis that are cut back to the ground each autumn or winter. Plant in well-drained, but moisture-retentive soil. Clematis are usually reported as favouring alkaline soils but they will grow equally well on neutral and acid ones, as long as the latter is not too extreme. They like a cool rootrun so it helps if the roots can be protected from direct sunshine by other plants. Their heads should be in the sun. *C. recta* and *C. durandii* really need support from pea-sticks at about 75–90cm (30–36in) high. They can be vigorous so make certain that the support is sturdy enough to take the weight. After flowering *C. recta* can be cut back by about half when it will reshoot with a fresh batch of leaves and possibly flowers. Other species can either be supported in a similar manner, or allowed to spill out across earlier-flowering plants. Cut down in the winter, being certain that the old stems have been removed before the next lot burst forth. They benefit from a mulch of manure or humsy compost in winter. New plants can be planted out in autumn or spring. Protect new spring growth from slugs and snails. The more commonly seen climbing forms all need supports. Their pruning regime is more complicated and specialist books should be consulted as to when and how to cut them back. They also appreciate a cool rootrun and organic mulch. Young plants can suffer from clematis wilt. If they are planted deeper than they were in their pots or nursery beds new shoots will form and plants that suffer from the disease will often recover the following year. Some clematis, especially those in the texensis group and cultivars such as 'Jackmanii', suffer from mildew. Spray with a fungicide.

Clinopodium (Labiatae). See *Calamintha*

Clintonia (Convallariaceae/Liliaceae). Woodland plants that need a moisture-retentive, humusy soil with plenty of leafmould, preferably in light shade. They spread by rhizomes but most are not particularly invasive. *C. uniflora* travels more than other species, particularly in light, sandy soils. Once planted leave in place as they resent being transplanted. Do not cut back after flowering as most clintonia are interesting in fruit.

Cobaea (Polemoniaceae). A small genus of tender plants from tropical parts of the world. The one mainly grown, *C. scandens*, is in fact a perennial although it is usually treated as an annual on account of the difficulties of overwintering it. It can be grown in a large pot and taken inside during the winter. Fresh plants are usually raised each year and are planted outside in a free-draining, but organically-rich soil. These are rapid-growing plants so do not allow them to dry out otherwise their growth will be checked. Seed can be sown directly into the soil in early summer for creating autumn-flowering plants. They need support, either from a trellis of some sort or by another plant. Unless attempting to overwinter in warmer areas discard in late autumn.

Cochlearia (Cruciferae). All species in this genus are too small to be considered in this book, the only eligible one, *C. armoracia* having been moved to *Amoracia rusticana*.

Codonopsis (Campanulaceae). These are climbing or scrambling plants that like to clamber up through or over other plants, especially shrubs. They will grow in any fertile garden soil as long as they are reasonably moisture-retentive. They appreciate a cool rootrun but can be planted in full sun as long as the soil is not too dry. They need some form of support, shrubs being ideal. Pea-sticks can be used but they can look rather ugly as they are not completely covered by the codonopsis. The climbing stems are somewhat fragile so do not break them while weeding or otherwise tending the border. They are not totally hardy and often need some form of winter protection, such as a sheet of glass. In milder areas shrubs will give them adequate protection. Do not damage the young emerging shoots in spring. Other species can either be supported in a similar manner, or allowed to spill out across earlier-flowering plants.

Colchicum (Colchiceae/Liliaceae). These bulbs will grow in most deeply-cultivated garden soils. They seem to do best on light, sandy soils. Most will grow in either full sun or light shade. Plant colchicums reasonably deeply, at least 10cm (4in) below the surface. The leaves appear at quite a different time of year to the flowers. In most garden forms the flowers appear in autumn, while the leaves appear in spring. At first the leaves form an attractive, glossy clump, but as with most bulbs they eventually turn yellow and look a mess. Once they have changed, cut them off at the ground. Alternatively they can be planted amongst other plants where they will not be noticed, and which will cover up the flower's autumn nakedness. However, the leaves must get light to build up energy reserves so do not smother them. *C. autumnale* and its various forms can be naturalized in grass, but other species prefer less competition and should be grown in drifts in cultivated soil. Plant new corms in autumn when they become available, transplanting should take place earlier, in summer. Slugs can attack the flowers so take evasive action, preferably as the flower emerges. Later they are liable to eat the leaves; again early action is needed.

Commelina (Commelinaceae). Spiderwort. *C. coelestis* with its bright blue flowers is a perennial but is sometimes treated as an annual because it is doubtfully hardy. In mild areas it will die back underground and will survive a winter. Elsewhere it can be lifted and stored in dry sand in a frost-free-place. *C. dianthifolia* is a self-sow annual but will thus perpetuate itself. It is not a nuisance. Plant out in any fertile garden soil as long as it is reasonably free-draining. A warm, sunny position is important.

Convallaria (Convallariaceae/Liliaceae). Lily-of-the-Valley. These will grow in a wide range of soils from acid to alkaline but do best in moist, woodland-type where the rhizomes can easily wander around in the damp leafmould. They grow in sun but look best in light shade. The best time to lift and split congested plantings is in autumn so that they are ready to perform again the following spring. In some areas where the plants will not have time to re-establish before winter sets in it will be necessary to leave division until spring, but this means that a year's flowering is likely to be lost. Plant where they can be seen in spring but where the leaves will be masked by other plants in summer when they can become rather tatty looking. They can become very congested to the point where flowering is diminished. Dig up, split and replant. They will appreciate a leafmould or humusy compost in autumn. To obtain a really good crop apply a liquid manure after flowering. They can suffer from botrytis or grey mould. You can try spraying affected plants with fungicide but it is probably best to burn the plants and start again elsewhere in the garden. Leaf spot, with red and brown spots, is another fungal disease from which they occasionally suffer. Spray with a fungicide.

Convolvulus (Convolvulaceae). A large genus of which many are invasive weeds. The two most commonly grown, *C. sabatianus* (*mauritanicus*) and *C. cneorum*, are both tender in most areas. They can both be grown in pots and taken inside during the winter or cuttings can be taken every autumn. Alternatively they will often survive if grown in a warm, sunny position, preferably with a warm wall behind. *C. althaeoides* is increasingly grown. This can be very invasive but in colder areas is cut back by the frosts each year so that it is more or less controlled. If the main plant is protected from the cold by a large rock it is likely to survive. They all need a well-drained soil, and do best in light, sandy ones. A sunny position is required.

Coreopsis (Compositae). Tickseed. These invaluable plants will grow in most garden soils as long as they are reasonably fertile and not too damp. They need a sunny position. The perennial coreopsis are spreaders, not particularly fast but they do spread, becoming congested and exhausting the soil. Split them up every few years, discarding the older material, and rejuvenate the soil. This will promote a longer flowering season. They tend to have stiff, wiry stems that need no extra support. The emerging shoots in spring are much liked by slugs and snails, which can prevent the stems developing, especially if there are weeds to keep the area moist and provide cover. Keep them weed free and baited. Top-dress in the autumn with a well-rotted manure. Deadhead to keep them flowering.

Coriaria (Coriaceae). This genus includes perennials and sub-shrubs. They are only hardy in warmer districts, but even here are often cut to the ground by frosts. They can be brought through a winter in other areas by providing some form of protection. Plant out in spring in any good garden soil. They like a sheltered, sunny position. The fruit of several species are poisonous.

Cortaderia (Gramineae). Pampas Grass. Provide a site that is furnished with well-drained soil and plenty of sun. Once planted they are likely to remain there indefinitely so make certain that the soil is free of perennial weeds. Plant out in spring. When splitting do not divide into too-small pieces. Cut foliage and stems to the ground each spring before growth starts. Traditionally, the tops are burnt off but this looks horrible for a long time before it is masked by the new growth, so avoid this method by cutting off the stems and leaves, as low to the ground as possible. Wear leather gloves as this grass can inflict severe cuts. For the same reason avoid putting any plants in close proximity to the pampas, otherwise the blades, swinging in the wind and acting as a scythe, will soon reduce them to tatters.

Corydalis (Papaveraceae). Most of this genus are best treated as alpine plants, but *CC. lutea, ochroleuca, cheilanthifolia* and the annual *sempervirens* are often grown in the open border. They must all have a well-drained soil but will grow in either sun or light shade. Most will self-sow (without being a nuisance), with walls being a favourite habitat. They need very little attention.

Cosmos (Compositae). This genus is mainly treated as annuals with the exception of *C. atrosanguineus*. This needs a well drained but fertile soil and a sunny position. It is not entirely hardy, with slugs and winter wet possible causing as many losses as frosts. The tubers can either be lifted and stored like dahlias or left in the ground and protected by a mulch. Plant them reasonably deeply, about 15cm (6in) should do. Another cause of winter loss is the lack of appreciation that this plant is very late to emerge, often not until early summer, so it is frequently either overplanted or disturbed in the spring. Label it clearly to avoid this. Deadhead.

Crambe (Cruciferae). Seakale. These need to have a free-draining soil otherwise their fleshy roots are inclined to rot off. On heavier soils add grit or sharp sand to the soil and make certain that there is no stagnant water likely to accumulate in the planting hole. Some forms of *C. cordifolia* wither after flowering and need cutting back, others produce a crop of seeds and remain presentable for some time. Cut *C. maritima* to the ground after flowering to get a second flush of leaves. Cabbage white butterflies lay their eggs on the leaves and the resulting caterpillars will completely wreck the foliage unless they are picked off (or the eggs are squashed). Slugs and snails can also be a menace, particularly as growth begins in spring. They are not the easiest of plants to move but if they need to be transplanted to another position do so in early winter as long as the weather is fine. Alternatively take root cuttings at the same time of year and start off with new plants.

Crassula (Crassulaceae). A very large genus of succulent plants that are generally tender, although they can be grown in warmer districts. It is essential to have a light, free-draining soil and a warm, sunny position. Winter protection, both from rain and cold, is usually needed. They can be grown in pots and moved under glass for the winter where they should be kept on the dry side.

Crepis (Compositae). Hawksbeards. A dandelion-like genus that likes well-drained soil and a sunny position. Regular deadheading helps to keep it flowering (unless you want to collect seed). Plant out while young as they resent disturbance. They are not long-lived and replacements should be kept on hand. Label so that they are not mistaken for dandelions when out of flower and weeded out.

Crinum (Amaryllidaceae). These like a deep soil, well treated with organic material to help keep it moist. Surprisingly some can also be grown in shallow water. Buy and plant out only those bulbs that are fresh; refuse dried-out specimens. Plant with the neck of the bulb level with the surface of the soil. They take a while to settle down and prefer not to be disturbed. An organic mulch applied during the winter is appreciated.

Crocosmia (Iridaceae). Montbretia. These are not too happy in the heavier soils and appreciate some grit or sharp sand added to make it free draining. However, they also dislike light soils that dry out so there should also be a good amount of organic material to create the proverbial moisture-retentive, free-draining soil. Some, especially *C.* 'Solfatare' (which is also not completely hardy), seem to be very particular about soil requirements and you may need to experiment in different places in the garden until they are happy. Plant out in autumn as they send out stolons early in the spring, which form new corms. In hot, dry summers they can suffer badly from red-spider mite. The foliage and seed heads of most crocosmias can be an attractive feature during autumn so do not be in too much of a hurry to cut them to the ground. Some crocosmia, *C. masonorum*, for example, can become very congested, to the extent of pushing each other to the surface and even out of the ground. Lift, divide and replant having rejuvenated the soil. When lifting for transplanting or division do not split away the underneath corms as they are storage organs for the main bulb. They are generally hardy and trouble-free, although in very cold areas they may need to be lifted and stored like gladioli.

Crocus (Iridaceae). A wide range of soils are tolerated as long as they are reasonably well-drained. Choose a sunny position, although a few, such as *CC. vernus* and *tommasinianus* and the large golden *C. flavus*, will tolerate light shade. Plant the corms about 5cm (2in) deep. They need dividing when they become overcrowded. If you have acute problems with mice, which adore crocus corms, try planting the yellow *C. korolkowii* which they seem to ignore. Besides mice, rabbits can also be a nuisance, eating off all the above ground parts. Another problem is from sparrows tearing the flowers apart. You can tie black cotton across the plants to deter the birds or they can be planted under deciduous shrubs which usually seem to afford protection. If naturalized in grass do not mow until the foliage has died down.

Crucianella (Rubiaceae). The main species, *C. stylosa*, has been moved to *Phuopsis*.

Cunila (Labiatae). Dittany. These aromatic herbs can be grown in any good garden soil, although they prefer them to be moisture-retentive. A sunny position is required. Cut back after flowering in the autumn.

Curtonus (Iridaceae). These are not too happy in the heavier soils and appreciate some added grit or sharp sand to make them lighter and freer draining. However, they should not become too dry and organic material may be added to remedy this. Plant in the spring at a depth of about 7.5cm (3in). They like a warm, sunny position. They are generally hardy but will require a winter mulch or similar protection in colder areas. In really cold areas lift and treat like gladioli.

Cyclamen (Primulaceae). If buying cyclamen try to buy those that are growing in pots. Never buy dried, shrivelled specimens. Most are essentially woodland plants and enjoy a leafy soil although it should be free-draining. Acid and alkaline soils are equally tolerated. They will in fact grow in surprisingly dry soils and are one of the few things that can be grown under *Aesculus hippocastanum* for example. They will grow in either sun or shade often quite deep shade. Shade is to be preferred in hotter areas. Plant the corms just below the soil surface of the soil. The best time for this is in early autumn. Transplanting or moving cyclamen can also take place this time of year. A light top-dressing of leafmould is beneficial, applied every year in summer after the cyclamen's leaves have died back.

Cynara (Compositae). Cardoon. A deeply-prepared soil, rich in humus but at the same time free-draining is required. They need a sunny, sheltered position. This should be well chosen as they resent disturbance and need not be moved for many years. *C. cardunculus* does not produce seed every year but when it does it is liable to self-sow. These self-sown seedlings need removing before they become too mature. The tall, flowering stems, up to 2.5m (8ft), are not very strong and will need support. Unfortunately canes are not likely to be man enough and stakes will be needed. The leaves are large and smother anything beneath so leave plenty of space around when planting; a good 90cm (3ft) is essential. They are hardy but it is a good idea to protect the crowns with a mulch of bracken in cold areas. Top-dress with well-rotted manure in the late winter before growth restarts. Watch out for blackfly in the early summer as they can attack the tips of the shoots. *C. hystrix* is a lesser plant which needs a very free-draining soil or it will rot off in winter. The globe artichoke, C. *scolymus*, is also smaller and generally needs no support but enjoys a rich soil.

Cynoglossum (Boraginaceae). Hound's Tongue. These are happy in any good, reasonably well-drained garden soil; either acid or alkaline will be suitable as long as they are not too impoverished. They also like a sunny position. Some tend to be short-lived so aim to replace them every two to three years. They are not keen on being disturbed so plant out while young or sow *in situ*.

Cypella (Iridaceae). These bulbous plants are only hardy in warmer areas. C. *herbertii* is the hardiest although this will need a warm, sheltered position. It also requires a light, free-draining soil. Plant out in late spring at about 7.5cm (3in) below the soil surface. In colder areas they can be lifted in autumn and overwintered. Any self-sown seedlings are likely to be killed in winter. Pot them up until big enough to plant out.

Cypripedium (Orchidaceae). Lady's Slipper Orchids. These rare orchids are not the easiest of plants to grow and should not be attempted if you are a beginner otherwise you may be confronted with expensive losses. Only buy plants that have origins in cultivation as those in the wild are rapidly being depleted by unscrupulous collecting. They like a cool, peaty soil in a light shade. The soil should be free-draining but should never dry out. Unfortunately they are rather finicky as to the precise soil composition and it takes experience to provide the correct mixture. Plant out in the autumn with the crown of the plant just beneath the soil's surface. Top-dress annually in winter with leafmould. Once established they resent disturbance.

Cyrtomium (Aspleniaceae). See *Phanerophlebia*

Cystopteris (Aspleniaceae). Bladder Ferns. These ferns like a well-drained soil in a shady position. C. *bulbifera* is a good plant for shade on chalky soil. It likes free-draining soil and grows well, along with other members of the genus, on walls.

Dactylis (Gramineae). Orchard Grass. A monotypic genus consisting of one grass of which there are several forms. They can be grown in most good garden soil as long as they are reasonably well drained. In sun is the preferred position but they will grow in a light shade. Cut back in the winter. They are clump-forming and do not run.

Dactylorizha (Orchidaceae). There are a few hardy species that are grown in the open garden (most of which have been transferred from *Orchis*). They like a deep, humus-rich soil that is moisture-retentive. Addition of leafmould to the soil before planting is advantageous. Top-dress in the winter with leafmould or well-rotted compost. Most prefer a light shade but will also grow in the open as long as they are not allowed to dry out. Every few years they can be split up if they are getting congested in a rich border, but can be left to their own devices in grass (they can be grown in grass but do better in deeply cultivated borders). However they are best left undisturbed if possible as the roots are brittle and tangled. Division should take place after flowering in late summer. Remove the flower stalks so that energy is not lost to seed production, but channelled into regeneration. Most orchids dislike any form of garden chemicals so do not spray on or near them.

Dahlia (Compositae). Dahlias will grow in any deeply-cultivated, fertile garden soil. It should have plenty of well-rotted organic material added to it, both to feed and provide moisture for the plants. They must be planted in a sunny position. Plant about 12.5cm (5in) deep. They are tender in most areas and need to be lifted in late autumn or around the first frosts and overwintered in a dry, frost-free place. They need to be dried off and dusted with fungicide. In warmer areas it may be possible to bring them through the winter by mulching with bracken but treat the area with slug pellets otherwise they will open up wounds that will let in diseases. If overwintered in the ground the soil must be very light and free-draining. Unless in a well-sheltered position, or of a dwarf nature, most dahlias will need staking. If growing quality blooms a certain amount of disbudding will be necessary but as a border plant they can be left; although deadheading is beneficial. Slugs are one of the worst enemies. Earwigs tear at the petals, ruining the flowers' appearance. They are also prone to a wide variety of viruses, and fungal diseases as well as attacks by aphids (which often bring in the diseases). If you just grow one or two in the border then burn anything with viral diseases and treat fungal ones with a fungicide. You are more likely to run into problems if you grow a lot of dahlias, in which case a book that includes treatment for all their problems will be a good investment.

Daiswa (Trilliaceae/Liliaceae). This is the resting place of several fugitives from the genus *Paris*, including *P. polyphylla*. They like a moist, woodland-type soil, with plenty of humus incorporated in it. A lightly-shaded position is also preferred but they will grow in sun if the soil contains enough organic material to keep it moist. *P. polyphylla* is late into growth and should be clearly marked so that it is not accidentally dug up or overplanted. Top-dress with leafmould during the winter. They do not seem to suffer from any specific pests or diseases, although slugs may be a problem with emerging growth.

Damasonium (Alismataceae). Starfruit. Waterside plants that can be planted into the mud surrounding a pond or shallow water. In water they can be planted in baskets or directly into the mud. In the latter case make certain that they are anchored down until they root or they may float away.

Darlingtonia (Sarraceniaceae). Californian Pitcher Plant. A genus of a single species of carnivorous plant that can be grown in warmer areas. Plant in a bed comprising peat and sphagnum moss that can be kept wet. A bog garden or a moist peat bed are both ideal. They should be positioned in light shade. In cold areas they should be grown under glass.

Darmera (Saxifragaceae). Umbrella Plant. This genus used to be known as *Peltiphyllum* and consists of only one species, *D. peltata*. It likes boggy conditions in either sun or light shade. Although it does well in waterside plantings it can be grown in any soil where there is sufficient organic material to keep the ground moist. Its large leaves and creeping habit make this a groundcover plant that should be kept away from any treasured plants that it might smother. Once planted no attention is required other than to keep it in check if necessary. An annual mulch of organic material will be beneficial but not essential, as its own dying leaves help to feed the soil.

Datisca (Datiscaceae). False Hemp. A small, two-species genus that can be grown in warmer areas. They like a rich, well-drained soil. It should be deeply cultivated with plenty of well-rotted organic material added to it. A sunny position is necessary. Top-dress in the winter with manure or compost.

Datura (Solanaceae). Thorn Apple. These are annuals and shrubs but the annual *D. stramonium* regularly self-sows making it an honorary perennial. It must have a warm, sunny position for the best results, indeed it is unlikely to grow unless it is warm enough. A free-draining soil is important, light sandy ones providing the ideal, although they will grow on chalk. If planted in containers they should be watered regularly, at least once a day in hot weather. The fruit is poisonous.

Davallia (Davalliaceae). Haresfoot Fern. These are mainly tender plants but *D. mariesii* can be tried outside in warmer areas. It enjoys a moist, woodland-type soil incorporating plenty of well-rotted humus, but it should also include grit so that it is free draining. A light, shady position is necessary. Their rhizomes run around just above the soil and should not be covered. If these ferns need moving or splitting do so before growth commences in the spring. Cut off the old leaves of the deciduous forms in winter as they break into growth early, although it may be beneficial to leave the old fronds as protection. Top-dress with leafmould in winter.

Deinanthe (Hydrangeaceae). The two species in this genus require a moist, but free-draining soil. They are susceptible to drought so ensure that there is plenty of humus in the soil to retain these conditions. A slow-release organic fertilizer also helps. The best plants to put out are pot-grown ones, as transplanted ones take a while to settle down and some may never satisfactorily do so. If you have to move an established plant, do so with the largest rootball possible. Plant out firmly, slightly below the level of that in the pot. Do not allow them to dry out at any point, even after they have flowered. Do not cultivate too deeply around a plant as this is likely to disturb the roots. Weed by hand, using a good mulch if possible. The taller delphiniums are likely to require staking. They can be either supported with one cane per spike or allowed to grow through a mesh of pea-sticks, strings or wires. Tie the base of the stems reasonably tightly but allow the tops to move in the wind if tied too tightly the tops are likely to snap off. After flowering cut off the flower spikes but leave the stems and leaves intact until they naturally die down, when they can be removed. If the stems are cut right to the ground a second flush of flowers may be induced, but this can affect the following year's flowering. Some cultivars have a natural tendency to produce two or more flushes of flowers do not discourage this, but on the other hand do not force the plants to do so. The second flush is often miserable anyway. The emerging shoots in spring are prone to slug and snail attack which can severely damage the stems. Take evasive action. The caterpillars of the delphinium moth can also be a nuisance. Pick the green caterpillars off by hand. Mildew and leaf spot are two fungal diseases that can affect delphiniums. Treat with a fungicide. Top-dress with well-rotted organic material in winter.

Dendranthema (Compositae). Chrysanthemum. These are the florist's chrysanthemums. Most are tender and need lifting for the winter. They should be stored in a frost-free place and either replanted the following year, or better still basal cuttings taken in mid winter from stools brought out into the light and warmth of a greenhouse,

83

and the resulting new plants planted out. Some varieties, such as the older *D.* 'Clara Curtis' and the relatively new *D. pacificum* are hardy in most winters but need cutting back so that new growth comes from the base. Deadhead as the flowers go over to prolong and improve later flowerings. Disbudding can be practiced on appropriate varieties if large show heads are required. Any reasonably fertile garden soil will do, but ill-draining ones are likely to cause losses during winter. Deeply cultivated ones incorporating organic material will produce the best results. Plant out or transplant in spring. Slugs can do a lot of damage to emerging shoots in spring, so take evasive action. Cut back the old stems in autumn. A light mulch of straw can be used in colder districts, but it is advisable to include slug bait. It is also advisable to take some plants inside to insure against losses.

Dennstaedtia (Dennstaedtiaceae). Cup Fern. A large genus of ferns of which one, *D. punctilobula*, is hardy. This is an invasive plant that should only be considered for the wild garden, or where its underground stems can be contained. It is very adaptable, and will grow in a variety of conditions including both sun and shade. It will also grow in dry soil as well as moist ones.

Dentaria (Cruciferae). Toothwort. Most garden-worthy species have been moved off to *Cardamine*.

Deschampsia (Gramineae). Hair Grass. These are clump-forming grasses that grow in a wide range of soils, although they seem to do best in moist ones. It is unusual in that it will grow in light shade in woodland conditions as well as in the open. Cut down during the winter. Plant out in spring.

Dianella (Phormiaceae/Liliaceae). Flax Lily. A medium-sized genus of plants that are mainly tender, but a few can be grown in cooler districts. They like a humus-rich, lime-free soil, that is reasonably free-draining. A warm, lightly-shaded, sheltered position is necessary. Lack of berries may be due to the soil being too dry. Their roots are rhizomatous and they do spread underground, but rarely to the extent of becoming a nuisance.

Dianthus (Caryophyllaceae). Carnations, Pinks. This is a very large genus with thousands of cultivars. The majority must have a free-draining soil that holds a certain amount of moisture. They do best in lightly alkaline soils, but will grow in neutral or even mildly acid ones. They can be seen growing in the light shade of a shrub, but they will be drawn and out of character. It is much better to grow them in full sun where they are not too crowded by other plants. They are all short-lived and it is essential to propagate new plants to replace any losses. It is a good idea to replace old plants every three years at the most. Some, such as the mule pinks, 'Napoleon III' for example, are so floriferous that they often flower themselves to death, and need replacing every year. Pinks benefit from a light dressing of bonemeal applied in early spring. Deadheading keeps the plants neat and will help to keep the modern varieties flowering through the summer and autumn. Slugs can hide under the plant and cause damage in spring. Rabbits love dianthus and can wreck a plant overnight, so protection is essential. Carnations will need some form of support. Many of the pinks, especially the doubles, are top heavy and also benefit from being supported but this is very difficult to do in a natural-looking way, and they usually look better being left. Alternatively avoid those varieties that are tall and floppy. The only other major problem is that many of the pinks split their calyces and allow the petals to spill out in a somewhat blousy manner. 'Mrs Sinkins' is one of the worst offenders. Unless you are thinking of exhibiting, do not worry about it; it is part of their charm.

Diascia (Scrophulariaceae). A surprisingly large genus of 150 species from South Africa. A few are relatively hardy and will stand a reasonable degree of frost. Younger plants seem to come through a winter better than older ones. Looking at the plants and knowing they come from South Africa one would naturally expect them to require a dry position, but in fact they grow in a damp habitat and prefer similar conditions, although they should not be waterlogged with stagnant water. Nor do they seem to appreciate stagnant air, so plant in a reasonably open position avoiding overcrowding with taller plants in a moisture-retentive, but free-draining soil. When the plants get leggy shear over, using some of the material as cuttings to raise new plants. They are not long-lived and should be replaced every three years. Some are likely to disappear suddenly over winter. This may well be due as much to the wet as the cold. It is advisable to take autumn cuttings of all your favourite species to ensure against winter loss. As the season progresses they become very straggly, with a few small flowers at the end of very long, sprawling stems. They will do better if they are cut back towards the end of summer. No particular feeding required. No special pests or diseases, although slugs may shelter under the plants.

Dicentra (Papaveraceae). Bleeding Hearts. Dicentra like to have a moisture-retentive soil that is free-draining but does not dry out too much. They will succeed in sun if the soil is reasonably moist, but they do best where they are protected from the hot mid-day sun. Cut the foliage to the ground as it begins to die back. This happens earliest with *D. spectabilis* which will need attention in the summer. The smaller species, such as *D. formosana*, will usually go on much longer. *D. spectabilis* is not very long-lived and may need replacing every five years by digging it up and replanting the more vigorous crowns after rejuvenating the soil. It is not the easiest of plants to divide and a knife is usually necessary. Split the clump up in such a way as to produce crowns each with a bud and roots. The white form *D.s.* 'Alba' seems to be longer lived. Many of the smaller forms are rhizomatous and spread, and occasionally can be invasive. *D. macrantha* is not a frequently seen plant mainly because it needs woodland conditions with a cool, moist, light-shaded position. The shade is required otherwise its leaves are likely to turn brown. These are hardy plants but the early growth of *D. spectabilis* may be burnt off by frosts or cold winds so some protection from these may be advantageous.

Dictamnus (Rutaceae). Burning Bush, Dittany, Gas Plant. *Dictamnus albus* is the only member of the genus although there are two forms. Both are plants that are slow to establish and dislike being disturbed; they will take a long time to settle down after transplanting. Avoid digging up and dividing it (use seed if you want to increase your stock). Plant out while still small. They like any deeply-cultivated, fertile garden soil as long as it is well-drained. They need to be planted in full sun. Plant out in the spring. It tends to appear quite late in the spring, so avoid damaging the emerging shoots. Slugs and snails like the young shoots so take avoiding action.

Do not be in too much of a hurry to cut back after flowering as the foliage remains attractive.

Dierama (Iridaceae). Angel's Fishing Rod, Wand Flower. Dieramas come from areas of summer rainfall and winter drought so should therefore be grown in soil that does not lie wet in the winter or become too dry during the summer. A deep, well-drained soil with some moisture-retentive organic material would be ideal. *D. pauciflorum* grows at the edges of bogs in the wild and will therefore probably prefer a wetter site. They like to be in an open position, not surrounded by other tall plants, this, of course, also suits them visually. The best time for planting out is during the spring, partly to avoid a winter, before they have established themselves and partly to avoid damaging the brittle roots that are formed after the plant has flowered. They resent being moved after they have been planted so get their positioning right first time. If they look tatty in winter do not shear them over but remove the dead, (brown) leaves by giving them a sharp tug with a gloved hand. If you are not strong enough, cut off just these dead leaves as low as possible. These are hardy plants but tend to be more tender while they are still young. For the first couple of years it might be an idea to give them some form of protection. They do not need supports and look best when the flowering stems are drooping and swinging free in the breeze.

Dietes (Iridaceae). Fortnight Lily. These are iris-like plants that spread by rhizomes into large clumps. A well-drained soil that is reasonably moisture-retentive, and a sunny position are required. Plant about 10cm (4in) deep. Not entirely hardy and can only be grown in warmer areas.

Digitalis (Scrophulariaceae). Foxgloves. Most of the foxgloves are perennial, even *D. purpurea*, which is generally considered an annual or biennial, is perennial in some of its native habitats. In the garden if plants are left in the ground after flowering they will often produce new basal shoots for the following year. However, these are not usually brilliant and the remains of the old plant can make them look scruffy. Since they are so easy to grow from seed, start again each year. They like a light, well-drained soil. Most grow in open situations in full sun, but *D. purpurea* are usually associated with woodlands. However, it is always in the clearings and margins where there is more light and sunshine that they are seen. Nearly all foxgloves seed prolifically. To prevent too many self-sown seedlings remove the annual varieties completely and deadhead the perennial forms once they have finished seeding. With *D. purpurea* the white forms can be identified at seedling stage by the main rib on the reverse of the leaf being a pale green as opposed to flushed purple in the purple forms. Any transplanting is best carried out at as early a stage as possible. They do not seem to have many problems, except one occasionally finds faciated plants in which the flowers are circular. There is no need to remove these plants. Although tall they rarely need staking, indeed they look ugly if they are supported. However it is best to give them a sheltered position if there are problems with wind.

Diphylleia (Berberidiaceae). Umbrella Leaf. This two-species genus prefers a cool, lightly-shaded position. The soil should be a leafy, moisture-retentive one, such as would be found in a woodland. Remove old stems and foliage when the plant dies down. They are spreading but do not need to be divided except for propagational purposes. They are hardy. Do not be in too much of a hurry to cut them back after flowering as the berries are rather attractive.

Diplarrhena (Iridaceae). Butterfly Flag. Plant these out in a well-drained but reasonably moisture-retentive soil in a warm, sunny position. They are not completely hardy and may need some form of winter protection. *D. moraea* is the most hardy and will survive even severe frosts but can suffer winter damp. A sheet of glass is usually sufficient to keep excess moisture at bay. Deadhead after flowering and cut back leaves in autumn.

Dipsacus (Dipsacaceae). Teasels. Monocarpic plants that tend to self-sow, giving the honorary perennial status. They grow in any good garden soil, even quite poor ones, but do best in deeply cultivated ground. A sunny position is best although they will grow in part shade. Do not cut back after flowering as the dried plants are attractive in their own right. The stems and leaves have sharp spines so be careful when handling them or when weeding nearby.

Disporum (Convallariaceae/Liliaceae). Fairybells. This is a genus of woodland plants that like nothing better than a moist, humusy soil and light shade. All spread by underground rhizomes, but most are rarely invasive. However *D. sessile* 'Variegatum' can become rampant, especially in light soils, and it may need to be checked. *D. smithii* can become a nuisance by self-sowing everywhere. Remove its orange berries before they spread, but they are rather decorative so leave them unless selfsowing becomes a real nuisance. Being woodland plants there is no need to cut them back, just let them die back naturally each year. A top-dressing of leafmould in the winter is advantageous.

Dodecatheon (Primulaceae). Shooting Stars. *DD. hendersonii, clevelandii, subalpinum* and *hansenii* all need to be kept dry during the summer, although they enjoy ample moisture during flowering time. Cover with a sheet of glass, grow in a frame or glasshouse, or grow in a very free-draining medium on a raised bed in full sun. The rest need to have moist growing conditions through the year and are best grown in a peat bed in a lightly-shaded position. They are all hardy. If they need transplanting or dividing, do so in early autumn.

Doronicum (Compositae). Leopard's Bane. Several species are grown in gardens all requiring a moisture-retentive soil, although they will tolerate drought once the leaves have died back. They grow in either full sun or light shade. Most gently colonize forming quite large groups but they are generally quite easy to control. Regular lifting and dividing every few years maintains the plants' vigour. Divide in summer after flowering when you can transplant, keeping them well watered; alternatively move in autumn so that they have re-established themselves in time to flower the following spring. Deadhead after flowering as this encourages a sporadic second flowering, and because it makes more of the reasonably attractive foliage. *D. pardalianches* dies right back after flowering, this is a good plant for woodland planting as it will tolerate shade, although it can become invasive. In winter they appreciate a top-dressing of well-rotted organic material.

Dorycnium (Leguminosae). See *Lotus*

Dracocephalum (Labiatae). This genus consists of plants that are botanically very close to *Nepeta* and that are horticulturally treated in a similar manner. They will grow in any fertile garden soil as long as it is free-draining and preferably light. Winter losses can occur on heavier soils. A sunny position is preferred. Some of the taller forms are in need of support, especially if in exposed positions.

Dracunculus (Araceae). Dragon Plant. Plant in a moist, woodland-type soil that contains plenty of humus. Their best position is in partial shade, although they will grow in sun in cooler areas. Before the flowers are pollinated they produce a foetid smell so do not plant near the house or places where you sit. These are rhizomatous plants and they can get congested so divide every few years when the plants are dormant to keep them vigorous. Top-dress in winter with well-rotted manure or other organic matter.

Drepanostachyum (Gramineae). Clump-forming bamboos that are well-behaved alth   bit on the tender side. They will grow on a wide range of soils but prefer a slig....., acid one. Cut out any tatty stems, as low to the ground as possible, and top-dress with organic matter to keep the clump healthy.

Dryas (Rosaceae). Mountain Avens. A genus of sub-shrubs that need space to sprawl and free-draining soil in the sun. As it is low growing it should be positioned so that it is not overcrowded by other plants. It requires little attention once it is established, other than keeping it weed-free.

Dryopteris (Aspleniaceae). Buckler Ferns, Male Fern. These ferns like a moist, humus-rich soil. They can be placed either in full sun or light shade. However, they self sow around the garden, usually indicating the sites they like best. Most are hardy, although *D. wallichiana* is not completely so. Top-dress in winter with well-rotted, organic matter. The deciduous forms should have the old fronds removed before the new ones start to unfurl.

Eccremocarpus (Bignoniaceae). Chilean Glory Flower. This is a small genus of mainly tender plants of which *E. scaber* is most frequently grown. It is often thought of as tender but it frequently survives the winter if planted against a warm wall and can become quite a mature plant. If planted in the open it is more likely to succumb to the winter. In colder areas it should be treated as an annual. It is not fussy about its soil as long as it is free-draining and reasonably fertile. A warm, sunny position is preferred. It can be grown by itself up a trellis but seems to prefer the support of another shrub or climber.

Echeveria (Crassulaceae). Hens-and-Chicken. A large genus of succulent plants that are on the tender side and can only be grown outside in the warmer areas. They are suitable for rock gardens or possibly the edges of borders or paths, but in colder areas they are best grown in pots and moved outside during the summer. They like a well-drained soil in a warm position in full sun. A spreading mat is formed that may need controlling if it is likely to grow into other plants. Cut off the old flowering stems in autumn.

Echinacea (Compositae). Purple Coneflower. These are easy plants to grow in any fertile garden soil and even in quite poor conditions. However they do not do so well on heavier soils. Full sun is preferred although they will take a little shade from neighbouring perennials. The stems are stiff and should not require staking except in exposed areas. They can self-sow and any seedlings that appear should be rogued out to keep the stand pure. If the stand becomes overcrowded or shows signs of diminishing it will need dividing. It is likely to need this anyway every four years or so, but if they look happy do not disturb them. Cut back in the autumn tidy-up. Echinaceae can suffer from mildew. Keeping the soil moist and by avoiding overcrowding the plants should help to mitigate this. Treat with a fungicide if necessary. Slugs may be a problem with new spring growth. In the US it is attacked by Japanese beetle. They are winter hardy.

Echinops (Compositae). Globe Thistle. Any soil suits these plants, even poor ones, but they obviously do better in fertile conditions. They should be given a light, sunny position. Staking should not be necessary except for some of the taller species if planted in windy positions. Seed heads develop quickly so deadhead immediately after flowering if you do not want a forest of seedlings developing. The post-flowering foliage is often very tatty so cut back once the flowers begin to fade is a good thing anyway. They are not easy plants to transplant so get their positions right first time, or start again with new plants. They suffer from mildew which can be treated with fungicide, but since this often happens after the flowering has finished cut the plant to the ground. Plants can suddenly die, often rotting off at the base. This is more likely to happen during wet weather. A well-drained soil helps. The commonly grown species are all hardy.

Echiodes (Boraginaceae). See *Arnebia*

Echium (Boraginaceae). Bugloss. Most of these tend to be annual, biennial or monocarpic. The perennial species are mainly tender and can only be grown in warmer areas, although an increasing number of gardeners are discovering that they can grow them in a sheltered spot. Even the perennials are short-lived. They are tap-rooted and are not easy to transplant so put in position when young. Some, such as the hardy biennial *E. vulgare*, self-sow and any seedlings that are required should be moved as soon as possible, the rest pulled before the roots get too deep. They need a well-drained soil and a warm, sunny position. Remove flowering spikes immediately they over over to reduce the amount of self-sowing.

Eichornia (Pontederiaceae). Water Hawthorn. A somewhat tender, floating water plant that is becoming increasingly popular. In milder areas where it overwinters it can become invasive. Elsewhere it is likely to require overwintering under glass. Select small plants for this and keep them in pots of fibrous compost which permanently stand in water. Plant out after the threat of frosts has passed.

Eleocharis (Cyperaceae). Hair Grass. Some, like *E. acicularis*, are carpeting pond weeds, related to the sedges. Others dwell on the banks. The carpeters are trouble-free plants that needs little attention once planted. They spread across the bottom of the pool where they make fine oxygenators. They need anchoring when first planted but so that they do not float away before they have put their roots down. Other species such as *E. caespitosa* are more sedge-like and will grow in boggy soil or shallow water.

Elsholtzia (Labiatae). Sub-shrubs with mint-like characteristics. Plant out in any fertile garden soil as long as it is reasonably free-draining. A warm, sunny position is best. Cut back hard in the early spring.

Elymus (Gramineae). Blue Lyme Grass. *E. arenarius*, the main species grown, is very beautiful, but spreads like greased lightning. Contain it in some way such as planting in a sunken bucket or other container. If it is allowed to run wild dig it up regularly, removing every bit of it and then replanting with selected pieces. It will grow in a wide range of soils and prefers a sunny position where it colours at its best. The best colour can be maintained by cutting it to the ground once flowering stems start to appear and allowing it to reshoot. It is hardy and useful for binding loose soils such as sand dunes. Others are not so invasive but equally easy to cultivate. *E. virginicus* is a woodlander and needs a shady position.

Endymion (Hyacinthaceae/Liliaceae). See *Hyacinthoides*

Eomecon (Papaveraceae). Dawn Poppy, Snow Poppy. The only species, *E. chionantha*, is a woodlander and likes a cool, moist, humus-rich soil and a lightly-shaded position. It has a creeping, rhizomatous rootstock that can become invasive and is best placed where it cannot swamp other plants. It may be necessary to keep it under control by constantly digging around it if it is planted where it can ramp. Do not plant the rhizomes too deeply, about 7.5cm (3in) will do. An annual mulch of leafmould will be appreciated. Cut back the foliage as it becomes tatty in the early autumn. When the roots are broken or wounded a reddish sap pours forth. This should not cause skin problems if you touch it. Winter protection may be needed in colder areas.

Epilobium (Onagagraceae). Willow Herbs. A large genus of plants of which quite a number are in cultivation. Some are invasive, others are well behaved. One of the worst offenders is the rose-bay willow herb which is very invasive, both by creeping and seeding. The beautiful white form is supposed to be less invasive but can still be a terrible nuisance. Avoid other native species as nearly all are invasive. They will all grow in any reasonable garden soil in a sunny position. Deadhead after flowering to reduce chances of seeding. Some species such as *E. glabellum* are short-lived and need regular replacing. They can be prey to flea beetle which perforates the leaves with many small holes, making the plants look very tatty.

Epimedium (Berberidaceae). Barrenwort. These are essentially woodland plants and appreciate the moist, humusy soil and a lightly-shaded position that they would find there. An annual top-dressing of leafmould will be appreciated. Although they prefer a moist soil they will grow in surprisingly dry situations. Cut off all leaves of the deciduous and semi-evergreen varieties in January or early February, before the new leaves or flower stems start to form. Many are creeping plants and most species will spread to create a good groundcover. However, if planted in a border they are not too difficult to keep under control, and besides there are several that form non-spreading clumps. This will reveal the splendours of the new leaves as they come into growth. There have been reports of sparrows stripping epimedium flowers, *E. pinnatum* in particular. Suspend a few strands of dark cotton over the plants to deter the attackers.

Epipactis (Orchidaceae). Helleborines. The garden forms like to have a moist, humusy soil and a lightly-shaded position. *E. palustris* and *E. gigantea* will grow in boggy conditions or on stream banks. *E. palustris* will grow in an open position as long as the soil is kept reasonably moist. It can become invasive, not a problem normally associated with orchids. An annual mulch of leafmould is beneficial. Do not cut down the old flower heads until they have seeded they may produce self-sown seedlings.

Eragrostis (Gramineae). Love Grass. A very large genus of which a few species are in cultivation. They are generally clump-forming and non-invasive, although they may well self-sow. Plant in spring in a well-drained soil in a light, open position. Cut back towards the end of winter.

Eranthis (Ranunculaceae). Winter Aconites. Creeping, rhizomatous plants that enjoy a humus-rich, but well-drained soil in light shade or sun, if the soil is not allowed to dry out. If buying new plants try and acquire them growing in pots. Packs of dried tubers are difficult to establish and should be avoided. They have died back below ground by late spring so mark them carefully if there is any chance that they may be accidentally overplanted or disturbed. Once established they self-sow.

Eremostachys (Labiatae). Plant out in any fertile, well-drained garden soil. They should have a sunny position. Cut back after flowering.

Eremurus (Asphodelaceae/Liliaciae). Foxtail Lilies. Plant in a well-drained, but fertile soil with the crown just below (10–15cm (4–6in)) the surface of the soil. Do not plant too close together as the roots from each crown become quite extensive. Traditionally they have been planted on beds of sand or gravel to improve the drainage and to deter slugs. If possible make a slight mound of this, so the crown sits on it with the roots hanging down on either side. (This is a good way of planting them even if they are planted directly onto soil.) They like a warm, sunny position, away from drying winds. Avoid buying plants that have dried out as they are difficult to establish. Indeed, be careful not to let roots dry out when transplanting. They are also very brittle so handle them carefully. Shoots can emerge before the last frosts. If possible protect them from these. Older plants are more susceptible as the crowns tend to rise to the surface as they age. As a matter of course these should be given a protection of bracken or something similar. If you need to move or split up established clumps do so in mid-summer after they have finished flowering and when the foliage has died down. Avoid disturbing in early spring as although there is nothing to see above ground, they are already stirring and can be fatally damaged. Try not to dig or hoe near as the roots are near the surface and can be easily damaged. Once they have flowered the foliage dies down and should be removed. Mark them clearly so that they are not damaged or overplanted in the autumn. The flowering stems are very tall and may need staking if the situation is exposed, but they look better if they can grow free. Slugs and snails can cause a lot of damage to emerging shoots, particularly after a mild winter.

Erica (Ericaceae). Heather. Although strictly a shrub these are often used as front-of-border plants. Heathers must have a lime-free soil, *E. carnea* is the one exception to this as it will tolerate mild alkalinity. Although they grow well in sandy, free-draining soils they are susceptible to drought so make certain that there is a reasonable amount of humus in the soil. A sunny position is best. They can be grown in light shade but the plants become very leggy and out of character. Even in the open these can get leggy but can be kept compact by lightly sheering them over after they have finished flowering. Cut no further into them than necessary to remove the dead flowers. Do not reduce to stumps or they will not survive. In winter a top-dressing of well-rotted organic material is appreciated.

Erianthus (Gramineae). See *Saccharum*

Erigeron (Compositae). Fleabanes. This is a large genus of relatively easy to grow plants. They will grow in any fertile garden soil, and will do well in quite dry soils, *E. karvinskianus* even growing in dry stone walls. A little shade is tolerated but they will do best in full sun. Cut back the large-flowered forms to the ground after flowering. The low-growing forms can be cut back in late spring if they are getting too leggy. The small-flowered *E. karvinskianus* blooms over such a long period that it is often considered an almost permanent feature, and as such little attention is given to it. However, if it is clipped over in spring it makes a much neater plant. It self-sows mildly but is rarely a nuisance, which is fortunate as there are too many flower heads to make it worthwhile deadheading. *E. philadelphicus* also sows very freely and should be cut back if possible. Some of the taller forms are rather floppy and need to be carefully supported with invisibly placed pea-sticks. Most are hardy and come through the majority of winters unscathed. There may be problems with slugs eating the young shoots, particularly after a mild winter.

Eriogonum (Polygonaceae). Wild Buckwheat. This large genus are mainly tender although a few can be grown in milder areas. Wet as well as cold is an enemy and is essential that the soil is free-draining. It is also important to have a warm sunny site. They are difficult plants to move as they have tap roots, so put them in their final positions while they are still young and avoid transplanting. A sheet of glass or a polythene light placed over the smaller ones may help them through the winter. Trim the plants after flowering.

Eriophyllum (Compositae). *E. lanatum* is the species usually grown. This likes a well-drained soil, and will often grow in quite poor conditions. It should be planted in a sunny position. A bit on the tender side and is best grown in warmer areas.

Erodium (Geraniaceae). Storksbills. A large genus of which the majority are probably too small for the herbaceous border. Some, such as *E. manescavii*, are eminently suitable. They all like a well-drained soil and a sunny position. Cut back the flowering stems after flowering as many of them have the habit of self-sowing, although not to the point of becoming a nuisance.

Eryngium (Umbelliferae). Sea Hollies. This is a very large genus of plants of which at least forty species and cultivars are in cultivation. Any fertile garden soil will do as long as it is reasonably well-drained. The soil should not be overfed otherwise growth becomes soft. In fact many seem to thrive on a spartan diet. A sunny position is required. These plants have deep tap-roots and should be placed in their flowering positions at an early age. Transplanting should be avoided. Wear gloves when handling or weeding near them, especially near some of the strap-leaved forms which have spines like razors. The young growth of some such as *E. tripartitum*, are prone to attack by blackfly and will need attention. Cut down during the autumn tidy-up. The monocarpic *E. giganteum* has a tendency to seed everywhere. Cut it back before it has a chance as the resulting seedlings are often difficult to remove. Most are hardy but they dislike winter damp which sometimes causes them to rot off at the base. Some of the taller forms may need discreet staking to prevent them flopping over. Even smaller species such as *E. tripartitum* can open up if they are not supported by pea-sticks. Grit will help to improve the drainage.

Erysimum (Cruciferae). Wallflowers. The most commonly known forms of wall-flowers are those that are treated as biennials. In fact the majority are perennial, albeit often short-lived perennials. Their life can be extended by growing them in a well-drained soil. Plants grown, for example, in a wall are not so large as those in a border but they live much longer. They also prefer a sunny site. Remove flowering stems as they finish flowering to keep the plant compact. Avoid the common problem of planting in a windy position where wind-rock forms a conical hole round the base of the plant which fills with water and kills the plant. Try not to plant Erysimum repeatedly in the same ground as they can suffer from club root. Burn any infected plants. As they are not long lived it is a good idea to take cuttings annually (in summer) of favourite plants to insure against winter loss.

Erythronium (Liliaceae). Dog-tooth Violets. Although some species grow out in the open these are essentially shade lovers and need to be planted in a humus-rich soil in semi-shade, reminiscent of their woodland homes. *E. dens-canis*, however, can be planted in the open where they will naturalize in a lawn or meadow garden. Plant vertically so that there is about 12.5cm (5in) of soil or leafmould above the bulb. If the tubers are not in growth the bottom can be determined by the rough scar of the previous year's roots. Do not buy bulbs that have dried out; success with these will be very limited. Only purchase from nurseries which offer bulbs that have been kept moist either by growing them in pots or stored under special conditions. Some clump-forming species and cultivars such as *E. tuolumnense* or *E.* 'White Beauty' become congested after two or three years and should be split up after this time during the early autumn. Feeding is not necessarily required but they like a free-draining, moisture-retentive soil containing a high humus level, so mulching with leafmould is advantageous. They prefer slightly acidic soils but will grow on chalk if sufficient humus has been added to the soil.

Eschscholzia (Papaveraceae). Californian Poppy. Although treated as an annual many of these are in fact tender or short-lived perennials. Even when treated as annuals they usually self-sow so that they come up each year and can be counted as honorary perennials (named cultivars and strains are unlikely to come true). They like a well-drained, even a poor soil and plenty of sunshine to perform at their best. They are tap-rooted and therefore resent disturbance, so if you need to transplant any, do so while they are still young. The same applies to seedlings. Seed can be sown in pots but it is better sown *in situ* to avoid disturbance. Deadheading prolongs the flowering period and prevents too much self-sowing.

Eucomis (Hyacinthaceae/Liliaceae). Pineapple Flower. Somewhat tender bulbs but they can be left in the ground under a layer of mulch where they will survive most winters. They must have a sunny position. They like ample water during the growing season but should be dry during dormancy, thus a well-drained soil is essential. A raised bed or rock garden will help with the drainage. A wall or rocks behind (or next) to the plants keeps them warm. They can suffer badly from slugs, and vine weevils can also cause problems.

Eupatorium (Compositae). Bone Set, Hemp Agrimony. These are mainly large plants and need plenty of space to grow, particularly as many are rhizomatous and can spread to form large colonies. They will grow in any fertile garden soil but prefer it to be moisture-retentive, so add plenty of well-rotted, organic material when the bed is being prepared. They make good plants to grow in any damp part of the garden or for naturalizing beside water features. *EE. cannabinum* and *purpureum* in particular are good for this purpose. They do best in a sunny position but tolerate a little light shade. They may need staking in exposed areas. Hidden pea-sticks topped to about

90–120cm (3–4ft) depending on species are best. *E. rugosum* benefits from staking in most situations. *EE. perfoliatum* and *rugosum* are poisonous to farm animals. Some, *E. cannabinum* in particular, self-sow, so cut off flowering stems before the seed is scattered. Cut back other forms after flowering or in the autumn/winter tidy-up.

Euphorbia (Euphorbiaceae). Spurge. Euphorbias generally like a warm sunny position although some, like *E. amygdaloides*, especially in its variety *robbiae*, will grow in shade, even dry shade – a useful characteristic. They like well-drained soils and do best in light ones. Transplant euphorbias as young as possible as they resent disturbance, try to keep a good root ball with them during this operation. Many euphorbia will self-sow, their explosive dispersal mechanism sending the seed some distance. This rarely becomes a nuisance, although some attention is required to prevent seedlings becoming too widespread. *EE. lathyris, hybernia, coralloides*, and *wallichii* seem to be amongst the worst offenders. Spreading by runners can, however, become a problem with some species, *EE. cyparissias* and *pseudovirgata* (*uralensis*) being two of the worst. Never allow either of these into a border without thought. They rapidly spread over a wide area and are very difficult to eradicate, making them possibly suitable for a wild part of the garden but not for an orderly border. Others, *E. griffithii* or *E. sikkimensis* also spread but at not quite such a rapid pace. They move faster in light soils, slower in heavy ones. I have *E.g.* 'Dixter' which has only reached the size of a dinner plate after 10 years in heavy clay. *E. amygdaloides robbiae* will grow in either quite dense shade or full sun. It has a habit of spreading, often dying out in its original position. Removing the old flower stems helps prolong the life of plants, thus preventing bald patches. Clear away the old foliage of the non-evergreen species as it dies back in the autumn or during the winter clear-up. Do not leave this too late as most euphorbias begin to shoot early in the year and are easily damaged when old stems are being removed. Many of this vast genus come from warm countries and are not suitable for outdoor cultivation (the poinsettia, *E. pulcherrima* for example) but with the exception of *E. mellifera* which needs a warm spot the majority of garden forms are hardy. *E. rigida* is sometimes thought to be a bit tender but seems to come through even extreme winters if planted against a wall. Some of the *E. amygdaloides* group, such as *E.a.* 'Rubra' and the hybrid *E. x martinii*, suffer from mildew. This can be treated with a fungicide but in the case of the former it usually occurs after the plant has had its moment of glory and when it is beginning to look tatty, so it can be cut down. Cut out the seeding stems of *E. characias, E.c. wulfenii* and any of the earlier-flowering euphorbias when they begin to look tatty in the summer or early autumn. However in some, *E. rigida* for example, the bracts stay colourful for a long time after flowering and the stems should be left as long as possible before removing. Some euphorbias can be left in the ground almost indefinitely, others such as *E. polychroma* and *E. seguieriana niciciana* need regular replacement to keep the clumps vigorous and fresh-looking. The white sap that oozes from a euphorbia, when it is cut or damaged, can cause irritation and rashes to some skins, so it is advisable to wear gloves when dealing with them. Sap in the eye is extremely painful so never rub them with sappy fingers or otherwise allow sap to come near them. When tidying up weed around the plants before cutting them back to avoid touching the cut stems.

Euryops (Compositae). These shrubby perennials are mainly tender but *E. acraeus* can be grown, even in cooler areas, as long as it has a free-draining soil and a sunny position. Sheer over to remove flower heads after flowering.

Evolvulus (Convolvulaceae). Sub-shrubs that are a bit on the tender side but can be grown in warmer areas in a protected site. The soil must be light and very free-draining.

Fallopia (Polygonaceae). A relatively new genus comprising species from *Polygonum* and *Reynoutria*. Most of these species tend to be either rapid spreaders (such as *F. japonica* (*P. cuspidatum*) or vigorous climbers (*F. baldschuanica* for example), both groups being invasive and requiring regular digging out and cutting back. Be certain that you want them before introducing any of them. They will grow (only too well) in any good garden soil and are happy in either sun or light shade. The spreaders need to be cut to the ground during the autumn/winter clear-up. Climbers will require cutting back if you need to contain them, otherwise just let them go.

Fauria (Menyanthaceae). See *Nephrophyllidium*

Felicia (Compositae). These daisy-like plants are generally tender in colder areas but can be perpetuated by taking cuttings in early autumn and overwintering under glass. *F. petiolata* seems to be quite hardy, especially if planted against a warm wall. They require good, fertile soil and a warm, sunny position. While most like a free-draining soil and will tolerate quite dry soils, an adequate supply of moisture is required for good flowering. Also, deadheading prolongs the flowering season. Cut back near the base during the autumn/winter clear-up to keep the plants compact.

Ferula (Umbelliferae). Fennel. These fennels are large and need plenty of space. They also require a deep, well-cultivated soil as they have very long tap roots. The soil should be moisture-retentive and well-laced with organic material. They can self-sow prodigiously, the tap roots making the seedlings difficult to extract, so deadhead after flowering before the seed is ready to drop. Cut to the ground in the autumn/winter clear-up. *F. tingitana* can be on the tender side and may need a protected site with a well-drained soil.

Festuca (Gramineae). Fescue. Tufted grasses that should not run or become a nuisance. Most grow in a sunny position but *F. gigantea* unusually for grasses, will grow in shade. Plant in well-drained, but fertile soil. The young leaves are the most attractive so pull out all the dead growth by raking the fingers through it in early spring. Alternatively, shear hard at the same time of year. The foliage is of a more brilliant colour if the plants are kept vigorous by frequent division (in spring).

Filipendula (Rosaceae). Meadowsweets. With the exception of *F. vulgaris*, which likes a dry situation, these are plants of moist, or even boggy soils. They must have a moisture-retentive ground and should be watered during dry spells otherwise they will begin to look sad with their leaves becoming scorched in the sun. *F. ulmaria* 'Variegata' has a tendency to revert to green and its seedlings are also plain. *F. u.* 'Aurea' is more stable but is liable to scorch in full sun. *F. vulgaris*, dropwort, can be a nuisance in borders; it is a rather floppy plant and needs support. However, its worst sin is that it has a habit of spreading. It forms brown tubers which are difficult to see in the soil, and some at least, invariably get left behind when a plant is moved. Since it is a native of dry, chalk meadows it is a plant to use in a wild garden but of this type, not in the border. It can look dreadful as it goes over so cut it back as soon as possible after flowering. In exposed positions some will need staking but *FF. palmata* and *purpurea* are generally strong enough to support themselves. Some forms can suffer badly from mildew, often brought about by being too dry. Cut back when they become tatty or during the autumn/winter clear-up. A winter mulch of organic material will help to preserve moisture around the roots.

Foeniculum (Umbelliferae). Fennel. Large plants that smell strongly of aniseed when touched. They will grow in any well-drained garden soil, even poor ones. A sunny site is best. These can self-sow prodigiously if the seed heads are not removed in time. Unfortunately they always seem to sow in other plants and their deep tap roots make them difficult to extract. If these seedlings are needed for transplanting, carry out this operation while they are still very young, before their roots have gone down too deeply. Another advantage of cutting down early (mid-autumn) is that a new growth of foliage will appear which will mask the stumps during the winter.

Fragaria (Rosaceae). Strawberries. These will grow in any good garden soil but prefer those that are relatively humus rich. The alpine varieties will grow in quite dry conditions including banks. The fruiting varieties need full sun but others, such as *F. daltonia* will grow in quite dense shade. Strawberries spread by runners and these can make them invasive. The smaller ones such as *F. vesca* 'Multiplex' (*F.* 'Bowles Double') can be particularly bothersome in borders as they are difficult to remove from amongst other plants. Weeding them out of Irises, for example, is tiresome and time consuming. They are best planted in wild or semi-wild areas where they can romp at will. Many will produce fruit of varying sizes. You will have to keep the birds away if you hope to harvest them.

Francoa (Saxifragaceae). Bridal Wreath. These are mainly tender plants but with care they can be overwintered outside in warmer areas. Elsewhere they need to be taken inside for the winter, or treated as annuals. To survive outside they must have a free-draining soil and a warm, sunny position. Cut off the stems when they have finished flowering.

Fritillaria (Lilaceae). A large genus of bulbous plants with a surprising number in cultivation. However many are grown either in pots or in a bulb frame. This still leaves quite a number that can be grown in the open garden. They will thrive in any good garden soil. *F. meleagris* even grow in quite damp soils and is ideal for naturalizing in water meadow-like situations. It will also grow in drier borders and meadows. The tall *F. imperialis* sometimes causes problems. It likes an open position where it is not shaded. The soil should not be too rich, and preferably neutral or alkaline. Add lime to the soil to bring the pH up to at least 7, preferably 7.5. Plant quite deeply 15–20cm (6–8in) is about right. It also likes a position that dries out in summer. This is difficult to achieve in the open in a temperate climate but try planting the bulbs near a thirsty bush which takes a lot of the moisture from the soil when it is in leaf. *F. camschatcensis* presents a different problem. The bulb often forms masses of bulbils ('rice') below ground rather than sending up a flower stem, and can remain 'blind' for several years. Make certain that it is planted in a moist, humusy soil in light shade. All these bulbs benefit from a light dressing of a potash-rice fertilizer in the early spring before growth commences. Any splitting or transplanting should be carried out soon after the plant has died down.

Fuchsia (Onagraceae). Fuchsias do not like drought conditions. Add plenty of organic material to the soil before planting and regularly top-dress it in order to keep the soil moisture-retentive. They like a cool situation, away from the baking sun, but resent overhanging trees. Frosts will kill off most top growth during the winter so they should be cut back in late winter before new growth begins. Some gardeners like to leave the dead stems on as long as possible to give some protection from the frost to the crown of the plant. Others are happy to remove it at anytime during winter. Hardy fuchsias, as well as those that have survived a mild winter, flower better if they are cut to the ground although they will flower earlier if they are left. Plant fuchsias so that the crown is below the surface as frost protection. A mulch of bracken or grit may also help in colder areas. Those that are grown in containers, including standard plants, can be overwintered under glass or in a frost-free shed. Fuchsias suffer from capsid bugs which damage the tips of the shoots. Spray with the relevant insecticide.

Gaillardia (Compositae). Blanket Flower. These are useful plants for gardens that are prone to droughts. They thrive in well-drained, even dry and poor soils. They are short-lived if the conditions are too heavy, moist or fertile. On clay soils they can be grown in raised beds. They must have a sunny position. Some form of support is usually required as they tend to be a bit floppy. Deadhead as the flowers pass over. It can be attacked by a downy mildew. The particular variety to which it is prone appears to be the same as that that attacks lettuces, so plant them away from the vegetable garden. Treat with a fungicide or discard affected plants.

Galanthus (Amaryllidaceae). Snowdrops. Few gardeners can resist these bulbous plants that flower in winter. They will grow in any good garden soil as long as it is not too dry or hot. A humusy, woodland-type soil is best. Plant at a depth of between 5–7.5cm (2–3in). They are probably best planted in light shade under deciduous trees or shrubs. They can also be grown amongst herbaceous plants that will shade them during the hot months. Avoid buying dried-out bulbs. They should always be transplanted without drying out. It does not matter when this is but the favoured time recently has been just after the flowers have finished and before the leaves disappear. This is probably not the best time (when they are dormant is best), but they are then easy to find at this time and also they are still there to remind you to do it. Do not allow clumps to become too congested otherwise they will force each other out of the ground. Divide at the first signs of overcrowding.

Galax (Diapensiaceae). Beetleweed. A monotypic genus represented by *G. urceolata*. This is a woodland plant that likes to have a moist, acid, humusy soil. As befits its habitat, it also likes a shady situation. It is evergreen with attractive winter foliage, so do not cut back.

Galega (Leguminosae). Goat's Rue. These fresh-looking plants which grow on quite a range of soils including quite poor ones. However, a deeply-tilled soil with the addition of well-rotted, organic material will produce the best plants. A sunny position is to be preferred. Plant out while they are still quite young as they do not like being moved at a later stage. They will last a good number of years in the same place. They form loose, open plants that usually need staking with pea-sticks to prevent flopping over. Cut back to the ground once flowering is over. *G. orientalis* has rhizomatous roots and can be invasive.

Galeobdolon (Labiatae). See *Lamium*

Galium (Rubiaceae). Bedstraws. Plant out in any good garden soil, but they do best if the soil does not dry out too much. They prefer a lightly-shaded position but will also grow in the sun if the soil is not too dry. They will form ground cover but always seem happiest if they can scramble up through other plants. However they can become invasive if they are too happy. Cut to the ground as soon as they begin to look tatty.

Galtonia (Hyacinthaceae/Liliaceae). Summer Hyacinth. These bulbs like to have a deeply-cultivated, fertile soil with well-rotted, organic material incorporated into it. They are not too happy on light sandy or heavy clay soils. They do best in a sunny position. Plant in spring at a depth of about 15cm (6in) and at least 30cm (12in) apart as they form quite big plants. They are hardy in most areas, but in places where the ground is likely to freeze solid it is best to lift and store in a frost-free place over winter. Do not let them dry out during the growing season, but they are best kept dry once they have died down. Although the flowering stems get quite tall they do not require staking. Cut off the flower spikes after flowering as they are liable to self-sow.

Gaura (Onagraceae). These are pretty, short-lived perennials that need a well-drained soil. They will tolerate quite dry conditions which makes them useful plants in areas afflicted with drought. A sunny situation is also required. They are a wiry plant that normally do not require staking. Gauras are frequently lost on heavier soils during a mild, wet winter. Remove the spikes as they finish and cut back the plant during the autumn/winter clear-up.

Gazania (Compositae). Treasure Flower. Must have a warm sunny position. Too tender to be left outside except in warmer areas, but can easily be perpetuated by overwintering cuttings taken in autumn. They will grow in any good, fertile soil, but it must be free-draining. A sunny position is essential. Plant about 30cm (12in) apart. They rarely need staking. Deadhead as necessary.

Gelasine (Iridaceae). A bulbous plant that will only overwinter outside in the warmer areas. Elsewhere it should be lifted and stored until the following spring. Plant out in a well-drained, moisture-retentive soil about 7.5cm (3in) below the surface. It does best in a warm, sunny position. Feed with a high potash fertilizer in spring.

Gentiana (Gentianaceae). Gentians. Like their smaller brethren, much beloved by alpine gardeners, the border gentians need a cool, moisture-retentive soil, made so by the addition of well-rotted organic material of some kind. Some, such as the willow gentian, *G. asclepiadea*, prefer a lightly-shaded position, while those from open meadows, *G. lutea* for example, prefer full sun. Once they are happy do not move them as they resent disturbance. Cut back in the autumn/winter clear-up, although the dead stems do have a certain quality that makes them attractive throughout the winter. If left, remove them before the new growth starts in the spring. Top-dress with organic matter such as leafmould in the winter or early spring. Do not allow them to dry out in the growing season.

Geranium (Geraniaceae). Cranesbills, Hardy Geraniums. This is a large genus with diverse needs. However most will grow in any fertile garden soil, but benefit by having plenty of well-rotted, organic material incorporated into the ground when it is dug. Most will grow in full sun, especially if they have a moisture-retentive soil, but nearly all will grow well in light shade. Those that do particularly well in shade include *GG. phaeum, macrorrhizum, sylvestris, nodosum, endressi, x oxonianum, psilostemon* and *versicolor*. A top-dressing of organic material helps. *GG. pratense, himalayense,* and 'Mrs Kendall Clark', and most of the other taller forms need to be cut hard back after flowering; they will make a neat hump of new leaves. *G. endressii* and *G.* x *oxonianum* also need a trim as soon as they get too floppy. It is no good waiting until they are out of flower as they go on producing them, even on the sprawled plant. Another advantage of cutting back is that it reduces the self-sowing, which both do a little bit too vigorously. Both these and *G. pratense* can get too large and formless and are better for dividing every few years. The latter is deep-rooted and deep digging is required to get it up without too much damage to the roots. In wilder areas they can be left to their own devices. *G. macrorrhizum* is an evergreen and unless it is getting over-vigorous does not require cutting back. However it can self-sow, so it is an idea to shear off the flower heads after they have flowered in spring. This also makes the plant look neater. It can become rather vigorous, starting to creep over other plants without it being noticed. Keep a check on the margins of the plant and cut back if necessary to prevent it swamping others. *G.* 'Russell Prichard' is a scrambling plant and need not be cut back. It may be sterile as it does not appear to seed and is not a nuisance. *G. procurrens* is late into flower and creates a great swathe of blooms, but it can be a menace. It roots wherever it touches the ground, sending down a deep tap root that once established is difficult to remove as any piece left in the soil will reshoot. It should only be admitted to wilder borders where it can ramp at will. *G. nodosum* can present the same problem. Clear away the old foliage of the non-evergreen species as it dies back in the autumn or during the winter clear-up. *G. malviflorum* has a strange life-cycle in that it comes into growth during the winter, flowers in spring and then retires below ground. Be careful that you do not forget it is there during its dormant period and overplant it or otherwise disturb it. Label it well to remind you of its presence. Some of the tall, vigorous or floppy plants, such as *G. psilostemon*, can be kept in check by lifting them in early spring, just enough to break a number of the roots, and then let them settle back again. This will check their growth, making them substantially smaller but not unduly affecting their flowering. A more conventional method to prevent flopping is to provide a pea-stick support at about 75cm (30in). *G.* 'Mrs Kendall Clark' desperately needs support as the stems are weak at the joints and splay outwards in the slightest breeze or shower of rain. Many others of a rounded, clump-forming habit are best staked at an early stage to insure against opening up. These are likely to include GG. *pratense, sylvaticum,* x *oxonianum, magnificum* and possibly *phaeum* in exposed areas. GG. *lambertii, procurrens, wallichianum* 'Salome' and 'Anne Folkard' are all scramblers and will scramble up through and over other plants. *G. thunbergii* self-sows in a most unacceptable way unless you want to use it as groundcover. *G. maderense* is tender and only survives outside in warmer regions. It can be grown in a large pot and moved outside for the summer. *G. traversii* can also be on the tender side and needs a well-drained soil and a warm position. Although there are some other tender species, the majority of the others that are grown in cultivation are completely hardy. Some of the *G. procurrens* crosses, such as 'Salome', have leaves which appear yellow in the early part of the year. This gives them an almost chloritic appearance but this is normal and they green up as the year progresses. Geraniums are generally disease and pest free, except for vine weevil grubs growing through their roots.

Gerbera (Compositae). Transvaal Daisy. These are somewhat tender perennials and can only be overwintered in the ground in warmer regions. They like an organic-rich soil well-drained, and a warm sunny position. Good drainage is important as they can be killed from rotting off round the neck and suffer badly in a wet summer. Do not plant too deeply. Plant out while they are still young as they resent having their roots disturbed. Deadhead as necessary. Watch out for slugs and snails, especially early in the season.

Geum (Rosaceae). Avens. Geum will grow well in any fertile garden soil as long as it is reasonably well-drained. On the whole they prefer a sunny position but will grow in light shade or the moving shade of other border plants. These can become congested and need splitting every few years to maintain vigour and health. A good time to do this is late spring in which case you will get a good display of flowers the following year. Do it later and flowering will not be so effective, do it earlier and you lose some of the current year's flowering (you will lose part of it anyway). When splitting throw away the old woody growth, use the young fresh material. Watch out for *G. urbanum*, this is a terrible weed and when it starts to seed around, it seems almost impossible to get rid of. Its flowers are tiny and it has no garden merit, but being a native, it sometimes finds its way into a garden. Unfortunately its leaves are difficult to tell apart from other *Geum* so it may become necessary to clear the garden of all of them until the weed has been cleared. Deadhead as necessary. The foliage is evergreen, so just remove any dead leaves. They can suffer from downy mildew at the end of the season. Treat with fungicide or cut back and burn.

Gillenia (Rosaceae). A two-species genus of which *G. trifoliata* is the most commonly grown. They will grow in any good garden soil, particularly acidic types, which should be reasonably moisture retentive (some gardeners even grow them in bog gardens). A sunny position suits them best but they will tolerate a little light shade, particularly in hotter areas. These take a while to grow to their full potential. Although it is possible to divide them, they are quite woody and really dislike it. In spite of their wiriness some gardeners find it necessary to stake these plants.

Gladiolus (Iridaceae). The species that grow around the Mediterranean are generally hardy and can easily be grown in cooler areas. Those that emanate from South Africa need to be dug up every autumn and replanted in mid-spring, having been stored in a frost-free place. They all like a well-nourished soil, although it should be free-draining. *G. byzantinus* will probably take the heaviest soils. They generally like an open sunny position, although *G. byzantinus* will grow in shade. This species is perfectly hardy and forms new corms below the existing one, slowly dragging the plant deeper into the soil, sometimes making it very difficult to extract. It can sometimes become a pest in a border (a beautiful pest) as it increases quite fast. If you try to move it from one area remember to search for the little brown corms below the main bulb otherwise these will be fully grown plants again in the following year. *G. papilio* can be left in the ground over winter but it spreads and forms clumps which can become congested, requiring to be regularly split up in early spring to retain its vitality. *G. tristis* will come through winters in sheltered situations. A few others are just about hardy but most others are too tender to be grown outside warmer areas. Lift these in autumn and store in trays of dry sand after dusting with a fungicide. Cut off flowering stems after blooms have faded to prevent seeding (especially important in *G. byzantinum*). Remove leaves as they start to die back. There is no need to support the hardier forms, the big blousy florist's gladioli from South Africa usually need staking.

Glaucidium (Paeonaceae). *G. palmatum* is the sole representative of this genus. It is a woodlander and likes a correspondingly cool situation in moist, humusy-rich soil and a shady position. It likes to be protected from the wind. A suitable situation is in a peat bed under deciduous shrubs or trees. Cut back when foliage dies down.

Glaucium (Papavaraceae). Horned Poppies. These are plants of well-drained soils; they are often seen on seashores for example. They should be planted in full sun. Some are annuals or biennial, while others are short-lived perennials. They self-sow around so there are always plenty of replacements unless the gardener has been too tidy. The long, curved seed pods are part of the charm of these plants, but if you wish to avoid self-sowing these will have to be removed before the seed ripens. Glaucium resent disturbance and should be planted in their final positions while young. Rather than attempt to transplant mature plants, start afresh with new ones.

Globularia (Globulariaceae). Globe Daisy. These are not difficult plants to grow although they are naturally not long lived and need regular replacement. Life is prolonged if they have a free-draining soil and a sunny position. Some self-sow providing replacement plants. Remove the flowering stems after flowering but do not cut back the evergreen rosette.

Glyceria (Gramineae). Reed Meadow Grass, Reed Sweet Grass. *G. maxima* is a bit of a thug, spreads rapidly and should be avoided except, perhaps, in a large, wild garden. The variegated form *G.m.* 'Variegata' is a bit better behaved, but can still be quite vigorous. It is generally grown at the edges of ponds, usually with its feet in the water, but it can be grown in any moist soil. In lined ponds it can be grown in baskets. A sunny position is preferred.

Glycyrrhiza (Leguminosae). Liquorice. These will grow in any fertile garden soil as long as they are not too dry. Adding humus to the soil will provide the right conditions. A sunny position is preferred. Top-dress with organic material in the winter. Cut back after flowering.

Goodyera (Orchidaceae). A few of these can be grown outside in the open garden, including, *GG. oblongifolia, pubescens*, and *repens*. They like to have a woodland-type soil rich in leafmould and pine needles. Added grit or sharp sand will help with drainage. Top-dress each winter with leafmould.

Grindellia (Compositae). These like a well-drained but fertile soil in a sunny position. Cut back in the autumn. These are rather floppy plants and do best if given the support of pea-sticks. The flower buds ooze a white latex. This is perfectly normal.

Gunnera (Gunneraceae). Chilean Rhubarb, Prickly Rhubarb. These are plants of moist, humusy soil. They like nothing better than to grow next to ponds or lakes where they can keep their toes moist. However, they can be grown in ordinary garden soil as long as it has had plenty of humus added to it, so that it does not dry out. They prefer a sunny position but will also grow in a little light shade. Gunnera forms a colony and gradually spreads outwards, so that after a period quite a considerable period fortunately in the case of the larger species (such as *G. manicata*), it will become bald in the centre and it may be necessary to start a new colony or try to re-establish growth in the centre. The smaller species are mat-forming and can be grown on a peat bed. The garden gunneras are frost-tender, so cover them each autumn with their own leaves. When winter is passed these will rot down and add to the humus in the soil. Late frosts will knock off any early leaves but this should not harm an established plant. Young plants should be protected against them if possible. Top-dress with manure or other rich compost each winter to feed the plants. In spite of their size they need no support.

Gymnocarpium (Dryopteridaceae). These ferns like a leafmould, woodland-type soil, preferably with good drainage, in light shade. They can become congested with individual plants getting smaller. Split them up before the growth starts in the early spring. If they need moving or transplanting, carry this out similarly in early spring.

Gymnospermium (Berberidaceae). These are summer-dormant, tuberous plants that need a summer drought to survive. This means that they are easier to grow in a bulb frame than the open ground. They will grow in the latter as long as it is free-draining and hot. They need little attention and do not need digging up as they do not divide. Being summer-dormant it is necessary to clearly mark their position so that they are not accidentally disturbed or overplanted.

Gypsophila (Caryophyllaceae). Baby's Breath, Chalk Plant. A rather large genus of plants of which only a few are in cultivation. They must have a deeply-cultivated, fertile, free-draining soil, preferably slightly alkaline, so add lime to acid soils to bring the pH to 7–7.5. They will grow on heavier soils but are generally not long lived. Plant out in spring while the plants are still young; being tap-rooted they dislike disturbance. If you want to move a plant, jettison it and start with a new young one. For forms that have been grafted, plant deeply so that the graft is below the level of the soil. In spite of their wiry stems some of the taller species can be prone to wind damage in exposed positions and may need to be supported by pea-sticks, although this is likely to look ugly and should be avoided if possible. They can suffer from brown spots of rust, but this is generally not serious and can be ignored. More of a problem is stem rot which takes place at ground level. Burn infected plants and start again in a different part of the garden.

Hacquetia (Umbelliferae). *H. epipactis* is the only representative of this genus. This likes a moist, humusy soil and a lightly-shaded position. It resents disturbance so plant out while young into its final flowering position and if you need to move it, do so with a generous rootball of soil. Cut off the leaves when they begin to look tatty, usually about the late summer.

Hakonechloa (Gramineae). This genus is mainly represented in the garden by *H. macra* and its various forms. These like a moisture-retentive soil. The species will grow in sun but the variegated varieties retain their colour better in light shade. Any planting or transplanting should be carried out in spring.

Haplopappus (Compositae). Not all of this genus are hardy by any means, but HH. *coronopifolius* and *spinulosus* are reasonably hardy and if grown in a free-draining soil should come through most winters. The soil can be quite poor and stony. They like a warm, sunny position. After flowering shear over to remove old flower heads. They are slow spreading, rooting where the stems touch the ground, but not invasive.

Hedychium (Zingiberaceae). Hedychium are probably hardier than hitherto believed, and the commonly grown ones should come through most winters as long as there is not prolonged periods below −10°C (14°F). They like a rich, moisture-retentive soil, with plenty of well-rotted, organic material incorporated into it. They prefer acid conditions but will tolerate a certain amount of alkalinity. It is essential that they are not allowed to dry out while in growth and should be copiously watered if necessary during times of drought. However, the soil should be relatively free-draining as they should not stand in stagnant water, especially during the winter. An open sunny position is best. Can be late into growth, so do not accidentally dig it up or overplant. Clearly labelling the plants can help prevent this. Cut off the spent stems when the flowering and growth finishes towards late autumn. If you have cause to move them do not do so during the dormant period otherwise they will rot. The best time is just as they are coming into growth in the spring.

Hedysarum (Leguminosae). Sweet Vetch. These like a deeply-cultivated soil that is reasonably free-draining. They prefer a sunny position, but can be grown in a light, dappled shade. Plant out while they are still young as they are not happy if their roots are disturbed. They are difficult to transplant, so either desist or start again with new plants if you want to move them. Cut back to the ground once the plant begins to look tatty in the autumn; alternatively wait until the spring. Hedysarum are not completely hardy although they will come through an average winter. To increase their chances give them a mulch of bracken or shredded bark in the late autumn. In the spring the young shoots may be attacked by slugs and snails.

Helenium (Compositae). Sneezeweed. Plant in any fertile garden soil, preferably moisture-retentive. In drier soils the flowers are likely to be smaller. They prefer a sunny position although they will take a little moving shade from other plants. They indicate as soon as they are short of water by allowing their leaves to drop. Water thoroughly when this happens. The shorter forms manage to be self-supporting in most gardens but if exposed to strong or turbulent winds they may need staking as do the taller varieties (usually the later-flowering forms). Deadhead the early-flowering forms such as 'Moerheim Beauty' so that they flower again later. Only remove the deadheads back as far as the next bud. In spite of their vigour helenium are susceptible to slug attack in the early spring when they damage young shoots and leaves. Use your preferred method to control them. They become congested and will need dividing and replanting every three or four years. Top-dressing with organic material helps to keep them vigorous.

Helianthella (Compositae). A small genus of clump-forming plants that will grow in a light, free-draining, even poor soil. They prefer non-acidic soils. Plant in a sunny position.

Helianthemum (Cistaceae). Rock Rose, Sun Rose. These are low-growing shrubby plants. They will grow in most soils. Whatever type, they must be free-draining, any waterlogging, especially in winter will cause the plant to die. A sunny position is also essential. Try to avoid other plants drooping over or growing through them. After the main flush of flowers is over (usually by mid summer), shear over the plant but do not cut right back into the old wood or the plant may not regenerate. This is particularly true of any winter cutting back. The double-flowered forms often go on flowering throughout the summer and need not be cut back until the spring.

Helianthus (Compositae). Sunflowers. These coarse plants will grow in any fertile garden soil. It should be reasonably moisture-retentive but well-drained. The soil should be fed as these are gross feeders but if it is too rich it is likely to produce a lot of foliage at the expense of flowers. They should be in full sun as far as a crowded herbaceous border allows. Their height usually necessitates some form of staking. They tend to spread and will need to be divided every few years to control them and to maintain their vigour. The more vigorous ones may need to be dug around every spring to prevent them travelling too far. In dry summers mildew can develop. Planting them in an open, airy position and preventing them from getting too dry will help to avoid this. Botrytis or grey mould can also be a problem, especially in wet weather. Make certain that plenty of air can circulate to help prevent this. Burn affected plants and spray the rest with a fungicide. They can be a martyr to slugs, especially after a mild spring.

Helichrysum (Compositae). Strawflowers. These all need a well-drained soil and a sunny position. *HH. microphylla* and *petiolare* are border stalwarts but are tender in most colder regions. However they can be perpetuated by taking cuttings in early autumn. Do not cut back the shrubby types after early summer or the wood may not have ripened sufficiently to get the plant through the winter.

Helictotrichon (Gramineae). Grasses that will grow in any garden soil as long as it is reasonably well-drained. They also want a sunny position. Pull out all the dead leaves in early spring with the gloved hand. Do not cut back close to the ground or the next season's flowering shoots will be sacrificed. Any planting or transplanting should be carried out in spring.

Heliopsis (Compositae). Ox-eye. These sunflower-like plants will grow in any good garden soil, including quite dry ones. In spite of their tolerance of drought they should be watered once the leaves are seen to droop. A sunny position is needed. The taller ones will need staking in some way. Deadhead as far down as the next bud will prolong the already quite long season. They slowly spread but do not need dividing as regularly as some similar plants. Top-dress with organic matter in the winter to help keep them vigorous. Slugs can be a nuisance at this time of year when they will eat most emerging shoots. Take avoiding action.

Heliotropium (Boraginaceae). Heliotrope. A large genus that consists of both annuals and perennials. The latter are mainly tender except in warmer areas. Elsewhere they need to be overwintered as cuttings and planted out in spring. As would be expected, they need a well-drained soil and sunny position.

Helleborus (Ranunculaceae). Hellebore. Hellebores will grow on a wide range of soils although they do best on those that are either neutral or just on the alkaline side of neutral. *H. niger*, in particular, does best in alkaline conditions. They grow in heavy soils in the wild but must have conditions that are neither waterlogged nor over-dry. They like a rich soil that has plenty of organic material added to it. They will grow in full sun if the soil does not dry out too much, or very light shade. They will grow in dense shade but the flowering is severely impaired. Plant out or transplant in the spring. Do not plant too deeply as this may impair flowering; just below the surface with the growing tips just on or above the surface is ideal. During winter, before the flower buds burst, cut off all the old foliage from *H. orientalis* and its hybrids. However, do not remove it from *HH. foetidus*, *viridis* and *argutifolius* otherwise they become leggy and their appearance spoilt. The stems of these die back after seeding and can be cut back to the ground after they have flowered or seeded. Hellebores often suffer from one of two black spot diseases on the leaves (*Phyllosticta helleborella* and *Conithyrium hellebori*). Remove all infected leaves and spray with a fungicide. Bordeaux mixture being a popular preventative. Greenfly are another problem, reducing the flower heads to a sticky mess. Treat with an appropriate pesticide. Hellebores appreciate a heavy manuring of well-rotting farmyard manure or compost, preferably as growth commences in early winter. Alternatively top-dress with bonemeal or a general fertilizer. *H. foetidus* can look jaded after a couple of years or so. However, there are usually sufficient seedlings to allow you to scrap the old plants and start afresh. Most happily self-sow, but be wary of *H. orientalis*'s hybrid seedlings as they are unlikely to resemble their parents (they may be better of course). Hellebores are generally perfectly hardy. The main exception is *H. lividus* which really needs winter protection, although it is much hardier in its hybrid form *H. sternii*. Another exception is the curious *H. vesicarius* from Turkey which may need covering during cold spells in the open garden, although Brian Mathew has successfully kept it through temperatures of −17°C (1°F).

Helonias (Liliaceae). Swamp Pink. A genus of a solitary species *H. bullata*. As its English name suggests it likes moist conditions and can be grown in a bog garden or on the margins of ponds or streams. It prefers an acid soil with plenty of humus incorporated in it. It should be planted in light shade. It is completely hardy. The flower spike can be removed but the leaves are evergreen and the rosette should be left to overwinter.

Heloniopsis (Melanthiaceae/Liliaceae). Rhizomatous plants that need a cool, moisture-retentive soil such as a peat bed. They also like to be protected from the hot, midday sun.

Hemerocallis (Hemerocallidaceae/Liliaceae). This is a large genus with hundreds of cultivars. Generally they will grow in most soils as long as they are not too dry. They obviously do best in fertile soils. Their versatility continues in that they can be grown in either sun or light shade. They form dense clumps which are self-supporting. Sometimes the flowering stems of the taller varieties with heavier blooms flop over, but there is no means of effective support which does not look ridiculous. The flowers only last a day. They shrivel and eventually drop off. There is no need to deadhead but the dead remains do hang on for a day or two and can look unattractive, so if you are feeling energetic pick them off. This genus presents few problems regarding pests and diseases, but it can become overcrowded and should be split up every five years or so and replanted in rejuvenated soil. Top-dress during the winter with well-rotted manure or apply a balanced fertilizer in spring. Remove the empty flower stems after the last blooms have faded, and the rotting foliage in the autumn.

Hepatica (Ranunculaceae). Liverleaf. Low-growing plants that are ideal for growing under deciduous shrubs in a mixed or woodland border. They like a cool, humusy soil and light shade. Avoid planting them with too much surrounding vegetation as they are not able to compete. Do not plant too deeply, the same depth as they are in the pot is best. Young plants often take a while to settle after being planted out or being transplanted. When happy they will self-sow but not in a way to become a nuisance. Cut off the old foliage in mid-winter before the flowers emerge otherwise the latter will be obscured.

Heracleum (Umbelliferae). Hogweeds. Most of this genus are weeds but *H. mantegaz-zianum* is sometimes grown as a garden plant (which does not stop it being a weed in other gardens). It is monocarpic and dies after seeding. It can take two or more years to reach this stage. It is a highly poisonous plant and should be avoided in gardens where there are children (bear in mind that seed could spread to neighbouring gardens). If the plant makes contact with the skin which is then exposed to sunlight a very bad rash or blistering can occur. When cutting it down or removing it do so on a rainy day and wear protective gloves and goggles, and be certain that your arms are covered. It is a very stately plant but you may think the risk is not worth it. A deep rich soil is best. It mainly grows in the sun but it will also grow where it gets shade for part of the day. It seeds about, forming large colonies if it gets the chance.

Hermodactylus (Iridaceae). Snake's Head Iris. A monospecific genus with creeping tubers that need a free-draining soil in a hot, sunny position, against a south wall is ideal. Plant in autumn at about 5–7.5cm (2–3in) below the surface.

Hesperis (Cruciferae). Dame's Violet, Sweet Rocket. *H. matronalis* is a biennial or short-lived perennial. It will regularly self-sow giving a display each year without any need to resow. However, it takes some time for the seed to ripen so do not be in too much of a hurry to dispose of the plants after flowering otherwise there will be an interruption in their appearance. Keep the white and purple varieties well apart if you want to keep populations pure. The double-flowered form is more difficult to keep in cultivation. The deteriorating stock has been cleaned up of bacterial infections by micropropagation in recent years, but it is still a plant that is short-lived and difficult to propagate. It will grow in any good garden soil. If deadheaded it can sometimes be persuaded to produce a second flowering.

Heuchera (Saxifragaceae). Alum Root. A large number of species and varieties of this genus are now in cultivation. They all like a well-drained soil that is laced with organic matter to keep it moist. They can be difficult on heavier soils. A light shade provides the best situation but they will grow in full sun as long as the sun is not too hot and the soil too dry. The best time to lift and split congested plantings is the autumn, so they are ready to perform again the following spring. In some areas where the plants will not have time to re-establish themselves before winter sets in it will be necessary to leave division until spring, but this means that a year's flowering is likely to be lost. Plant quite deeply. They benefit from a winter mulch of well-rotted organic material (which can be spread over their crowns without detriment). Cut off flowering stems after the flowers have finished.

X *Heucherella* (Saxifragaceae). These bigeneric hybrids between *Heuchera* and *Tiarella* are treated in the same manner as the above.

Hibiscus (Malvaceae). Rose Mallow. A genus of annuals, perennials and shrubs. The perennials are mainly plants that require moist, humusy soil, although they will thrive in any reasonable garden soil. They will flower in full sun, or light shade in hotter areas. A warm position is needed. Tidy-up during autumn/winter clear-up. They are somewhat tender and can only be grown in warmer areas. Elsewhere it is worth mulching them with shredded bark or bracken.

Hieraceum (Compositae). Hawkweeds. Many of these are weeds that can cause quite a nuisance, but there are some garden-worthy species. They generally need a well-drained soil and will often grow quite well in poor soils. They should have a sunny position. Most will self-sow if given half a chance so deadhead as soon as flowering is over unless you want a few seedlings.

Hippocrepis (Leguminosae). Horse-shoe Vetch. Edge of border plants that will grow in any good garden soil, preferring it to be well-drained. They like a sunny position. Plant out while plants are still young as the roots do not like disturbance. Similarly avoid transplanting, but use new plants if necessary. Cut back as soon as the plant looks a bit tatty which is usually soon after flowering.

Holcus (Gramineae). This genus is mainly represented in cultivation by the variegated form of *H. mollis*. It will grow in most garden soils, preferably in full sun, without much trouble. Plant or transplant in the spring, and cut back in the late winter as they have an attractive winter presence.

Hormium (Labiatae). *H. pyrenaicum* is the sole representative of this genus. It will grow on any good garden soil, especially calcareous ones, in either full sun or shade. It is evergreen and only needs to have the old flowering stems removed.

Hosta (Funkiaceae/Liliaceae). A large genus with many species and hundreds of varieties in cultivation. They do best in a deep, rich soil that has had plenty of moisture-retentive humus added to it. They will grow in the sun if the soil is not allowed to dry out, otherwise they are best in light shade. They probably form better plants in the sun. Plant out at any time when they are dormant with their noses just below the surface of the soil. Clear away the old foliage as it dies back in the autumn. The biggest scourge of the genus is slugs. These must be kept under because if they nibble the emerging buds the leaves will be scarred for the whole of the following season. Hailstorms also play havoc with the foliage, leaving it in tatters. They can become very congested but there is no reason to lift them unless you want to propagate from them. Top-dressing with an organic mulch in the winter plus a light dressing of a general fertilizer in spring will keep them vigorous. Water in times of drought, particularly if the leaves go limp.

Hottonia (Primulaceae). Water Violets. Submerged aquatic plants that should not be introduced to a pond until it has been established for sometime and has settled down. They can be planted into the bottom of a natural pond or in lined baskets. Anchor newly-planted plants to prevent them floating away. Anything appearing yellow is likely to become detached from its soil.

Houttuynia (Saururaceae). The single species, *H. cordata*, likes a moist, shady place and when satisfied it will ramp about at speed, creating groundcover if you want it. The variegated form 'Chameleon' is not so fast a spreader but still forms a carpet. Neither travels so fast if given a drier, sunnier position. Hard winter frosts can cut them back, otherwise they need to be kept in check by digging around them to remove questing roots. Best for groundcover in a wilder part of the garden, or somewhere where it can be contained.

Humulus (Urticaceae). Hop. This genus is mainly represented by the golden form, *H. lupulus aureus*. This is a vigorous scrambler and unless given a support up which it can climb it will scramble over the surrounding plants. It is likely to do this anyway unless it is trained up the supports. If space is restricted reduce the number of climbing stems to just three or four and no harm will be done. It likes a fertile soil, rich in organic matter and a sunny position. Top-dress with a humus mulch in winter. Slugs can attack the emerging shoots, and aphids can be a problem on the growing tips. If the plant wilts, dig it out and burn it. Cut back to the ground every autumn.

Hyacinthus (Hyancinthaceae). Hyacinths. Although there are several hyacinths, it is the large-headed plants derived from *H. orientalis* that are mainly grown. They will grow in any ordinary garden soil, preferably in full sun, but they will take a little light shade. Plant the bulbs in autumn about 10cm (4in) below the surface. Any bulbs that have been grown indoors can be planted out as soon as they have finished flowering. These will be exhausted and may take a couple of seasons to come back to flowering. Remove flowering stems as soon as the flowers are over. A light sprinkling of a potash-rich fertilizer in early spring helps to keep them vigorous.

Hyacinthoides (Hyacinthaeae). Bluebells. Still also known as *Endymion* or even *Scilla*. These will grow in any good soil as long as it is not too dry. A moist, woodland-type soil suits them best. They prefer to grow in the shade but will also grow in sun if the soil is not too dry. Although bluebells are very attractive plants they have their problems. In the first place they spread rather rapidly both by seed and offsets, preferring it would seem to grow up through some other precious plants. Once established they are very difficult to eradicate. The other problem is that they look so awful when they go over, the leaves turning to a terrible mush. They are usually so prolific that any harm caused by premature removal of the leaves does not seem to inhibit them, so I am inclined to remove all vegetation after flowering and before seed is set. When buying avoid dry, shrivelled up bulbs. Plant about 10cm (4in) below the surface.

Hydrastis (Ranunculaceae). Goldenseal. A genus of two species of which *H. canadensis* is sometimes seen in gardens. This is a creeping woodlander that likes a deep, moist, humusy soil and a position in light shade. Plant out in the spring with the rhizomes just below the surface (about 5cm (2in) deep). Top-dress with leafmould each winter.

Hylomecon (Papaveraciae). *H. japonicum*, the only member of the genus, is a beautiful plant for woodland conditions: light shade and moist, humus-rich soil. Plant out in spring. Clear up any remains in autumn or simply let them return to the leaf litter. Mulch in winter with leafmould.

Hymenocallis (Amaryllidaceae/Liliaceae). Spider-lily. Quite a large genus of mainly tropical bulbous plants, of which *HH. amanceaes, caroliniana, narcissiflora* and one or two others are sometimes grown in warmer districts. Unlike most bulbs *H. caroliniana* likes a moist soil and will grow well in a bog garden or next to a water feature. The others can be grown in any good garden soil as long as they have a warm, sunny position. They can be lifted and kept quietly in pots during winter in cooler areas. Plant deeply, about 15cm (6in) will do.

Hyoscyamus (Solanaceae). Henbane. This pretty-flowered biennial will grow in most soils as long as they are not too wet. It prefers a freshly-tilled position and not too much competition. Remove the whole plant after flowering. It will self-sow and any seedlings should be planted out while still young as the plant resents disturbance. Note that the plant and its seed are poisonous, so avoid if children are likely to be around.

Hypericum (Guttiferae). St John's Wort. It is usually the shrubs that are grown in cultivation although a number of the native herbs are used in wild gardens. They will all grow in any garden soil, even quite dry ones, although they obviously do better in fertile conditions. Most will grow in either full sun or light shade. Cut the herbaceous varieties to the ground in the autumn. The groundcoverer *H. calycinum* (which will grow in the shade) will be in better condition and flower better if it is sheared over during the late winter. This also gives you a chance to remove any litter that invariably seems to become embedded in it. This is a vigorous colonizer so keep in check if planted in an area where it can not run free.

Hypolepsis (Dennstaedtiaceae). Deciduous ferns that are very invasive. Only plant them where they can ramp about. They like a moist, woodland-type soil in full sun or light shade. Cut back the dead fronds in winter. Top-dress with leafmould at the same time.

Hypsela (Campanulaceae). Creeping plants from the southern hemisphere that die back every winter. They are completely hardy and it is best to take rooted cuttings to overwinter under glass until you are certain that they will survive your conditions. They grow in any garden soil, preferably a humusy one. Hypsela prefer a light, shady position although they will grow in full sun as long as it is not too hot or if they are shaded at midday.

Hyssopus (Labiatae). Hyssop. The main species grown is the well-known herb, *H. officinalis*. This forms a shrubby plant which should be cut back into old wood in the late winter or early spring, leaving a framework of old stems about 15–23cm (6–9ins) long. It will grow well in any garden soil, preferably one on the dry side, in a sunny position.

Hystrix (Gramineae). Bottlebrush Grass. This small genus of grasses of which *H. patula* is the one normally seen in gardens is clump-forming and will grow in any good garden soil, preferably a moist one. They grow best in a lightly-shaded position. They tend not to be too long lived but if allowed to they will self-sow. Plant or transplant seedlings in spring. You may like to cut back this grass as soon as it begins to fade as it is a rather untidy plant.

Iberis (Cruciferae). Candytuft. Candytufts need a well-drained soil. They will even grow in walls, which shows just how well-drained they will take conditions. While they will grow in acid conditions they seem to prefer slightly alkaline ones. They grow best in full sun but will grow in shade, although this is likely to make the plant open and leggy. After flowering, shear over to keep the plant compact.

Impatiens (Balsaminaceae). Balsams, Busy Lizzies, Touch-me-nots. The Impatiens normally grown in the open garden are all annuals and should be raised afresh each year, either from seed or overwintered cuttings. Some vigorously self-sow, giving them perennial status. They like a moist, but well-drained and reasonably rich soil, and do best in areas with a moist atmosphere. Even localized dampness such as situations near ponds is appreciated. Some such as *I. glandulifera* can become pests so be certain that you want to introduce them before you do so. *I. tinctoria* can be brought through a winter outside in milder areas if given a warm spot. On the whole they prefer a shady position. They can be grown in full sun but it is essential that the soil remains moist. The busy lizzies used in containers and for bedding need to have the tips pinched out to promote bushiness. Clear away annual forms as first frosts start.

Incarvillea (Bignoniaceae). Trumpet Flower, Hardy Gloxinia. These attractive plants like a deeply-cultivated, well-drained soil that does not dry out while the plant is in growth. A sunny, warm position is also required; avoid shade. Plant the large tubers in the spring at a reasonable depth, about 15cm (6in) below the soil surface. Once planted try not to disturb it as it does not transplant very easily. They are just on the border of hardiness and it is safest to give them a mulch of bracken or shredded bark in the winter. No supports are required. Watch out for slugs, which can cut right through the stems. Plants can also suffer from nematodes. Use an appropriate spray.

Indigofera (Leguminosae). This is a large genus of shrubby plants, some of which are hardy and are treated like herbaceous perennials by cutting to the ground each winter. It is important to plant them in a well-drained, but reasonably moisture-retentive soil, and to give them a warm, sunny position either backed by a wall or by more permanent shrubs. Some are likely to be cut back by the frosts but will reshoot from the base. These can be treated like fuchsias and cut back in the late winter or early spring. Others remain in growth but, like *Cestrum*, do best if they are cut to the ground. If left the latter group are often late into leaf, usually giving the appearance of being dead; don't throw away.

Inula (Compositae). Like so many of the daisies the inulas are an easy-to-grow genus. They will grow in virtually any soil, although they prefer it reasonably moisture-retentive. *I. magnifica* will even grow in boggy ground. A sunny position is best although some such as *I. ensifolia* will tolerate just a little shade. Some including *I. hookeri* and *I. racemosa* can become a bit rampant and need to be kept in check. *I. hookeri* can also suffer from later spring frosts, with the emerging shoots all being cut back. It usually reshoots. Some of the taller forms may require staking. A winter mulch of organic material will pay dividends.

Ipheion (Alliaceae/Liliaceae). Bulbous plants that can spread to form quite a large colony, although they are not invasive. Plant out in the autumn in well-drained soil, in an open, sunny position. About 5cm (2in) is the right depth. They can become crowded and may need dividing if their vigour drops off. Lift and replant while they are dormant. Leaves appear in the late autumn or early winter, but they are usually hardy and need no protection. A light dressing of a potash-rich fertilizer in autumn is beneficial.

Iris (Iridaceae). This is a very large genus of thick rhizomatous, thinner creeping, and bulbous species. The thicker rhizomes bearded irises (*I. germanica* and similar species) require a well-drained soil that is reasonably enriched with well-rotted, organic material. Avoid heavy or waterlogged soils unless they can be improved. They like an open, sunny position. Plant these irises with the rhizomes only half in the soil. Spread out the old roots as an anchor on either side and cover with earth. These will soon die off but in the meantime they will hold the plant upright in the soil. Reduce the fan of leaves to about one third to prevent from being top-heavy and making it liable to topple over, especially in winds, before the new roots have firmly anchored the plant. Overcrowded clumps of irises should be dug up in mid-summer, after flowering. They should be split up with the older pieces being discarded and the new young pieces being replanted. Irises are not too happy about being disturbed and often take a year or two to settle down once they have been replanted. Irises like to have their rhizomes exposed to the sun. This means that it is virtually impossible to grow anything in close association with them as they are likely to act as a sun screen. A few diaphanous plants, such as *Nigella* or *Omphalodes linefolia* may work but generally it is best to keep the exposed rhizomes completely clear of other plants and weeds. Give bearded irises a light sprinkling of a general fertilizer in early spring, just as they are coming into growth. One of the worst problems facing irises is soft rot which can spread through the rhizomes killing them. It is most easily noticed by the yellowing and dying of the leaves. The rhizomes should immediately be dug up and the rotten part completely cut away. The cut surface should be treated with a copper fungicide. It should be replanted in fresh soil. Iris leaves can be despoiled by leaf spot, a fungal disease which starts with small brown spots eventually spreading with the leaf dying back from the tip. All affected leaves should be removed and burnt, the remainder being sprayed with a copper fungicide or Dithane. Some authorities recommend that an annual dressing of superphosphate to the soil will help prevent the problem. It is more prevalent during wet summers. *I. unguicularis* prefers to be left undisturbed and takes a while to settle down if moved or divided. If it is necessary to move them do so after flowering in the spring. The leaves can look ugly at flowering time (winter) if they have not been cut over near to the ground in late spring or early summer (some extremists set fire to the foliage). The flowers are treated as a feast by slugs so preventive measures must be taken. Plant in well-drained soil against a warm wall and cover the rhizomes with soil. The soil can be quite poor, some gardeners deliberately include rubble in it, too rich conditions will produce too much leaf at the expense of flowers. They seem to like limey soils (perhaps mortar in the old rubble helps) but they grow and flower very well on neutral soil. They are very hardy and should not suffer from severe winters, although the flowering may be impaired. *I. lazica* is very similar and is often confused with *I. unguicularis*. This, however, prefers a lightly shaded position although it grows perfectly alright in full sun, and the top of its rhizomes should be exposed. The flower buds of both can suffer very badly from slugs. Split *I. japonica* every three years or so, otherwise it becomes congested and unable to stand up in the wind. It likes a sunny position. The Californian or Pacific coast irises, surprising, like a light dappled shade and a moisture-retentive soil, preferably a well-drained peat bed. Some, *I. douglasiana*, in particular will also grow in full sun. Some irises will grow in shallow water or moist soil. *II. laevigata, missouriensis, pseudocorus, sibirica* and *versicolor* will all do this. The sibiricas and spurias will grow happily in an ordinary border. Both need moisture-retentive soil that is not allowed to dry out in periods of drought. The beardless irises will mix much more readily with ordinary border plants, unlike the bearded irises. They form dense clumps which tend to die out in the middle. When congested the flowering also suffers, so it is a good thing to split them up every few years having rejuvenated the soil. When planting, unlike the bearded irises, the rhizomes should be covered with soil. Most irises should be grown in open, sunny positions but *I. foetidissima* will grow in shade. It grows on chalk soils in the wild, although it will grow on a wide range in cultivation. The larger bulbous irises will grow well in a mixed border and like a well-drained but rich soil. They do especially well on alkaline soils, but will grow in a wide range of conditions. The English iris, *I. latifolia*, must have a moisture-retentive soil so that it does not dry out. Most increase well, both by offsets and seed. They are generally trouble-free and apart from cutting back to the ground once the leaves start fading, little attention is required. The smaller bulbs of the reticulata group are also easy to grow. These are seen at their best on rock gardens or raised beds, but can be used in a variety of positions where summer plants are yet to emerge. They should be lifted and the bulbs separated every two or three years, depending on how fast they clump up. The small bulbous irises of the reticulata type suffer from ink spot which will wipe out a complete clump. To a certain extent it can be avoided by regularly digging up clumps and splitting them so that the bulbs are not touching. If you suspect the disease dig up the infected bulbs which will have inky-looking black marks and burn them. Do not replant in the same area, or change the soil. *I. danfordiae* can be shy-flowering after the first year in the ground. It seems to help if the soil is enriched with bonemeal and the bulbs planted deeply (about 15cm (6in) below the soil).

Isatis (Cruciferae). Woad. *I. tinctoria* is an annual but sows so copiously that it can be considered a perennial annual. It will grow in any fertile garden soil, preferably in a sunny position. Can be rather floppy, especially in exposed areas, so it is safest to give it some support with pea-sticks. The self-sowing can become a nuisance but it is easy to remove the seedlings while they are still young. Alternatively, remove the plants as soon as they have finished flowering. *I. glauca* is a short-lived perennial that is usually treated as a biennial if it is grown. Conditions as above.

Isopyrum (Ranunculaceae). This is a small genus of creeping woodland plants that enjoy a humusy soil and a light shade typical of its habitat. A peat bed or a position under deciduous shrubs or trees are ideal. It disappears below ground in the spring soon after flowering and seeding, so mark it carefully to avoid accidental disturbance.

Isotoma (Campanulaceae). Usually treated as an annual although it is in fact a perennial. In warmer areas it might be possible to treat it as such. It requires a reasonably rich, but well-drained soil where it is not shaded or overgrown by other plants.

Ixia (Iridaceae). Corn Lilies. Plant in a sunny position in a light, well-drained soil, about 7.5cm (3in) is the depth to plant. On dull days the flowers are unlikely to open. These bulbs are of doubtful hardiness and should be lifted in colder areas in autumn and stored in dry sand in a frost-free place. Dust with a fungicide before storing. Alternatively new bulbs can be purchased each year.

Ixiolirion (Ixioliriaceae/Liliaceae). A small genus of bulbous plants. They will grow in any well-drained soil. The bulbs are likely to rot if they are wet in winter. Preferably site in a warm, sunny position. Plant in the autumn about 7.5cm (3in) deep. Top-dressing with a phosphate-rich fertilizer in the winter will help to keep the bulbs vigorous, but it is not essential as the bulbs tend to grow in quite poor soil in the wild. In colder areas the bulbs may be tender and they can be lifted and stored in a frost-free place.

Jaborosa (Solanaceae). A small genus of plants of which *J. integrifolia* is sometimes grown in gardens. In spite of coming from a damp habitat it is usually grown in a well-drained soil. A warm, sunny position is essential. Can be a bit tender so give it a winter mulch of shredded bark. It can become rather invasive so either take measures to control it or let it ramp in a wilder part of the garden.

Jasione (Campanulaceae). Sheep's Bit. A delightful genus of plants that like a light, generally lime-free soil. They prefer to grow in a sunny position. An open rock garden or raised bed makes an ideal site. Deadhead after flowering.

Jeffersonia (Berberidaceae). Twinleaf. Both the two species of this genus are wood-landers and prefer a cool, semi-shaded situation. They like a leafy woodland soil, that is rich and moisture-retentive. Remove old foliage when the plant dies down. They appreciate a top-dressing of leafmould in the winter, both to feed the soil and to keep it moist.

Juncus (Juncaceae). Few of these are grown in the garden. They will grow in moist soil but do best as a marginal plant for ponds. Both *J. effusus* 'Spiralis' and *J.e.* 'Vittatus' should be regularly lifted and divided, throwing away any pieces of either that have reverted; straight-stemmed pieces in the first case and green in the second. Some can become a bit invasive, seeding in any damp patch. Try and remove them at an early stage as they are difficult to extract once they have formed a good clump.

Kentranthus (Valerianceae). See *Centranthus*

Kirengeshoma (Hydrangeaceae). Yellow Waxbells. A single species genus, repre-sented by *K. palmata*. This plant must have a moist, acid soil to perform of its best. Deeply-cultivated ones, with plenty of incorporated organic material are ideal. It will grow in sun if the soil is kept moist, but light shade is preferred. It is a hardy plant, but the late flowering can be impaired by early frosts. Top-dress with organic matter in the winter. It slowly spreads to form a large colony but is not invasive. In a sheltered position it does not require support, but elsewhere it is best staked. Slugs often attack young shoots, particularly on young plants. Established clumps should not be so vulnerable.

Knautia (Dipsacaceae). A large genus of which *K. macedonica* is the one usually seen in gardens. Plant in any fertile garden soil, preferably reasonably well-drained. It should be given a sunny position. The plant is rather floppy and is best given a pea-stick support. As the season progresses so the flowers become smaller. Dead-heading, if you have the time for such a momentous task, will help to keep the size of the remaining flowers. The old stems pull away very easily in late winter, not damaging the new, emerging shoots and foliage. A top-dressing of manure in the winter will help to keep the plants vigorous.

Kniphofia (Asphodelaceae/Liliaceae). Torch Lilies, Red Hot Pokers. A large genus of plants that will grow in any good garden soil as long as it is moisture-retentive. Ideal conditions would be a free-draining soil with plenty of well-rotted humus added to it. A sunny position is required. There is much debate about winter treatment of kniphofia. The rotting leaves can be removed to prevent the rot spreading into the crown, or they can be left to give protection against frost. Some advocate lifting the foliage and tying it to form a protective water-proof, cold-proof 'cap'. Others reduce the leaves by half (removing the dying and dead ones), but leave the remainder until spring when new growth begins, arguing that as long as the leaves remain green they are providing the plant with food. I am not so happy about leaving them on since by the end of winter the old leaves are often very rotten and smelly forcing the new ones to try and push through, but at least they come away easily, causing little damage to the new growth. In colder areas they may be tender and a winter mulch of bracken, straw, or shredded bark is useful. They are usually happy remaining undisturbed for up to 10 years so long as perennial weeds do not infest them. *K. caulescens* benefits from being split up every three or four years. When you want to move or split them do so in the spring, reducing the foliage by two thirds. Kniphofias can suffer from violet root rot which has wiped out several collections. Treatment with fungicide is urgently required at the first sighting.

Koeleria (Gramineae). This medium-sized genus of grasses contains a few that are garden-worthy. They grow in any garden soil that is not too rich, including dry and calcareous. A sunny site is required. They form tufted clumps and do not have any tendency to run. Shear over in the late winter. Plant or transplant in the spring.

Lactuca (Compositae). Blue Lettuce. Several of these blue-flowered plants are grown in gardens, but they are all a bit invasive and some, *L. bourgaei* in particular, very invasive. Unless you have a large garden which includes an area for thugs, they are really best avoided. The better behaved include *L. alpina* (now *Cicerbita alpina*). Should you wish to give them a try (and the flowers are rather pretty), plant them in any garden soil in either sun or light shade. Cut off the flowering spikes after flowering.

Lamiastrum (Labiatae). *L. galeobdolon* seems to have finally settled back in *Lamium*.

Lamium (Labiatae). Deadnettles. These will grow in any fertile garden soil, mainly in full sun but some prefer shade. Some, *L. orvala*, in particular can be mistaken for the weed white deadnettle, *L. album*, when out of flower so label clearly to prevent them being weeded out. *L. galeobdolon* is an invasive plant, although it is not too difficult to cut back. However, it should not be put in a bed of choice plants. It is usually grown in the variegated form although this, like the type, will seed around; the seedlings retaining the silver splash on the leaves. It looks better if the old leaves and runners are sheared off to the ground in late winter before new growth starts. It does best in a leafy soil in light shade. Some, *L. maculatum* particularly, can suffer from mildew. Plant in an airy position and do not allow it to become too dry. Spray if necessary. Alternatively, shear the plant over and let it re-emerge with new foliage. This is a good practice with this plant anyway to prevent it from becoming too straggly. Cut it back after the first flush of flowering is passed. Tall clumps of *L. orvala* can be opened up by the wind, so stake with hidden pea-sticks in exposed areas.

Lapeirousia (Iridaceae). See *Anomatheca*

Lathyrus (Leguminosae). Peas like to have a well-drained soil that never completely dries out. On the whole they like a sunny position, but *L. grandiflorus* and *L. vernus* will take a little shade. Most members of this family need some form of support as they are either climbers or scramblers. They can be grown either through shrubs or up pea-sticks. Sometimes they can be allowed to scramble over herbaceous plants that have finished flowering. Some, such as *LL. vernus* and *luteus* 'Aureus', are low-growing, clump-forming plants that need no support. *L. grandiflora* is a scrambler that likes to grow amongst shrubs, although it can be free-standing if you do not mind it flopping over other plants. It has a tendency to run and should be dug around every year, during the winter tidy-up, to keep it in check.

Lavandula (Labiatae). Lavender. Strictly shrubs but these are frequently grown with herbaceous plants. They need to have a free-draining soil that is reasonably rich. A sunny position is also important although they will grow in places which are shaded for part of the day. Shear over after flowering or as growth starts in spring to keep them compact. If plants get old and leggy scrap them and start again.

Lavatera (Malvaceae). Tree Mallow. A free-draining soil is best for all the species in this genus. A sunny position is essential. If planted in containers they should be watered regularly, at least once a day in hot weather. *LL. olbia* and *thuringiaca* can be cut back hard, almost to the ground, like a *Buddleja* if they are getting rather big. Smaller plants need less drastic action and can just have the weaker stems removed. Totally cut-back plants will obviously flower later than those only lightly pruned. Wind can break or crack stems at the base; remove and tidy-up the wound if this occurs. In exposed areas reduce all the branches by about half in autumn to prevent winter wind-damage. Some coloured forms, especially *L. thuringiaca* 'Barnsley', can revert to bright pink. The stems bearing these flowers need to be cut out before the whole plant reverts. They tend to be short-lived plants and need replacing every three or four years. *L. arborea*, especially in its variegated form, can become very ugly and leggy after its first year and it may be considered best to grow fresh plants each year rather than perpetuate it. This species likes a well-drained soil and will often be seen growing near the sea in almost pure shingle. *L. maritima* is tender; as a safeguard against winter-loss cuttings should be taken in the autumn. *L. cachemiriana* needs to be cut to the ground every autumn or during the winter clear-up. Some lavateras are attacked by the same rust as attacks hollyhocks. Spray with a fungicide.

Leontice (Berberidaceae). A small genus of which only *L. leontopetalum* is in cultivation. It is a summer-dormant tuber and requires to be kept dry during this time, which really makes it a plant for the bulb frame rather than the open garden. It can, however, be grown here as long as it is a hot, well-drained position and the tuber is planted deeply at least 20cm (8in) below the surface. It does not require division so needs no disturbance. It needs little attention apart from removing leaves and stems when it dies back. As it is summer-dormant be certain to label clearly to avoid overplanting or accidental disturbance.

Leontopodium (Compositae). Edelweiss. These like a well-drained soil that is not too rich. Calcareous soils are preferred. If difficulty is found in growing them it might be an idea to add lime to the soil, taking the pH to about 7.5 As with all silver, felted-leafed plants these require full sun. Some tend to be short-lived.

Leonurus (Labiatae). Motherwort. Tall herbs that are increasingly seen in gardens, especially *L. cardiaca*. It grows in any well-drained garden soil, preferably in full sun. It spreads and can become quite invasive, especially if well fed, so keep in

115

check. The wiry stems do not need pea-stick support unless in an exposed position. Cut to the ground in autumn.

Lespedeza (Leguminosae). Shrubs and sub-shrubs that die back and need to be cut to the ground each winter or early spring. They need well-drained soil and a sunny position. Being only just hardy give a winter mulch of bracken or straw in colder areas.

Leucanthemella (Compositae). A new genera following the split up of *Chrysanthemum*. It comprises *L. serrotina*, previously known as *C. uliginosum*. This is a very tall plant in which the flowers tilt vertically and follow the sun. This means it must be planted on the south of the garden otherwise the flowers will point over your neighbour's fence. It will grow in any fertile garden soil and prefers a sunny position. It slowly spreads to form a large clump but is not invasive. It also occasionally self-sows, but not with any conviction. This dense mass of stems benefits from a winter top-dressing of well-rotted organic matter in winter. If it becomes congested, split it up but it can stand many years (up to 10) without this being necessary. Cut back in the winter (the plant does not flower until late autumn).

Leucanthemopsis (Compositae). This is another refuge for outcasts from *Chrysanthemum*. In particular it includes the low growing *L. alpina* and *L. radicans*. These are plants for a well-drained rock garden, raised bed or front of border. Neither is long lived, especially on heavier soils, and need regular replacement. Deadhead.

Leucanthemum (Compositae). Shasta Daisy. The third of these confusingly, similarly named genera that contain the remains of *Chrysanthemum*. The main species here are the shasta daisies, *L. maximum* and *L. x superbum*. These will grow in any good garden soil, but do best in a reasonably rich one. They will grow in either full sun or light shade, although they do best in the former. In spite of their apparently stout stems they do tend to flop and need some form of hidden staking. Alternatively cut them down when they are about 30cm (12in) high and this will shorten them when they re-grow. However, this method usually means smaller flowers as well. Deadhead to the next bud and cut back after flowering is completed to get a fresh crop of leaves. Top-dress in winter with well-rotted organic matter. They can look distressed if short of water during the summer. Watch out for slugs, especially in the spring.

Leucojum (Amaryllidaceae). Snowflakes. *L. aestivum* does best in a moist woodland-type soil or beside water. It will also, surprisingly perhaps, grow in a few inches of water. *L. vernum* likes a humusy soil. They will grow in either sun or light shade, possibly under deciduous trees or shrubs. Transplant and divide clumps of bulbs after they have finished flowering and before the leaves die back. Avoid buying dried out bulbs. Since they are below ground for much of the year mark them clearly so that they are not accidentally disturbed. The bulbs are hardy but harsh frosts can turn the leaves to mush.

Lewisia (Portulaceae). An increasing popular genus of small plants that can either be grown in pots or in the open garden. They like a well-drained soil that does not dry out completely. It is important that water is not allowed to accumulate in the crown of the plant so they are usually planted on their side in a crevice in a rock garden, or in a gap in the wall of a raised bed. A lightly-shaded, north-facing wall is usually advocated. Avoid getting water on the leaves when watering. They also dislike water remaining around the neck so whatever position you plant in, make certain of free-drainage. If they become too dry in summer they go dormant until autumn. Do not throw them away as they are not dead.

Liatris (Compositae). Blazing Stars, Kansas Gay Feather, Button Snakeroot. Most liatris are reasonably drought-tolerant and are good for growing on light, fertile soils. They need to be split up every four years or so to keep the plants vigorous and to prevent the flower spikes shrinking in size. Divide in early spring. Cut off the old flower stalks as the blooms go over (unless you want the seed) as this may well promote a second flush. They like a sunny position. Liatris are generally hardy but they do not like winter wet and can suffer on heavier soils. Some of the taller forms such as *L. aspera* may need staking.

Libertia (Iridaceae). Clump-forming evergreen plants that need a well-drained soil, although it should not dry out completely. Any good garden soil should be ideal. A sunny site is preferred although it will take a little light shade. These plants gradually form large clumps which can begin to look tatty after two or three years but it is difficult to tidy-up without destroying the shape of the plant. It is better to replace them with new plants. They can be deadheaded but removing the fading flowering spikes will deprive the garden of the attractive seed pods, so leave until the winter although this does mean that they are likely to self-sow.

Ligularia (Compositae). This genus of mainly tall plants needs a moist soil with plenty of humus added to it. Several will happily grow in marshy conditions and are ideal for growing in the bog garden. At the slightest hint of being dry at the root the leaves begin to sag, indicating it is time to water. They prefer a light, dappled shade. In full sun the leaves again droop but they will come up again as they cool. They can be deadheaded, but if the old stems are left until late winter they pull away very easily, not damaging the new, emerging foliage. Slugs can be a problem as ligularias are one of their favourite foods and they will soon make the leaves look like paper doilies.

Lilium (Liliaceae). Lilies. Planting levels vary from bulb to bulb and it is best to consult a specialist book for the correct depth. *L. candidum* needs only about 4cm (1.5in) of soil above it but a better depth for most is about 12.5cm (5in). A deeply-cultivated soil with plenty of organic material and added grit or sharp sand for good drainage is required. The soil should generally be on the acid side, about pH6 is perfect. If lilies are dug up they like to be re-planted in different soil. *L. regale* push up their noses early but they are frost-tender so cover temporarily if they are threatened. Do not let lilies dry out too much in a hot summer otherwise their growth becomes weak and stunted. This will not only be unattractive but will also leave them open to disease. One of the most serious problems in recent times has been the spread of the lily beetle. This insect with a red body and a black head, also red at egg and laval stages. They eat all parts of the lily plant and can be really devastating unless action is taken to eliminate them. The best method seems to be vigilance, squashing the eggs and removing larvae and beetles on sight. An alternative is to resort to a general pesticide such as malathion, but the excrement that covers the larvae acts as a waterproof and spraying is not very effective. A more common problem is that of slug and snail attack in spring. Control them by your preferred method. Cut back at the beginning of autumn to prevent botrytis getting into the bulbs. Before discarding the stems remove any bulbils from the axils of the leaves and 'sow' these like seeds to produce new plants. If lilies need to be moved do so while the foliage is still green, and while there is still enough warmth in the soil for them to re-establish themselves before winter sets in. Some are floppy and need staking. This always looks clumsy so if possible plant them among other plants where they will become self-supporting.

Limonium (Plumbaginaceae). Sea Lavender, Statice. Any good garden soil will do as long as it is reasonably deep and free-draining. A sunny position is essential. Plant out while the plants are young and avoid transplanting, starting with new plants if necessary. Some limonium, *L. latifolium* for example, are prone to mildew, especially after a severe, dry spell. Avoid by keeping the soil moist during droughts. Spray with fungicide if all else fails. They can become a bit floppy but they cannot be staked satisfactorily, so put up with it if you can. The spent flower sprays are attractive and can be left for the winter, cutting them back in the early spring. Several species will withstand salt so are ideal for seaside gardens.

Linaria (Scrophulariaceae). Toadflax. On the whole these prefer a light, well-drained soil, but will grow in most garden conditions. Most like a sunny position. They can be invasive either by seed or by runners. Certainly think twice about introducing the native yellow toadflax *L. vulgaris*, pretty as it may be. It runs underground on very thin roots which are impossible to extract. Grow it in a wild garden by all means but keep it out of the borders. *L. dalmatica* can also run but not quite so badly. This is a floppy plant and will need some support unless it can be grown through other plants. Cut back after flowering. *L. triornithophora* is a bit on the tender side and should be grown as an annual in colder areas. Where it survives it can also be invasive.

Lindelofia (Boraginaceae). These will grow in any good garden soil, preferably with good drainage. A sunny position is needed. Cut back in the late autumn once flowering has finished. Can be short-lived, especially on heavier soils, where they dislike the winter wet.

Linum (Linaceae). Flax. These are short-lived perennials that need regular replacement. If happy with the conditions they will provide self-sown seedlings to facilitate this. They like a well-drained soil and a sunny position. Plant out in the spring while the plants are still small. Avoid trying to transplant, replace with young plants if positional changes are required. Some gardeners like to stake *L. narbonense* and *L. perenne* at about 30cm (12in) high or so. The light, airy stems are still attractive when in seed but they do self-sow, so cut back if you wish. Cutting back the stems before energy is spent on seed production may help to prolong the life of the plant.

Liriope (Convallariaceae/Liliaceae). Lilyturf. Liriope will grow in any reasonable garden soil, including quite dry ones. Although they perform best in a sunny position, they have the advantage of growing well in shade. Protect from slugs, especially when in new growth. Cut back the foliage in spring, just before new growth starts. They are spreading plants, some quite vigorous and may need to be kept in check. This is not too difficult a task. Although they form large clumps this does not seem to impair their vigour and they need not be divided unless for propagational reasons.

Lithospermum (Boraginaceae). See *Buglossoides*

Lobelia (Campanulaceae). Most lobelias like a rich, moist soil with plenty of organic material. They generally grow in sun but nearly all will also grow in light shade. Most are short-lived and need regular replacement. *L. cardinalis* 'Queen Victoria' likes to be split every other year to prevent it dying out in the middle. They should be split in the spring, but do not leave it too late as the new shoots are rather brittle and can easily be broken off. Discard any of the central, woody portion of the plant. It is possible to move them even as they come into flower as long as they are well watered. If planted in containers they should be watered regularly, at least once a day in hot weather. In colder areas it may be expedient to dig them up and replant them in a coldframe over winter. Many of the lobelias, especially *L. cardinalis*, are poor at fighting for territorial space so plant in beds where there is not too much competition. They are all on the tender side, and cuttings should be overwintered under glass as a precaution. A mulch of shredded bark helps against the cold but watch out for slugs. Lobelia can suffer from leaf blotch which causes white spots on the leaves, often killing them. Pick off the affected leaves and burn. It is mainly confined to *L. syphilitica. L. fulgens* is reported to suffer from cucumber mosaic; for which the only treatment is to burn the affected plants.

Lotus (Leguminosae). This is a genus of shrubby plants that now also includes what was *Dorycnium*. They need a well-drained soil in a sunny position and dislike heavy soils, especially if they are associated with wet winters. Extra drainage material, such as grit will help. A sunny position is also essential, preferably near a warm wall. In colder areas they may be cut to the ground by the winter. If so cut off all the dead material and they should reshoot from the base unless they have been killed below ground as well. They are quite drought resistant.

Lunaria (Cruciferae). Honesty. *L. rediviva* is the perennial grown in gardens. The biennial *L. annua* is inclined to self-sow making it an honorary perennial. They will both grow in any fertile garden soil, but prefer a moisture-retentive one. Either sun or shade provides a suitable position. Move any seedlings, especially those of *L. annua*, that require transplanting at an early stage in their life. Occasionally cabbage white butterflies lay eggs on the leaves and the resulting caterpillars need removing by hand or by spraying before they reduce the leaves to tatters. Although the dead stems of *L. annua* make a very decorative plant in the garden for winter, it must be remembered that it self-sows so vigorously that it may be preferable to cut down most, if not all, immediately after flowering. Keep the different forms of *L. annua* separate otherwise they will cross and the resulting plants will not come true.

Lupinus (Leguminosae). Lupins. These like a deeply-cultivated soil. The species prefer it to be light and free-draining but the hybrids much prefer a rich, moisture-retentive soil. When top-dressing the hybrids avoid putting manure in contact with the roots, especially if it is fresh. Well-rotted manure can be used as a mulch. Cut out old flower heads leaving any secondary side buds which will produce new flowers. Once this secondary growth has finished cut out the complete flowering stem and with luck new shoots will develop. Some strains go on producing flowers well into the autumn when this technique is used. Watch out for the grey lupin aphids that turn the flower heads and shoots into a slimy mess. Spray at first sight or the lupins will suffer. If they get a hold and leaves start dying back, cut the plant to the ground. They also suffer from mildew. They are not long-lived and should be replaced regularly. Transplant in the autumn when the plants are still quite young. Avoid transplanting after this stage as they resent disturbance.

Luzula (Juncaceae). Woodrush. These present no problems as they can be grown in any reasonable garden soil. They will tolerate sun if the soil is moist, otherwise they prefer shady, woodland conditions.

Lychnis (Caryophyllaceae). Catchflies. These do best in well-drained, but fertile soils. A position in full sun is to be preferred. Most of the taller forms need support. Cut down to the ground after flowering to prevent the copious self-sowing that most seem to provide. *L.* x *arkwrightii* and *L.* x *haageana* are prone to bad attacks of slugs and snails in the spring. Take evasive action. *LL.* x *arkwrightii, coronaria* and x *haageana* are both short-lived and need regular replacement.

Lycopus (Labiatae). Bugleweed, Gypsywort, Water Horehound. A small genus usually grown as medical herbs, or in the wildflower garden. They like moist conditions, growing well beside a pond or stream. They prefer full sun but will also grow in light shade. Cut back to the ground in the autumn or before if you want to avoid the aggressive self-sowing.

Lycoris (Amaryllidaceae). These are bulbous plants that are on the tender side. Plant in a well-drained soil in a warm, sunny position. Do not plant too deeply, the neck of the bulb should be level or slightly above the surface. Mulch in the winter with straw or bracken. Should be kept moist while the leaves are in growth, but drier when in flower. There is a gap between the leaves dying down and the flower stems appearing, so do not think they have died. Poor flowering is induced by cool summers. They prefer not to be disturbed. Top-dress in winter with a potash-rich fertilizer.

Lysichiton (Araceae). Skunk Cabbage. Both the species in this genus like a damp soil and grow well in a bog garden or beside a water feature. They will grow either in full sun or partial shade. A top-dressing of manure or leafmould in the winter is beneficial. The flowers stink so do not plant near a house or sitting place. Let them die down naturally in the autumn.

Lysimachia (Primulaceae). Loosestrife. A very large genus of which a few are grown in cultivation. Most can be a bit invasive (*L. ephemera* being the main exception), so be careful where you plant them. They need a large border or wild garden. In drier soils they are slightly better behaved and do not spread so quickly. Any good garden soil, preferably moisture-retentive will be suitable. They prefer a sunny position but can be seen growing in a light shade, especially *L. nummularia*. Apart from in exposed areas most are self-supporting, except for *L. ciliata* which is rather floppy unless growing through other plants. Cut back after flowering or during the autumn/winter clear-up.

Lythrum (Lythraceae). Purple Loosestrifes. These will grow in any fertile garden soil but are happiest if they are moisture-retentive. They grow best (and look best) by water features. A sunny position is preferable but they will take a little light shade although the performance is not so good. Support is not usually required. Clear away the old foliage as it dies back in the autumn or during the winter clear-up.

Macleaya (Papaveraceae). Plume Poppy. (Formerly known as *Bocconia*.) Two-species that need plenty of space. They spread rapidly by underground stolons. *M. cordata* is reputedly less invasive than *M. microcarpa*, but I have not noticed much difference in them. If necessary dig round them at least once a year and remove all questing roots. These can run deep so they are not easy to restrain by planting in a bottomless container. The roots and stems produce a yellowish sap that should not cause skin complaints if touched. Macleaya seem happy in most soils but prefer a rich and well-drained one. They also prefer a sunny position but will take light shade. Top-dress in the winter with a rich compost or farmyard manure. They are gross feeders and some authorities in the past have advocated weekly liquid feeds during the growing season, but this is being a bit excessive (it is not surprising the plants have the energy to run). Although both species are tall they do not need staking except in very exposed areas. Cut the tall stems to the ground as part of the autumn or winter clear-up.

Maianthemum (Convallariaceae/Liliaceae). May Lily, Twin-leaved Lily-of-the-Valley. *M. biflorum*, the only member of the genus that is regularly grown in gardens, is a low woodlander that likes a cool rootrun in a moist, humusy soil and a lightly-shaded position. It is rhizomatous and spreads around underground. This is not too much of a problem where there is plenty of space but it can become a nuisance in a small border.

Malephora (Aizoaceae). This is a tender genus really only suitable for warmer areas. They grow in well-drained soils and are able to withstand drought conditions for a short time. A warm, sunny place is also required.

Malva (Malvaceae). These will grow in any deep, fertile soil. If it is too dry or tired the plants will be small. A sunny position is best. Most are not very long-lived but usually self-sow to provide replacements. *M.* 'Primley Blue' can suffer from rust similar to hollyhocks. Spray with a suitable fungicide. If you regularly have problems with this disease spray the plants as a matter of course before they get it. If not try it without spraying. As well as being a prostrate plant it can be trained up through plants or even against a wall. Most malvas self-sow quite vigorously and some, such as *M. moschata*, need to be cut back before they seed and have at least some of the seedlings removed before they put down their deep tap roots. *M. sylvestris mauritanica* is often sold as an annual in seed catalogues but it is a short-lived perennial and can be left for a second year. Again, it self-sows. Being tap-rooted any transplanting should be carried out while the plant is still small. Later movement should be avoided and new plants started instead. Cut back after flowering.

Mandragora (Solanaceae). Mandrake. A small genus of which *M. officinarum* is sometimes grown as a medicinal herb or out of curiosity. It likes a deep, light, well-drained soil in full sun. In cooler areas it may need winter protection in the form of a mulch of bracken or straw. Plant out while young and start with new plants rather than try to move older ones.

Marrubium (Labiatae). White Horehound. Few of this genus are in cultivation. *M. vulgare* is the most frequently seen as it is sometimes grown as a herb. In the borders *M. incanum* is grown for its silvery leaves. Most of this genus seem to thrive on poor, free-draining soils and a sunny position. They are likely to seed around so cut off flowering stems once they have finished flowering.

Marshallia (Compositae). Barbara's Buttons. A small genus that is not much grown except for *M. grandiflora*. It needs planting in a damp or moisture-retentive soil and a sunny position, although it will also grow in light shade.

Matricaria (Compositae). This genus has lost a lot of its species, but *M. recutita* (*M. chamomilla*) remains. This is an annual that in most gardens is considered to be a weed, but it has also been used as a herb for centuries and so has a cultivated place in many gardens. It will grow in any good garden soil, usually in full sun, in shade it becomes very drawn. Do not let it seed otherwise you will rue the day you introduced it.

Matteuccia (Aspidiaceae). Ostrich Fern. These are invasive plants that like a cool, moist (even wet), woodland-type soil in a shady position. Moisture in the soil is important as they do not like to dry out. They are deciduous so cut back the dead fronds towards the end of winter. Only plant where they can run about without becoming a nuisance. Unfortunately the roots are near the surface making it difficult to weed round them.

Matthiola (Cruciferae). This is a genus of mainly annual or biennial plants. What perennials there are tend to be short-lived. They will all grow in any good garden soil as long as it is reasonably well-drained. They all like full sun. Take cuttings or collect seed from all perennial forms in case they are lost during the winter. One suspects that it is the dampness as much as the cold that kills them. Cut back the flowering stems before seed is ripe if you want to prevent them self-sowing, although this is a painless way of ensuring their continuance.

Meconopsis (Papaveraceae). Blue Poppies. These popular plants are not perennials. Some are monocarpic and die back after flowering, others are simply short-lived. A rich soil with plenty of manure dug into it is essential for most of them. They all need moisture but *M. horridula* and one or two others can be grown in somewhat drier conditions if necessary. A moist, shady atmosphere helps considerably, and gardens with a wet maritime climate stand the best chance of having good stands of meconopsis; hot, dry areas the least. *M. cambrica* is the exception, this will grow virtually anywhere. It can become a pest and it is important to deadhead it to prevent it seeding everywhere. The cut stems ooze a nasty sap that can stain clothes, so take care. For those meconopsis that over-winter as rosettes remove any dead leaves to prevent them infecting other leaves and to improve the plant's appearance. If grown amongst shrubs they should be self-supporting, but in an exposed position they may need individual staking, although this can look quite ugly.

Meehania (Labiatae). Japanese Dead Nettle, Meehan's Mint. This is a small genus of woodland plants that like a moist, humusy soil and a light shade. They are creeping plants with overground runners, but are not thuggish. They naturally die back for the winter and if planted in a woodland or wild setting there is no need to clear them up. Protect from slugs.

Megacarpea (Cruciferae). This is a small genus of perennials of which MM. *bifida* and *polyandra* are the most important. They take a long time to reach flowering stage and then often die, making them probably monocarpic. They need a reasonably rich, free-draining soil and an open, sunny position. They have deep roots and should therefore be planted out while young and not moved.

Melanthium (Melanthaceae/Liliaceae). This is a small genus related to the *Veratrum*. They like conditions similar to their relatives, namely a deep rich, humusy soil and a light, shady position, although they will grow in sun if the soil is moist enough. They take several years to reach flowering size. Cut back the tall flowering stems after flowering. A top-dressing of leafmould can be applied in winter.

Melianthus (Melianthaceae). Honeybush. These require a fertile garden soil and a warm, sunny position. *M. major* is a much loved plant for its foliage quality. It is usually treated as annual and grown from seed each year, but it is possible to overwinter it from cuttings taken in autumn or by covering it with some form of winter protection, such as bracken or fern fronds, or even a hessian sack. After its first two years the chances are that it will be tougher and able to survive subsequent winters more easily, although the bits above ground may be frosted. If it does survive it is likely to flower in its second year. However, it is a plant that can get leggy and it can benefit from being cut back if the frosts do not do it for you. Can be transplanted in winter, before the spring growth recommences. Avoid bruising the leaves as they do not smell very nice.

Melica (Gramineae). Melick. This is a large family of clump-forming and creeping grasses. Most need a moisture-retentive soil, preferably one that is on the calcerous side. They are happy in either sun or part-shade. Cut back in late winter. Plant out or transplant in the spring.

Melissa (Labiatae). Balm, Lemon Balm. A small genus of which only *M. officinalis* is in general cultivation. This is a somewhat leggy herb that either needs supporting with pea-sticks or cutting back before it flowers so that a fresh crop of shorter shoots are produced. Cutting back also helps prevent the plant from self-sowing everywhere. It will grow in any good garden soil, but can become mildewed if it is too dry. The best situation is an open, sunny one but *M.o.* 'Aurea' needs to be planted in light shade to prevent its golden leaves scorching.

Melittis (Labiatae). Bastard Balm. The sole representative of this genus is the attractive *M. melissophyllum*. It is a woodland plant that likes a typical, moist, humusy soil and light shade. Unlike many of this family it is not a spreader and can safely be used in any border situation where it can be afforded a little shade. Cut back after flowering once it begins to look a bit tatty.

Mentha (Labiatae). Mint. These will grow in any fertile garden soil, although a moist one is preferred. They will grow in either sun or light shade. Most are extremely invasive. The roots rarely go deep and thus are not too difficult to remove (they are also quite thick which also helps). This also means that they can be controlled by planting into a sunken, bottomless container such as an old bucket. Alternatively they can be dug up every year, every other year at the most, in spring and a few strands replanted. Make certain that all stray pieces are dug out so that only the area you want is planted. A number (*M. longifolia*) in particular will also self-sow prodigiously so cut them back before they seed. They can be little floppy but look better if they are not staked.

Menyanthes (Menyanthaceae). Bog Bean, Buckbean, Marsh Trefoil. A marginal plant for ponds or streams that grows in shallow water or in boggy soil. It tends to spread but is rarely a nuisance as it is easy to control. Every few years remove it and chop the thick stems into lengths and replant them. The best time is after flowering.

Mercurialis (Euphorbiaceae). Dog's Mercury. This is a small genus of one *M. perennis* which is sometimes grown in a wild flower or woodland garden, although it is considered a weed by most gardeners. It is a bit of a spreader and should not be introduced into ornamental borders. Any moist, woodland soil is suitable, and it will even grow in leafmould over pure chalk. A shady position is required. No attention is required once planted.

Mertensia (Boraginaceae). Bluebells, Virginian Cowslip. An interesting genus of plants the number of which in cultivation seems to increase every year. Their requirements vary considerably. The most popular (taller) group headed by M. *virginica* like a cool rootrun in a woodland-type soil in light shade. Many of the others, MM. *asiatica* and *maritima*, like a well-drained, gritty soil in full sun. The young shoots are much appreciated by slugs so take evasive action. M. *virginica* and some of the others retire below ground early in the year and should be marked to avoid accidental disturbance. These are deep-rooted and should be planted in their final positions as soon as possible. They are not easy to transplant so it may be easier to start again with young plants.

Meum (Umbelliferae). Bald Money, Spignel. A single-species genus of which M. *athamanticum* is the sole representative. It is undemanding, requiring any fertile garden soil and a position in the sun. Cut back once it begins to look unattractive.

Michauxia (Campanulaceae). These monocarpic plants dislike wet conditions and have done very well in the recent years of drought. Add grit or coarse sand to the soil before planting if the soil is at all on the heavy side. It may also be necessary to cover in the winter, but only protect from the rain, allow air to circulate freely over the plant. An open, sunny position is required. Grow the plants in their first year in pots, and overwinter in a covered coldframe. Plant out in the spring of their second year. When flowering these are tall plants and usually require individual staking to prevent them falling over.

Milium (Gramineae). Millet. A small genus of grasses of which the most frequently met in cultivation is M. *effusum* in its form *aureum*, commonly known as Bowles' Golden Grass. This will grow in any garden soil but does best in a rich, moist one. Light shade is preferred. Don't give it too much shade or the leaves will turn green rather than golden. It will seed. Remove flower heads before seeding if it becomes a nuisance.

Milligania (Asparagaceae/Liliaceae). M. *longifolia* is the only one of the four species that is in general cultivation. It likes a fertile garden soil that contains plenty of organic material and a place in the sun.

Mimulus (Scrophulariaceae). Monkey Flower, Musk. A large genus of plants of which quite a number are in cultivation. One of the essentials for these plants is a moist soil. Many will grow in boggy conditions, even standing in shallow water, but few will tolerate dry soil. Add organic matter to drier soils to make them moisture-retentive and more fertile. Most will grow in either sun or light shade. Cut back once they begin to look straggly or tatty. Some taller species such as M. *lewisii* (which will take drier conditions than most) will need staking with pea-sticks to keep them from flopping. They are not all hardy by any means. Some need winter protection, others are treated as annuals. They tend to hybridize so self-sown seedlings can not always be depended on to give replacements. M. *luteus* can become invasive but generally can be controlled by pulling it up. Others may self-sow. M. *glutinosa* is hardy in warmer areas but can be grown in a container elsewhere and moved inside for the winter. It has brittle stems so it should be given a sheltered position and staking if necessary. Top-dress in winter with an organic mulch.

Mindium (Campanulaceae). See *Michauxia*

Mirabilis (Nyctaginaceae). Four O'Clock, Umbrella Worts. *M. jalopa* is usually considered to be an annual and is treated as such, but its fleshy tubers can be lifted and stored over winter like dahlias. *M. multiflora* is slightly hardier but not so frequently seen. They will grow in any fertile garden soil and should be given a warm, sunny position. Plant out new plants or old tubers in spring. Remember that these flowers do not open until late afternoon, so plant them where they can be appreciated.

Miscanthus (Gramineae). A genus of very garden-worthy grasses. They will grow in a variety of garden soils, but do best when organic matter has been incorporated. They are versatile in that they can be used in a variety of positions: the border, the water's edge, or the margins of a woodland garden. They do best in full sun, getting weak and spindly in shade. Cut back to the ground every winter. If you want to leave for winter effect cut back in spring, but before the new growth starts. A mulch of well-rotted humus, applied each winter, helps to keep the plant vigorous.

Molinia (Gramineae). Moor Grass. A small genus of grasses that are happy to grow in wet, even boggy conditions. In cultivation it can be grown in any good garden soil but benefit from plenty of organic material. It prefers an acid or neutral soil, but is unhappy on chalk. Grow in a sunny position. They are clump forming and non-invasive. Cut back in late winter.

Molopospermum (Umbelliferae). Striped Hemlock. *M. peloponnesiacum* is the only species in this genus. It likes a deep, well-drained, but fertile soil and a sunny position. Cut back when its attractiveness begins to fade. Set out while the plant is still young and avoid transplanting.

Moltkia (Boraginaceae). A small genus of perennials and sub-shrubs. They all need a fertile, but well-drained soil, preferably on the limy side although this is not essential. They do best in full sun but in areas where the summer sun is very hot, a situation where there is light shade around midday is to be preferred. *M. doefleri* is a rhizomatous plant but does not spread to the extent of becoming a nuisance.

Monarda (Labiatae). Bee Balm, Bergamot, Oswego Tea. An increasing number of these are coming into cultivation. They all require a rich, moisture-retentive soil and an open, sunny position. The soil must be well fed or the monarda will become less vigorous after a couple of seasons. It is advisable to dig it out at least every three or four years, rejuvenate the soil and replant. In any case it should be carefully top-dressed with manure or compost every winter. Although the soil should be moisture retentive it should also be reasonably free-draining as some forms resent heavy soils and can die out over winter. Neatness will be improved if they are deadheaded as they fade. Monardas can be very prone to mildew, especially during a dry spell. Make sure that there is plenty of moisture-retentive, organic material in the soil, and water copiously. Spray with a fungicide if the attack is likely to become severe. Some of the modern varieties can be severely weakened by mildew and will often be lost in the following winter. Strong winds can open up a clump of plants and in exposed areas a discrete support of pea-sticks will be an advantage. The clumps are likely to spread but since they are shallow-rooted they are very easy to control and rarely become a nuisance.

Monardella (Labiatae). To all intents a smaller version of the previous genus. However, it tends to be less hardy and it is important that they have a warm, sunny position and a well-drained soil. A rock garden or raised bed makes an ideal site.

Montbretia (Iridaceae). See *Crocosmia*

Moraea (Iridaceae). Butterfly Irises. The majority of this genus of iris-like plants are tender although one or two, *M. spathulata* in particular, are hardy in many areas. They are helped if they are planted in a warm, sunny position, by a wall for example. The soil should be reasonably rich, but it must be well-drained. Plant out at about 10cm (4in) below the surface, deeper on heavier soils. They are best if they are left undisturbed but it may eventually be necessary to lift and divide the clump in order to maintain its vigour. Carry this out in spring. Top-dressing with a potash-rich fertilizer in the spring will also help to keep them vigorous.

Morina (Morinaceae). Only a few of the 17 or so species are in cultivation but they all like a damp, humusy soil that will not dry out. In the wild they often inhabit light woodlands but in cultivation they seem to prefer an open situation as long as the soil is not too dry. They are long-lived if these conditions are met. They are likely to dwindle if not, especially in recent drought years. Conversely they do not like wet conditions and a cold, constantly wet winter soil will spell disaster. These can be mistaken for thistles and weeded out, so label clearly.

Muhlembergia (Gramineae). This is a large genus of grasses of which one, *M. mexicana*, is hardy enough to be grown in some of the warmer areas. It grows mainly in moist woodlands and should therefore be given a moist, humusy soil in a light shade. Plant out or divide in spring.

Mukdenia (Saxifragaceae). *M. rossii* (previously *Aceriphyllum rossii*) is the single member of this genus. It is a creeping woodland plant that likes a cool, moist, humus-rich soil and light dappled shade. It will take a little sun if the soil is moist enough. Top-dress with leafmould during the winter.

Muscari (Hyacinthaceae/Liliaceae). Grape Hyacinths. A genus of small bulbous plants that are often used between herbaceous plants. The beauty of them is that they will group in virtually any soil, unfortunately too well in some cases as they can become a bit invasive. They will grow in a light shade but prefer a sunny position. Plant out in the autumn as they come into growth very early and carry their leaves through the winter. Plant about 5cm (2in) deep, slightly deeper for the larger species. One of the problems with this bulb is the lank leaves that seem to hang around for ages after the flowers are over. In theory you should leave the leaves on until they naturally die back, but with the more vigorous ones it does not seem to do any harm if the foliage is removed as soon as it begins to look tatty. They are all hardy but *M. comosum* and *M. moschatum* prefer a warm, sunny position such as up against a wall. These two also appreciate being left undisturbed for as long as possible. The most vigorous will eventually thrust themselves to the surface and need replanting every so often. Do not plant these more vigorous ones in a border unless you really want them as they are very difficult to eradicate once introduced. *MM. armeniacum* and *neglectum* are two of the worst spreaders. *M. botryoides* is less invasive.

Mysotidium (Boraginaceae). Chatham Island Forget-me-not, New Zealand Forget-me-not. This genus is closely related to *Myosoitis* and consists of just one species, *M. hortensia*. This is a beautiful plant but, unfortunately, it is not the easiest one in the world to grow as it is only marginally tender. It seems to like a moist, warm, but not over-hot climate, and does well in the west of Britain and Ireland. The best results seem to come from planting it in a compost made up of seaweed, but it will also grow in a moist, loamy soil that is not too heavy. It is evergreen and stays above ground during the winter. In most areas it is advisable to give it some form of protection, such as a cloche, during this time of year, covering it only when cold weather or particularly wet conditions are threatened.

Myositis (Boraginaceae). Forget-me-nots. It is difficult to imagine any garden without these plants. Some of those most commonly seen in gardens are in fact annuals, but they sow themselves around and rarely seem to die out. They will grow in any soils. *M. scorpioides*, the water forget-me-not, will grow in boggy conditions, even in shallow water. They will all grow in either full sun or light shade. Most, especially the annuals, will self-sow quite prodigiously. Remove any unwanted seedlings, particularly those appearing in or up against the crowns of other plants, and thin others to get the best result. The thinnings can be used elsewhere if so required. Remove any old plants in late spring as soon as they have finished flowering and before they become prey to mildew.

Myriophyllum (Haloragiedaceae). Water Milfoils. A valuable genus of submerged water plants. Some are perfectly hardy, cuttings of others may need to be overwintered inside. They will grow in water up to 90cm (3ft) deep, but most prefer a much shallower position than this. When planting out make certain that they are anchored in the mud or they float away. Can be used in lattice pots. They do spread making a veritable underwater forest that is ideal for spawning fish but which can take up all available space.

Myrrhis (Umbelliferae). Sweet Cicely. *M. odorata* is the only member of this genus. It is a herb that is widely grown in herb gardens and can be seen growing wild in many northern areas. It will grow in any deeply cultivated, fertile soil. It also grows in the light shade of a hedgerow but prefers a sunny position. Plant out while it is still quite young as, being tap-rooted, it does not like being disturbed. Similarly it is better to start with a new plant than to try and transplant it. It produces copious amounts of seed which are part of the attraction of the plant but it does self-sow and it may be prudent to deadhead it before the seed spreads. Cut back in autumn.

Narcissus (Amaryllidaceae). Daffodils. A genus of very popular bulbous plants. Most like a well-drained soil in a sunny position. They all like moisture during the growing season but prefer it dry while they are dormant. Many will tolerate a little shade such as under or amongst deciduous trees and shrubs. *N. cyclamineus* and its various cultivars and hybrids prefer a somewhat damper soil and will even grow well in quite heavy conditions. A lightly-shaded position with a humusy woodland soil is ideal for this species. Plant in mid-autumn at about 15cm (6in) deep. Leave the foliage until it has died down. Avoid tying it in knots or cutting it off until its work has been completed or the bulb will be weakened. Lightly top-dress in the early spring with a potash-based fertilizer. Mark all clumps while still in leaf so that they can be divided later when they are dormant. Clumps become congested and need dividing every four years or so.

Nardus (Gramineae). Mat Grass. A single-species genus represented by *N. stricta*. This will grow in any garden soil, even quite poor or boggy ones, and likes an open, sunny situation. Any division or transplanting should be carried out in spring. Cut back in the late winter.

Nectaroscordum (Alliaceae/Liliaceae). The one or two species (depending which taxonomist you follow) of this genus used to belong to *Allium* and are still listed there by some nurseries. They will grow in any soil, preferably in full sun, but they will take a little shade. Plant in autumn at a depth of about 15cm (6in). They will often pull themselves deeper and you may have to dig a long way down to remove them. The seed pods on these plants are very attractive but when they discard their seeds they can become an invasive nuisance. You will have to make up your own mind whether to keep or remove them, most who have had experience of the seed rooting in unwanted places will doubtless advocate removal after flowering. They also spread underground and can become a menace in this way too. They are attractive plants but they are best banished to the wild garden. The foliage has a very pungent onion smell and should be removed as soon as it begins to look tatty.

Nepeta (Labiatae). Catmint. A large genus of which an increasing number are coming into cultivation. All grow in any fertile garden soil as long as it is well-drained. A sunny position is also essential except for *N. govaniana* which will grow in light shade. Some nepetas are likely to self-sow and should be cut down before they seed. *N. x faassenii* is sterile. Shear over the nepetas in late summer or early autumn to tidy them. If you leave them beyond this they begin to look sad, especially in rainy weather. Few nepetas are strong, upright plants, they all tend to flop to varying extents. Some of the taller forms can be supported with pea-sticks but the *N. x faassenii* types look more natural if allowed to sprawl. Make allowances for this when planting.

Nephrophyllidium (Menyanthaceae). Deer Cabbage. A single species (*N. crista-galli*) that will grow in a moist, even boggy soil in a cool position such as besides a water feature. It will grow in sun or partial shade. It is a creeping plant that makes dense carpets and should be kept in check if necessary. Previously belonged to the genus *Fauria*.

Nerine (Amaryllidaceae). A genus of bulbous plants. The species most frequently grown is *N. bowdenii*. These may be reluctant to break into flower after a dry summer so give them a good soaking if they seem delayed. They appear to grow well in most soils but a well-drained one that is rich in organic material seems to be preferred. Do not plant too deeply. The top of the bulbs should be level or just above the surface. Colonies are liable to become congested, often with bulbs being pushed above ground, and will need dividing every five or six years. This is best done between the leaves dying back and the flowers appearing, ie in early autumn or between the flowers and the leaves, ie winter if the weather is suitable or early spring. *N. bowdenii* is generally quite hardy as long as it is planted deep enough, but the white form is much more tender than the type. Other species are less hardy and should be given protected sites if they are to be left in the ground. *N. bowdenii* will also appreciate such a position in colder areas.

Nicotiana (Solanaceae). Tobacco Plant. A genus of about 70 species of annuals and perennial plants. Many of the perennials are tender and are in fact treated as annuals, although their rootstock will persist below ground throughout the winter. They will grow in any fertile garden soil, preferring those which are free-draining but moisture-retentive. They will grow in sun or light shade, in hot areas the latter is to be preferred. They generally have large drooping leaves that need a generous amount of moisture, so water in dry weather if necessary. Most will self-sow, *N. sylvestris*, quite copiously, so deadhead if necessary. Cut back the plants after the first frosts. The taller forms may need discrete staking.

Nierembergia (Solanaceae). Cupflower. This genus includes perennials that are often treated as annuals. Plant in a moist but well-drained soil. They will grow in sun or light shade. The latter is preferable in hotter climates. Deadhead as the flowers fade to promote a long season, and cut back during the autumn/winter clear-up. If kept as perennials take cuttings as an overwinter insurance.

Nigella (Ranunculaceae). Love-in-a-Mist. The nigella are strictly speaking annuals but they self-sow themselves about in such a way that once they have been introduced to the garden they are likely to remain. Do not hurry to clear them up as they are interesting for the shape of their seed pods as well as the flowers, which will also give them time to self-sow before being relegated to the compost heap. They are hardy, and autumn seedlings will survive most winters to flower in the following spring. They will grow in any fertile garden soil and prefer an open, sunny position.

Nipponanthemum (Compositae). Nippon Daisy. *N. nipponicum* used to be in *Chrysanthemum* but now has a genus to itself. This is a sub-shrub which likes a well-drained soil and a warm, sunny position, preferably against a wall. It may need winter protection. Pinch out growing tips after planting to get it to bush out.

Nomocharis (Liliaceae). These are closely related to the lilies. They must have cool woodland conditions to succeed. The soil should be moist but well-drained and contain plenty of humus such as leafmould. It should be lime free. They do not like hot, dry atmospheres and do best in areas that have a relatively high rainfall and high humidity. A partially shaded position should be provided. Plant the bulbs 7.5–10cm (3–4in) deep. Top-dress with leafmould in winter. Do not allow soil to dry out and spray the plants with water during dry hot spells. Watch out for slugs and snails.

Nonea (Boraginaceae). This genus is very closely related to *Pulmonaria* and should be treated in a similar manner. They prefer a cool, semi-shaded position, with a leafy, moisture-retentive soil. They will grow in a more open position as long as the soil is not allowed to dry out. Remove flower stems after flowering unless seed is required. Remove foliage after it has died down. It is a hardy genus but some are annuals.

Notholirion (Liliaceae). A genus of bulbous plants closely related to lilies. It should be given the same treatment as *Nomocharis*. One respect in which it differs is that it is monocarpic and dies after flowering and seeding. However as it dies down it leaves offsets behind. It is difficult to flower as the bulbs often break down into a mass of bulbils, much in the manner of some *Fritillaria*. There is no one way to ensure flowering other than giving the best possible conditions.

Nothoscordum (Alliaceae/Liliaceae). This is a medium-sized genus of bulbous plants that are related to the onions. They require a well-drained soil and a warm, sunny position. They are not completely hardy and can really only be grown in warmer areas. Plant deeply, at least 15cm (6in), and cover if necessary. The main problem with them, as with so many onions, is that they produce masses of bulbils that spread everywhere.

Nuphar (Nymphaeaceae). Brandy Bottle, Spatterdock, Yellow Pond Lilies. A small genus of pond plants. They will grow in ponds or slow streams, either directly in the mud or in a lattice pot if the pond is lined. They are vigorous plants and spread quite rapidly so may need to be kept in check. Be warned that new plants in their first year are likely to make only underwater growth. This is normal. If planted directly in the bottom of the pond make certain that the plant is anchored until its roots get a hold. Plant out in late spring or early summer in water that can be as deep as 2m (7ft) or more. For feeding plants in pots see *Nymphaea*.

Nymphaea (Nymphaeaceae). Waterlilies need warmth for growth and should be planted out in summer between, say, May and August. Either plant in lattice containers or directly into the mud of a pool. They prefer a sunny position although they will tolerate a little dappled shade. If planting in mud tie the roots to a stone or brick so that it sinks to the bottom and comes into contact with the soil. The tops of the crowns should just be exposed when planting, and nymphaea planting depth varies according to the variety, so check this when purchasing. The roots of *N. odorata*, *N. tuberosa* and their various forms need to be planted horizontally in the mud or compost. Hybrids of *N.* x *marliacea* and *N.* x *laydekeri* should be planted vertically. If they are planted in containers in a lined pool they will need feeding. One way of doing this is to mix up a paste of bonemeal and clay and roll it into small balls. These can be pushed into the soil around the plants, if they can be reached, or dropped onto the crowns of the plants. Alternatively use a John Innes base fertilizer mixed into a paste. Many are often very vigorous plants, with a strong root system and will need to be thinned annually to keep them in bounds. Only a comparative few waterlilies are hardy.

Oaksiella (Convallariaceae/Liliaceae). See *Uvularia*

Oenothera (Onagraceae). Evening Primroses. This large genus appreciates a well-drained soil. They will often grow wild in very sandy soils and seem to be drought-resistant. They like a sunny position, although they will often sow themselves in light shade. Many of the perennial members of the genus seem to be short-lived, but most produce enough self-sown seedlings to perpetuate the line. Self-sowing can be a problem with some species and cutting back early might help. This is not quite as easy as it sound as Oenothera flower over a long period and ripe seed will be found on stems that still have plenty of flowers to come. Deadheading is the alternative but this is not a very easy proposition with this plant. Many are tap-rooted so plant out while they are still young and take a large lump of soil with them if you attempt to transplant them at a latter stage. *O. speciosa* can become invasive as it sends out rhizomes in all directions, so either avoid or place with care and keep under control. (It is a beautiful plant and worth the effort.) Not all species are hardy. *OO. acaulis, fruticosa, missouriensis, perennis, speciosa, stricta*, and *tetragona* are amongst the hardiest.

Omphalodes (Boraginaceae). Creeping Forget-me-not. Navelworts. Most of the perennials can be grown as a ground cover in light woodland or under deciduous shrubs. They like a moist, humusy soil. Set out young plants in autumn, or spring in colder areas. They prefer not to be disturbed but any division can take place at the same time of year. Although they spread they are not particularly invasive and are easy to keep under control. *O. linifolia*, a beautiful annual, self-sows vigorously but is rarely a nuisance. This likes a sunny position. Top-dress the woodlanders during the winter with a well-rotted mulch. Cut back when the foliage begins to look jaded. Watch out for slugs when the leaves first break through.

Omphalogramma (Primulaceae). This is a small genus of Chinese plants closely related to the primulas, that are not easy to grow. They like a humusy, moisture-retentive soil but one that contains enough grit to ensure adequate drainage. Place them in a shady position, preferably where the air is moist and humid. They grow best in cool, maritime-type climates. They are not very large plants so avoid planting them where they might be swamped by larger neighbours. A peat bed would be ideal.

Onoclea (Aspleniaceae). Sensitive Fern. A single-species genus consisting of *O. sensibilis*. This fern likes a moist, humusy soil that never dries out, beside water is ideal but not in it as they are not happy about being submerged. It can be grown in a boggy situation. Plant out with the rhizomes just covered in soil. The best time for this is in the spring. It is mainly grown in shade under trees or bushes but it can also be grown in the open if the situation is moist enough and the sun not too hot. It is hardy but the fronds die back at the first frosts. Leave fronds to protect the crowns and remove in the late winter. It forms a dense mat of rhizomes below the surface which spread to create a large colony.

Ononis (Leguminosae). Rest Harrow. This is a large genus of annuals, biennials and perennials, several of them having a shrubby growth. They all like a well-drained soil and will even grow in quite poor conditions. Most prefer a calcareous soil. They must have full sun. Being quite deep-rooted they must be planted out when young and transplanting should be avoided. Trim over in autumn to keep them compact. They may be on the borderline of hardiness in colder areas. Provide winter protection if necessary.

Onopordum (Compositae). Cotton Thistle, Scotch Thistle. A genus of biennials that are frequently seen in herbaceous borders. They need a well-drained soil in full sun. Although they will grow in quite poor conditions they do best if the soil is reasonably fertile and deeply cultivated. Plant out or transplant while they are still young. Avoid moving once they are established. Being very tall they may need staking in more exposed areas but they generally manage to stand on their own, especially if placed at the back of a border. Like most thistles they self-sow, so deadheading will be needed to preempt this.

Onosma (Boraginaceae). A large genus of plants suitable for growing on large rock gardens or on the top of retaining walls where they hang down. It is important they have a free-draining soil. Put a layer of grit or small stones under the plant to keep the leaves from contact with moist soil. They may need protection in the winter as much from the wet as the cold. The bristly hairs on some species can cause skin complaints for some people so wear gloves when handling them if necessary.

Ophiopogon (Convallariaceae/Liliaceae). Lilyturf. This genus requires a well-drained soil but one that contains a reasonable amount of moisture-retentive humus. They will grow in either part shade or full sun, but the black leaves of *O. planiscapus nigrescens* are likely to change to green in shade. Ophiopogons can get congested and need to be split up every few years. *O. japonicus* can cause mild panic because it produces stolons that very closely resemble couch grass, but it is not at all invasive. Tidy the plants by removing old flower spikes and dead leaves.

Ophrys (Orchidaceae). Bee Orchid. These are very tricky plants to grow in the garden. If they like you they may well turn up of their own accord and appear in the lawn. In cultivation the easiest way of growing them is in pots. Do *not* dig them up in the wild, they are almost one hundred per cent certain to die and you are depriving the natural flora. All-in-all they are probably best not attempted in the garden.

Orchis (Orchidaceae). A few hardy orchis remain in this genus but the rest have moved to *Dactylorhiza*. *OO. morio* and *mascula* are the two most commonly grown. These are British natives but should *not* be dug up from the wild. Both thrive in borders but seem to do best in grass meadow-like conditions, perhaps in an old orchard, where they are left undisturbed and free to seed about. They can be left to their own devices, indeed they seem to thrive better without man's interference.

Origanum (Labiatae). Marjoram, Oregano. These all need a sunny position and any reasonable, well-drained garden soil. *O. vulgare* 'Aureum' retains its golden colour much better if it is split up every three years, preferably in autumn. Small pieces can take a long time to become established so replant using sizeable clumps. The golden form's leaves can be scorched in hot sun, so it is best planted in light shade. It is likely to lose its colour anyway as the season progresses turning to green, although there are forms about that remain golden. Trim over in the late autumn or during the winter clear-up, if you have not done so immediately after flowering to prevent self-sowing. The smaller forms are not keen on competition and can be smothered by larger plants. *O. laevigatum* and its cultivars seem to be able to stand much better up to the rigours of border life. Those of the amaracus section, *AA. amanum*, *dictamnus*, and *tournefourtii* for example, are much less hardy and require a sharp-draining soil in a warm site, perhaps backed by rocks, to allow them to survive outside in milder areas.

Ornithogalum (Hyacinthaceae/Liliaceae). Star-of-Bethlehem. A very large genus of bulbous plants, of which a few of the larger ones are suitable for borders. Plant out in any good garden soil in either sun or a light, dappled shade under deciduous shrubs. They multiply rapidly and can become congested, producing leaf but little or not flowers. Lift and divide every two or three years to prevent this. The leaves can become very tired looking before they finally disappear. Cut them off if you want to. It is generally not good practice to cut off leaves before they die down naturally, but it does not seem to affect these bulbs adversely. Cut off flowering stems before seed is produced to prevent self-sowing.

Orobanche (Orobanchaceae). Broomrapes. This is a large genus of parasitic plants. The main problem in growing these is that the plants must be brought into contact with their correct hosts. Thus Ivy Broomrape, *O. hederae*, needs to grow on the roots of Ivy. The only really successful way of getting these plants established is to scatter their seed around a suitable host. If successful do not cut down until seed has been shed.

Orontium (Araceae). Golden Club, Water Dock. *O. aquaticum* is a water plant that should be grown in about 30–45cm (12–18in) of water in a pond or lake. It can be planted directly into the mud or planted in a lattice pot if the pool is lined. In the latter case use a compost with plenty of humus added to it. It should be in a sunny position. This plant is hardy as long as the pond does not freeze as far as the mud. Plants in pots should be fed as described under *Nymphaea*.

Orostachys (Crassulaceae). A small genus of succulent plants that can only be overwintered outside in warm areas. *O. iwarenge* is one of the hardiest. They need a well-drained soil and a warm, sunny position. The rosettes of leaves die back after the flower has seeded, leaving just a dormant winter bud. Protect in cooler areas.

Orthrosanthus (Iridaceae). Morning Flag, Morning Flower. This is a small genus of quite tender plants that are related to the *Sisyrinchium*. They can only be grown in warm areas or with winter protection afforded by a greenhouse or conservatory. These plants need a moisture-retentive soil and a position in a light, dappled shade.

Osmunda (Osmundaceae). Royal Fern. *O. regalis* is the best known and hardiest of this small genus, although others are appearing in nurseries. These must have a moist soil that does not dry out and contains a supply of organic material. A lime-free soil is preferred. They do best near a pond or stream, or growing in the bog garden, but they are not keen on having their roots submerged in water. They will grow in sun if the soil is kept moist but prefer a lightly-shaded position. If the latter is under shrubs make certain that their lower branches are high enough to accommodate this tall fern; at least 1.5m (5ft) is required. Plant out in spring. Make certain that the removal of the old fronds is accomplished by the time the new ones start to emerge in spring. Top-dress with organic material in winter.

Osteospermum (Compositae). Star of the Veldt. A large genus of mainly tender plants of which a few are suitable for cooler areas. Osteospermum like a well-drained, but reasonably fertile soil and should be placed in a warm, sunny position. Deadhead to help keep the plant tidy and vigorous. They are evergreen and may well last through a mild winter without being cut back, in which case they will flower early and long. They can get rather sprawling and may need cutting back. They may well get cut back in the winter or, even more likely, killed, so take cuttings in the autumn and overwinter them under glass. However, more and more hardy forms are appearing that seem to come through most winters unscathed. If flowering seems impaired in spite of reasonable top-growth it might be due to capsid bugs attacking the shoots.

Ostrowskia (Campanulaceae). Giant Bellflower. *O. magnifica* is the single member of this genus. It requires a deeply-cultivated well-drained soil. It needs a hot, sunny position where it can enjoy a backing. Plant out with the shoot about 15cm (6in) below the surface and once planted avoid disturbing or transplanting it. It will have retired back below ground by the end of summer so mark it carefully so that it is not disturbed during any tidying up or weeding. They do not flower until they are several years old, and the younger plants may die back even earlier than a flowering one. Cover in the winter with a cloche to protect from rain and cold. Late spring frosts might damage emerging shoots so take care at that time of year and cover if necessary.

Ourisia (Scrophulariaceae). The one or two taller species in this genus like to have a cool, humusy, moisture-retentive soil that is lime-free. Give them a lightly shaded position. A peat bed is ideal but they must not get too wet during the winter months, when cloche protection may be needed. Plant out in spring.

Oxalis (Oxalidaceae). Wood Sorrel. An amazingly large genus of over 800 low-growing species. Some of them have become established in gardens as pests and should be avoided at all costs. *O. acetosella* can be a pest in the wrong place but it is an ideal plant for a large woodland garden where it will make mats of attractive, dainty flowers. It grows in quite dry conditions but prefers a typical woodland soil of moist leafmould. It should be lime-free. Most of the other species that are grown in cultivation are really for the alpine bed. Avoid *O. corniculata*, *O. stricta*, *O. pes-caprae* and *O. rubra*.

Oxypetalum (Asclepiadaceae). See *Tweedia*

Oxytropis (Leguminosae). Locoweed. A large genus related to *Astragalus* of which a few are in cultivation. They will grow in any good garden soil but prefer one that is light and free-draining. A sunny position is required. Plant out in the spring while the plants are still young, and avoid transplanting as they dislike being disturbed. Many, especially the silver-haired forms, dislike the winter wet and should be given the shelter of a pane of glass or a cloche in wet areas if they are to survive.

Paeonia (Paeoniaceae). Peonies will tolerate light shade or full sun but flowers will last longer in shade but the plants will flower less freely. The single-flowered varieties seem to do better in the shade than doubles. They will grow in most soils as long as they are not too wet, however they do appreciate humus in the form of well-rotted manure or leafmould incorporated into the soil to keep it moisture-retentive. Peonies resent root disturbance and will take a couple of years to settle down if moved without care. Care in this case means including a large enough root ball of earth in the move, to prevent the roots being disturbed. The best time for moving and planting is as soon as the leaves die back, although any time when the plant is dormant will do. Do not plant them too deep, the eyes should be just below the surface. Too deep a planting can result in the plants languishing and producing no flowers. They are hungry feeders and require to be given a top-dressing of well-rotted manure each winter. Be careful this does not build up so the plant becomes too deeply buried. A top-dressing of bone meal is a good alternative and it might be an idea to alternate this with the manure every winter. Plants can eventually become too old to flower and should be dug up and any vigorous-looking plants replanted once the soil has been rejuvenated. However, with judicious top-dressing and prevention of weed penetration, peonies can be left *in situ* for many years. The flowers can become top-heavy, especially when wet, so stake, preferably with ring type supports. Remove leaves when they die back.

Mulch with manure or leafmould in the autumn. They can suffer from peony wilt, peony leaf spot, and botrytis. Spray with a copper fungicide.

Paesia (Dennstaedtiaceae). A small genus of ferns of which *P. scaberula* is occasionally grown in cultivation. They will grow in any garden soil, including poor ones, but would do best in a fertile one. In the wild it grows in full sun but will also grow in light shade. It is rhizomatous and can become invasive so either plant it where it can ramp, or where it can be controlled.

Pancratium (Amaryllidaceae). This is a small bulbous genus of which *P. illyricum* and *P. maritimum* can be grown in warmer areas. They like a well-drained soil that is reasonably rich in organic matter. They must have a warm, sunny spot where the bulbs get a good baking otherwise flowering is a bit shy. Avoid too much vegetation round the bulbs which may prevent the sun reaching them. Plant about 15cm (6in) below the surface of the soil. Mulch with bracken or straw in winter to help with protection from frosts.

Panicum (Gramineae). Panic Grass, Switch Grass. One of the largest genera of grasses with over 600 species, but with surprisingly few in cultivation. They will grow in any good garden soil but most will also cope with light, dry, even poor soils. They need a sunny position. They are only marginally hardy and may require a winter mulch to give them some protection.

Papaver (Papaveraceae). Poppies. This is a large genus of both annual and perennial plants. For best results they need a deeply cultivated, well-drained soil. It should not be too well fed, indeed many thrive in very poor soils. An open sunny site is required for all species. Plant out while the plants are still young and avoid transplanting as the deep roots make this difficult. If you do move them, any roots left behind, especially of any of the *P. orientale* group, are likely to sprout into new plants, so clean the ground thoroughly. Many *P. orientale* need supports of some kind, preferably short pea-sticks that will not show. One or two varieties, such as the true *P.o.* 'Beauty of Livermere' (not 'Goliath' with which it is often confused) are sufficiently upright not to need staking. Both the flowering stems and leaves need cutting back to within an inch of the ground. Within a couple of weeks a new flush of leaves will have appeared, much fresher and neater than if the old leaves were left on. One or two cultivars may put up a second flush of flowers but this is not a frequent phenomenon. All species tend to produce copious amounts of seed and should be deadheaded to prevent too much self-sowing.

Paradisea (Asphodelaceae/Liliaceae). St Bruno's Lily. A small genus of two species. These are tuberous plants that form clump-like plants. They need a well-drained soil that does not remain too wet during the winter. A sunny position is best but they will take a little light shade. The roots are quite fleshy and can be damaged if the plant is moved, so take care. *P. liliastrum* is hardy in most areas, whereas *P. lusitanica* may need protection in all but warmer gardens.

Paris (Trilliaceae). Plant in a moist, humus-rich, woodland soil in light shade. They do not seem to have any specific diseases or problems. *P. quadrifolia* is a British native and seems to grow best in woods on calcareous soils. When suited its creeping rhizomes form extensive colonies, but it is reasonably easy to contain. See also *Daiswa* to which some of the better known species, such as *P. polyphylla* have been relegated.

Parnassia (Saxifragaceae). Grass-of-Parnassus. *P. palustris* is the most commonly seen species in cultivation of this genus of moisture-loving plants. Plant in a humusy, moist soil in full sun if soil is wet enough, or in part shade. The ideal position would be in a bog garden or beside a water feature. Watch out for slugs and snails.

Parochetus (Leguminosae). Shamrock Pea, Blue Oxalis. This is a genus of only one species, namely *P. communis*. It is a low, mat-forming pea which roots at the nodes. It spreads rather rapidly and can become a nuisance but fortunately it is often cut back in the winter which restrains its activities. However it can also get killed completely so it is worth while potting up a few rooted stems to overwinter under glass; alternatively it can be covered with a cloche or pane of glass. It will grow in any good garden soil but prefers a relatively moist, humus-rich soil and is happy in full sun or part shade. In milder areas it will be necessary to keep it in check.

Patrinia (Valerianaceae). Stoloniferous or rhizomatous plants that slowly form large clumps. They are very accommodating plants and will grow in any good garden soil, and are happy in sun or shade, though they do prefer a cool rootrun, perhaps created by the shade of neighbouring perennials. If in sun they will do better if the soil contains a reasonable amount of humus so that it remains moist. They have the advantage of a long flowering period and even look attractive as they fade, so do not be in too much of a hurry to cut them back.

Pelargonium (Geraniaceae). Most pelargonium species and cultivars are tender and need overwinter protection. However, there are a few species that are hardy enough to withstand some winters, especially in warmer areas. They will do best in a well-drained soil and sunny position. It should be warm but not too hot. Species often prefer a modicum of shade during the hottest part of the day, especially in warmer areas. During the winter it is the wet as much as the cold that does damage so protect plants with a sheet of glass or cloche. However avoid stagnant, damp air being trapped under the glass as pelargoniums are very susceptible to botrytis. Remove flowering heads once blooming is finished. The brasher bedding and container plants need similar conditions, but must be taken inside for the winter. If planted in containers they should be watered regularly, at least once a day in hot weather, but be careful not to overwater.

Peltandra (Araceae). Arrow Arum. This is a small genus of two or three species of bog-loving plants. They can all be grown in either a bog garden or in the shallow water at the margins of ponds or streams. They are not completely hardy and are likely to need some form of winter protection. They are rhizomatous and form large clumps. Do not remove flowering stems once they are over as they later bear red or green berries.

Peltiphyllum (Saxifragaceae). See *Darmera*

Pennisetum (Gramineae). Fountain Grass. Pennisetum is a large genus of which some very attractive species are in cultivation. They are not completely hardy and may need protection in colder areas, especially the beautiful *P. orientale*. Ideally they need a well-drained soil but they do require a certain amount of moisture in the soil. Some, *P.*

villosum, in particular will do well on even quite heavy soils. A sunny position is necessary. They all tend to remain attractive during the winter months so do not cut back until early spring. However, do not leave it too late or the new growth will have started. Plant, transplant and divide in the spring.

Penstemon (Scrophulariaceae). A large genus of plants of which an increasing number of both species and cultivars are coming into cultivation. They all like a fertile, well-drained soil and a sunny position. Many are completely hardy but others are borderline. As a rough rule of thumb the larger the trumpets the more tender the plant. Penstemons do not like cold, drying winds and these can often kill them in exposed areas. They are very easy to increase from cuttings so it is good insurance to take some in the autumn and overwinter them under glass. Many will remain evergreen throughout the winter. They can be left to grow on or can be cut back to the base in the spring to get new, vigorous growth. If they are left on they flower much earlier in the summer beginning around June. They can then be cut off after the main flush of flowering is over. Lightly feed in spring, but do not overdo it otherwise the growth can be too lush, reducing flowering and making them more prone to die during the winter.

Pentaglottis (Boraginaceae). Alkanet. *P. sempervirens* is the only member of this genus. It needs a moist, humusy soil and a lightly-shaded position, although it will grow in full sun if the soil is not too dry. A bit unruly for borders but can be grown in woodland or wild-flower gardens.

Perezia (Compositae). Although this is quite a large genus, few species are in cultivation. Those that are require a well-drained soil (especially during the winter) in sun or light shade. They are best grown in the front of a border or on a rock garden or raised bed.

Perovskia (Labiatae). Russian Sage. Although this is a genus of shrubs and sub-shrubs they are often found in the herbaceous border. They like a well-drained soil and need to have a warm to hot, sunny position. Some gardeners feel that perovskias do better on limey soils. They look very miserable in damp, shady conditions. To ensure vigorous and neat plants cut back the previous year's growth almost to the woody stems in early spring, before new growth is made. The young growth can be early in mild winters and can be caught by late frosts. The plants usually recover.

Persicaria (Polygonaceae). Knotweeds. This is one of the new genera that has evolved out of *Polygonum*. Although the smaller ones of these are often grown as rock garden plants they do not really like drought conditions. They do best in a soil that has had a reasonable amount of organic material added. Some, such as *P. bistorta*, revel in moist, even boggy conditions. They will grow in either full sun or light shade but in the former it is important that the soil is moisture-retentive. *P. vivipara* tolerate quite dry conditions. Most of this genus are spreaders and need a certain amount of control to keep them in check, but they are not as rampant as some of the previous members of *Polygonum* that are now listed under different genera. Several of the genus, *P. affinis* in particular, are attractive during the winter so do not be in too much of a hurry to tidy them. Most are completely hardy but *P. capitata* is on the tender side and will often be cut back during the winter, as it frequently self-sows it rarely disappears completely. *P. campanulata* is also tender in colder areas and is best given some form of winter protection.

Petasites (Compositae). Butterbur, Coltsfoot. A genus of winter- or early spring-flowering plants that tend to be very invasive. It is strongly recommended that you do not plant them in borders; the wild garden or waste ground are the only suitable situation. They will grow in a wide variety of soils including quite poor ones. Most, however, do best in moist conditions. They are not difficult to grow and need little attention, apart from keeping an eye on their invasiveness.

Peucedanum (Umbelliferae). A large genus of plants of which a few are in cultivation. They will grow in any good garden soil in either full sun or very light shade. They are tap-rooted and should therefore be planted out while young and should not be subsequently transplanted. *P. verticillare* is monocarpic, taking several years to reach flowering size and then dying. It will often self sow. Others are biennial.

Phanerophlebia (Aspleniaceae). Holly Fern. A genus of ferns that now includes the *Cyrtomium*. Most are tender but *P. falcata*, *P. fortunei* and *P. macrophyllum* are reasonably hardy, especially if given some winter protection. Give them a reasonably moist soil and a sheltered position. Cut back in winter and mulch.

Phlaris (Gramineae). Gardener's Garters. This is a rampant grass that most gardeners do their best to avoid. However, it has a very attractive, fresh-looking leaf and in many ways it is desirable. It can be controlled by planting in a restricted position, such as an area cordoned off by a path or drive, or by putting it in a sunken container such as a bucket without a bottom. An alternative is to lift it every other year, removing every piece of wandering root and replant it. Plant in any fertile garden soil, including moist ones. Although usually seen on land it can be grown in shallow water at the edge of ponds. It will grow in either full sun or light shade, although it is a bit sparse in the latter. Plant or transplant in spring although if a large enough clump is lifted it can be moved at other times of year. Do not cut back until the early spring as it is attractive during the winter.

Phleum (Gramineae). Cat's Tail, Timothy Grass. A small genus of annual and perennial grasses that are often used in wild-flower gardens and, occasionally, in borders. They will grow in any garden soil and should be planted in full sun. Plant, move or divide in the spring. Cut back when they begin to look tatty.

Phlomis (Labiatae). Jerusalem Sage. This is a large genus of perennial and shrubby plants that has been increasing in popularity. Although they all like a well-drained soil, they also like it to be reasonably moisture-retentive. They will quickly show, with drooping leaves when they get too dry. A warm, sunny position is necessary. Remove old flowering stems and leaves as they die or become tatty. The shrubby ones should have about a third of the old wood removed each year to keep them vigorous and flowering well.

Phlox (Polemoniaceae). Different conditions are required for the different groups of phloxes. The carpeting rock garden types such as *P. douglasii* or *P. subulata*, need a reasonably well-drained soil. The low-growing woodland types, such as *P. divaricata* and *P. stolonifera* like a moist, humusy woodland-type of soil, while the tall border phloxes based on *P. paniculata* will grow in any fertile garden soil but should not be allowed to dry out. Water them during dry weather and at any other time that they look limp. The woodlanders grow best in light shade, the rest preferring a sunny position. Remove the heads (just the tops of the plant) of vigorous, early-flowering varieties to encourage a second flush of flowers. Growth starts early so that any cutting back of old stems or division to rejuvenate the plants ought to be carried out in autumn. If you move phlox do not replant in ground just vacated by other phlox. This is not on medical grounds but aesthetic ones, as the previous incumbents are bound to have left roots behind which will come up and confuse your new colour scheme. Any ground that has had any of the *paniculata* type that suffer from eelworm should not be replanted as there is the risk of re-infection. Eelworm or nematodes will distort leaves and stems. Any plants so suffering should be burnt. However, the pest is not transmitted through the roots, so root cuttings can provide new, pest-free plants. Phlox, especially the *divaricata* types, can be devastated by slugs and snails in early spring. Take evasive action before too much damage occurs otherwise flowering will be heavily impaired. A problem that afflicts both woodland and border types is mildew. To help with prevention, ensure that the plants do not dry out, and plant in a position where plenty of air can circulate. Reducing the number of stems on the border types will help with circulation of air and also the vigour and flowering of the plant. Divide the border plants every three or four years to help keep them vigorous. Discard the older material from the centre of the plant. Mulch the woodland types with leafmould, and the border varieties with well-rotted manure or compost during the winter.

Phormium (Agavaceae/Phormiaceae). New Zealand Flax. These are increasingly being grown in spite of their being on the tender side. These are likely to come through most winters but can be cut to the ground by stiff frosts, from which they will take several years to recover. They can be protected with straw covered by polythene, but as always with this sort of protection allow air to circulate through the base. Siting in a warm sunny position will also help. The soil should be well-drained but moisture-retentive, mulch around the plant in winter with leaves or other organic material. Do not cut back after flowering as the seed heads are attractive in their own right. Dead leaves are very tough and will need cutting off.

Phragmites (Gramineae). Spire Reed. This is a small genus of very invasive reeds suitable only for planting in large ponds or lakes of which *P. australis* is the one commonly seen. If grown in smaller ponds plant in a container so that its rhizomes cannot spread. The variegated form *P.a.* 'Variegatus' is slightly better behaved and is easier to contain, as well as being more attractive. Plant in the mud in shallow water of the pond or lake.

Phuopsis (Rubiaceae). *P. stylosa* (formerly known as *Crucianella stylosa*) is the only member of this genus. It is an attractive plant, although some gardeners object to its smell. It spreads, rooting where stems touch the soil, but it is not too invasive as it is reasonably easy to control. It will grow in any fertile soil, including dry ones, but prefers one that is moisture-retentive. It grows best in full sun but will also grow under a north wall. If you do not want it to spread too far cut back to the original plant in autumn, removing any rooted pieces in the process.

Phygelius (Scrophulariaceae). Cape Figwort. A small genus of two species of sub-shrubs with numerous named cultivars and hybrids. Although from South Africa they are reasonably hardy. Frosts will often kill off the leaves and stems above ground, but they will shoot again in the following spring. Plant out in spring after the frosts are finished. In the wild both inhabit wet areas, but in cultivation they seem happiest in well-drained but not-too-dry soil. They prefer a sunny position, but will survive on a north wall. In warm areas they are likely to survive a winter and can become very large (up to 6m (20ft) at Sizergh Castle for example), particularly if sheltered by a warm wall. But in most areas it is best to treat it as a herbaceous plant and cut it back to the ground (as with a fuchsia) in the autumn or early spring. Deadheading helps to keep the plant tidy and to keep it flowering through the summer into autumn. No special feeding required. Do not let them get too dry. They are generally pest free but occasionally attacked by figwort weevil which causes mayhem. In a bad attack the plants lose all their flowers as the slimy, rather unpleasant grubs eat the buds, giving the plants a very forlorn look. The eggs are laid in the leaf which swells up like a blister. Spray with permethrin-based chemicals as soon as the grub or adults are seen.

Phyllitis (Aspleniaceae). See *Asplenium*

Phyllostachys (Gramineae). Golden Bamboo. This bamboo benefits by being thinned out from time to time, removing any dead wood as well as weak stems. Cut them out as close to the ground as possible. Top-dress with compost, well-rotted farmyard manure or mushroom compost. A light winter dressing of a nitrogen-rich fertilizer will also be of benefit. The golden form *P. aurea* needs to be in sun if it is to retain its colour. It will become green in shade. They will grow on a wide range of soils but prefer a slightly acid one. They prefer a warm sunny position. Phyllostachys are clump-forming but can become invasive under some conditions. Plant out in the spring. Any dividing or transplanting should also take place at this time of year.

Physalis (Solanaceae). Chinese Lanterns. Winter Cherry. A large genus of some 80 species, of which only one, *P. alkekengii*, is in general cultivation. It is an invasive plant that spreads by underground runners somewhat in the manner of mint. Plant the rhizomes in any good garden soil, about 7.5cm (3in) below the surface. It will grow in sun or part shade. It is not a plant for a favourite border rather somewhere where it can ramp at will or can be contained. It is a rather floppy plant and does look best when growing through low shrubs or even given some form of twiggy support. Do not cut back after flowering as its main attraction is after it has been dried.

Physostegia (Labiatae). Obedient Plant. Although there are about 15 species, *P. virginiana* and its various forms is the main species in cultivation. They will grow in any fertile garden soil but have a preference for moist, slightly acid ones. On some light soils they tend to be short-lived. They grow best in full sun although they can be grown in light shade. If the plants are grown on a rich soil, so that they become quite tall then support is required. Shorter-growing plants can normally look after themselves. They are clump-formers but they can spread beyond bounds and need splitting up to control them, and to keep them vigorous and not congested. Top-dress with organic matter during the winter.

Phyteuma (Campanulaceae). Horned Rampions. The majority of this genus are grown in the rock garden, but a few are suitable for growing at the front of a border or in odd corners. They will grow in any fertile garden soil but prefer it reasonably moisture-retentive although well-drained. They perhaps do best on alkaline soils but can successfully be grown on neutral or acid ones. The taller species are generally woodlanders and enjoy that type of soil. They do best in full sun but will tolerate a little light shade. Deadhead before seed is formed, otherwise they may self-sow and become a nuisance.

Phytolacca (Phytolaccaceae). Pokeberry, Pokeweed. The members of this genus are all big shrubs or shrubby perennials. They like a rich, moisture-retentive soil in either sun or light shade. They have an unpleasant smell and all parts of the plant are poisonous. Some authorities claim that *P. americana* acts as a reservoir for all kind of virus diseases. They can self-sow over vigorously, and are apt to make rather large invasive clumps, so ensure you have plenty of room. All in all these are plants to treat with caution.

Pimpinella (Umbelliferae). Anise. This is a large genus of plants of which only a few are in cultivation. They will all grow in any fertile garden soil, even quite dry ones. They will grow in sun or in the light shade of an edge of a wood or hedge. *P. major* is happiest in this type of light shade. Plant out while still young and avoid transplanting as they resent disturbance.

Plantago (Plantaginaceae). Plantain. Many gardeners think of this genus as weeds and most are just that. However, of the 265 species there a few are grown for their decorative qualities. They will grow in any fertile garden soil, even quite dry ones. A sunny position is needed. Keep an eye that they do not become too invasive, especially by seed. They can suffer from mildew particularly towards the end of the season.

Platanthera (Orchidaceae). Butterfly Orchids. These are best left to grow in the wild, and under no circumstances should they be dug up from their natural habitat. If you are able to buy cultivated plants, plant them in a woodland-type soil in very light shade. A peat bed would be a good choice. They are not easy plants to grow and are probably best left to the experts.

Platycodon (Campanulaceae). Balloon Flower. There is only a single species, *P. grandiflorus*, in this genus, although it does have several cultivars. They are clump-forming and like a fertile soil that is well-drained but also moisture-retentive. However if it is too damp and heavy the fleshy roots are likely to rot. It likes an open, sunny position, but will take a little light shade. Clear away the old foliage as it dies back in the autumn, or during the winter clear-up. The young shoots in the spring are brittle and can be easy broken. They are also susceptible to slug and snail damage, against which they should be protected. The new shoots are quite late emerging so do not accidentally dig them up or otherwise disturb them. As a precaution they should be well marked. The fleshy roots are not too keen on being disturbed.

Pleioblastus (Gramineae). This genus of bamboos will grow on a wide range of soils but prefers a slightly acid one. They grow best in an open, sunny position, but some are woodlanders and prefer light shade. The rhizomatous root system is invasive in some species (*P. chino* and *P. humulis* for example), particularly if well suited. *P. auricomus* (*Arundinaria viridistriata*) has better coloured foliage if the colony is cut to the ground in early spring. It appreciates being well fed and should never be allowed to dry out completely. If grown in the shade the leaves turn green. In warmer areas it may well need to be kept in check as it runs. In cooler parts it is better behaved and can be safely used in borders.

Pleiones (Orchidaceae). These are generally treated as plants for the alpine house but *PP. formosana* and *limprichtii* can be grown outside in milder areas. They need a well-drained, humusy soil. They are best grown in lightly-shaded position under trees, a peat bed or a humus-rich rock garden being ideal situation. Do not allow them to dry out. Mulch in the winter with leafmould or composted bark.

Plumbago (Plumbaginaceae). This is a small genus of annuals, perennials and shrubs of which the main contender, *P. larpentiae* has been moved to *Ceratostigma*.

Poa (Gramineae). Blue Grass, Meadow Grass. This is a large genus of grasses a few of which are in cultivation, several being used in lawns or meadows. They can all be grown in any good garden soil, preferably those on the light side. An open, sunny position, reflecting their meadow origins, is required. Cut back in late winter before new growth starts. Plant out, divide or transplant in spring. They all tend to be clump-forming and even those with creeping rhizomes are reasonably well-behaved.

Podophyllum (Berberidaceae). Mayapple. They seem to prefer a moist, shady position although several also grow in the open in the wild. A cool moist atmosphere (that of parts of Scotland for example) produces the best results. The soil should be deep, leafy, and moisture-retentive. This is a hardy genus the late frosts can burn off early growth in spring. Remove old foliage and stems when the plant dies down. Although these are rhizomatous plants and tend to spread forming dense colonies, there is no need to lift and divide except for propagational reasons, or to prevent them from spreading too far. Top-dress with organic material to keep soil moisture-retentive and to add nutrients unless they are situated in a woodland and are subject to leaf-fall. Although the fruit is edible the plant itself is poisonous. They are quite tall but no support is generally required.

Polemonium (Polemoneaceae). Jacob's Ladder. This delightful genus of cottage-garden flowers will grow in any fertile soil, although it does prefer one that is moisture-retentive. *P. viscosum* is a calcifuge and will not grow on alkaline soils. Some of the other rarer species may also have this tendency. Either full sun or light shade will be suitable, the latter is to be preferred in really hot areas. Cut back hard after flowering. *P. caeruleum* can be grown in grass and is good for naturalizing. They can suffer from mildew. Fortunately this is usually after they have finished flowering and so the disease remains should be cut off and burnt. The taller species are likely to need staking in any area where a wind has access. They tend to be short-lived and need regular replacement although some, such as *P. caeruleum* and *P. reptans*, regularly self-sow providing more than ample seedlings.

Polygonatum (Convallariaceae/Liliaceae). Solomon's Seal. This is a genus of woodland plants and their liking for a moist, humusy soil reflects this. They must have a cool rootrun in light, dappled shade, although they will grow in a more sunny position as long as there is ample moisture at their roots. The best time to lift and split congested plants is in autumn so that they are ready to perform again the following spring. In some areas where the plants will not have time to re-establish themselves before winter sets in it will be necessary to leave division until spring, but this means that a year's flowering is likely to be lost. In summer the leaves often appear tatty and full of holes. This is caused by the caterpillars of a sawfly. Slugs and snails can also cause problems especially to emerging growth. They can be handpicked or sprayed. The rhizomes form a dense colony which can become invasive in small gardens, but they are easy to control by digging them up. Although some species are tall, their strong stems rarely need to be supported. Top-dress in the winter with well-rotted organic matter.

Polygonum (Polygonaceae). See *Fallopia* and *Persicaria*

Polypodium (Polypodiaceae). Polypody. This is a large genus of rhizomatous ferns. They like nothing better than a moist, humus-rich soil, preferably in a light shade. Although liking a moist soil, they also like it to be free-draining and in the wild they grow in stony areas and will also happily grow on walls or trees in areas that have a damp climate. Do not cut back the old evergreen foliage, which begins to look tatty, until the new foliage begins to appear as it does not do so until summer. Alternatively wait until it dies, turning brown and then pull off the individual dead leaves.

Polystichum (Aspleniaceae). Shield Ferns. A lime-free, moist, humus-rich soil is required for this group of evergreen ferns. They also like a lightly-shaded position. If they need moving or splitting do so in spring before the new growth commences. Remove all the evergreen fronds in late winter or early spring to allow the new growth to show up and not be masked or spoilt by the presence of battered, older material. Top-dress with leafmould in the winter.

Pontamogeton (Pontamogetonaceae). Pondweed. This is a large genus of submerged, aquatic plants with floating leaves. They are good oxygenators but are probably too vigorous for small pools. Plant directly into the mud or in a lattice pot if the pond is lined. They prefer cool, deep water up to 60cm (2ft) in depth, although some *P. lucens* for example will grow in up to 1.8m (6ft) of water.

Pontederia (Pontederiaceae). Pickerel Weed. This is a small genus of aquatic plants suitable for shallow water round the margins of ponds and lakes. They can be planted directly into the mud in the bottom of the pool or in a lattice container if the pond is lined. They can be grown in water up to about 30cm (12in) deep. The thick rhizomes spread and may need to be controlled if space is limited. They are generally hardy as long as the rhizomes are below water assuming the water does not freeze solid. A sunny position should be chosen.

Potentilla (Rosaceae). Cinquefoils. This is a very large genus with 400–500 species (depending on which taxonomists you follow) and quite a number of varieties. Not many are grown in the garden, the most probably on the rock garden although a number are grown in open beds. Some are rank weeds and should be avoided. *P. anserina*, for all its attractive, silver leaves, is the worst of these and should be avoided at all costs, as it is not the easiest of plants to get rid of once it has established itself. Most tend to have a creeping habit, although few are as bad as this. Although some members in the wild seem to grow in quite boggy situations, the majority in cultivation like free-draining soils, even quite impoverished ones. Although there is the temptation to enrich the soil this tends to produce a lot of leaf at the expense of flowers. Better flowering specimens are usually found on the poorer soils. They tend to prefer a sunny position but many will take a little shade, especially the scramblers which will climb up through shrubs and other plants. Many hybridize so if you wish to get pure seed do not plant different species or forms in proximity to each other. Cut to the base in the autumn or winter clear-up. They do not seem to be prone to any specific pests or diseases.

Preslia (Labiatae). *P. cervinia* is the only member of this genus. It is grown as a marginal plant for ponds. It will either grow in the surrounding mud or, preferably, in shallow water only a few inches deep. It can also be grown in moist soil as long as it does not dry out. It has a prostrate habit but is not invasive.

Primula (Primulaceae). Cowslips, Polyanthus, Primroses, Primulas. A well-loved genus of plants that have long been grown in gardens. They must have a soil that does not dry out, preferably one that is not too light. Add well-rotted organic material to help with moisture-retention. Some, such as *P. florindae* will even grow in water on the edge of a pond or stream. They will grow in sun if there is enough moisture in the soil, but do best in a light shade, especially in hotter regions. Remove all yellowing leaves from around the plant. They appreciate a mulch of well-rotted farmyard manure, compost or crushed bark, not only to keep to help retain moisture but also to provide nourishment. Most will self-sow but will not necessary come true in colour to their parents. They will also often hybridize, so deadhead or keep plants separate if you wish to keep a colony pure. Many of the smaller varieties are incapable of surviving the hurley-burley of the border and are more the province of the alpine gardener as they need specialised conditions that can be only provided by the rock garden, peat bed or alpine house. Vigorous colonies of some species and cultivars regularly need to be divided. Some, such as *P. vialii*, are short-lived and need regularly replacing, often every year. Vine weevil grubs can cause havoc by chewing through the roots, and any stunted primulas should be dug up and the soil around them examined for these white, horseshoe-shaped larvae. Primulas grown in the same area year after year can suffer from soil sickness. Polyanthus are particularly prone to this. Replant elsewhere should the colonies start to deteriorate.

Prunella (Labiatae). Self-heal. Not all of this small genus are suitable for growing in the border. *P. vulgaris* is certainly one that should be avoided as it is often a pestilent weed. Even the more attractive types have a tendency to self-sow or creep, and can become a nuisance. They will grow in any fertile garden soil, including dry ones. They will grow in either full sun or light shade where the flower spikes are usually longer, especially if the soil is moist. Shear over before seed is cast to prevent self-sowing which can introduce inconsistent plants amongst cultivars.

Pteridium (Dennstaedtiaceae). Bracken. This is a name to produce fear in the hearts of most gardeners as the single species *P. aquilinum* is a real pest and one difficult to eradicate. It is strongly recommended that you do not introduce it to the garden unless it is into a large wood where it can spread to its heart's content. The best way to get rid of it if you have got it is to keep cutting it back every time you see a frond appear. It will soon have to give up through starvation. However, if you want to grow it you must have an acid soil. It will grow in either sun or shade. Transplantation is very difficult. You need to dig up a large lump of soil to ensure that you have enough root. Bracken produces a carcinogenic dust, so when cutting it wear a mask. Cut back in the autumn or spring before the new growth starts.

Pteridophyllum (Fumariaceae). *P. racemosum* is the only member of this genus. It is a prime candidate for growing in a shady peat bed. It likes a cool, humus-rich soil and a light shade. It is hardy but can be cut back by late frosts. Although it is usually deciduous the foliage may remain evergreen in favoured positions. Top-dress with leafmould in winter.

Pulmonaria (Boraginaceae). Lungwort, Soldiers and Sailors. This popular garden genus needs to be planted in a cool, lightly-shaded position. It will take an open position if the soil is kept moist but any drought will immediately cause signs of stress. The soil should be a humus-rich, moisture-retentive one. The leaves make attractive groundcover throughout the summer if the plants are not allowed to become too dry. Remove old flower heads before they seed. Keep a watch that self-sown seedlings do not appear as these can introduce impure strains into named varieties. For example *P. officinalis* 'Sissinghurst White' is liable to produce pale blue seedlings which will soon take over if they are not rogued out. One year's leaves are likely to die just before the next emerges; the old, blackened ones can easily be removed in winter to reveal the new growth. As well as removing flower heads, shear over the foliage in late spring so that a new crop of fresh ones appear. I know of one gardener who goes over his pulmonarias in the late spring with a rotary mower and gets a beautiful crop of new leaves. The soil can get a bit tired and should be top-dressed, or the plants removed every four to five years and replanted after the soil has been revitalized.

Pulsatilla (Ranunculaceae). Pasque Flowers. A small genus of plants that are not always easy to tell apart, especially as they have hybridized in cultivation. Fortunately they generally all need the same treatment. They like a well-drained soil that is reasonably fertile. A sunny position is also required. They are not very big plants and should not be allowed to be overcrowded by other inhabitants of the border. The seed heads are very attractive in their own right but they will allow the plants to self-sow, so remove them just before they disperse if this is likely to be a problem. They are best left undisturbed. Some, such as *P. vernalis* are short-lived and should be regularly propagated. Remove the dead foliage before the new growth starts in the spring, otherwise it is difficult to avoid damage. Some have the annoying habit of suddenly rotting off at the neck and dying when in full flower. A top-dressing of gravel or small stones may help to prevent this.

Puschkinia (Liliaceae). A small bulbous genus of which *P. scilloides* is the main species grown in cultivation. Plant in autumn in any well-drained garden soil. They should be set about 5cm (2in) below the surface. Like most bulbs they like a sunny position. They do not clump up very fast but should they become crowded, lift them and divide.

Puya (Bromeliaceae). This is a large genus of mainly tender plants, of which one, *P. alpestris*, may be capable of being grown in warmer districts. It is important to give it a well-drained light fertile soil and a sunny, warm position, preferably sheltered by a wall.

Pyrethropsis (Compositae). A new genus that has come about since the demise of *Chrysanthemum*. The main plant of interest here is *P. hosmariensis* which has had so many changes of name that it must be quite dizzy. It is a low-growing plant that likes a well-drained soil in full sun. An ideal position would be on a rock garden, raised bed, or front of border. It is evergreen so only requires deadheading and the occasional light shear to keep it trim.

Pyrethrum (Compositae). See *Tanecetum*

Ranunculus (Ranunculaceae). Buttercups. There are a large number of species in this genus, some are worthy of being grown in the border, others are rank weeds and should be avoided except in wild-flower meadows. Being a large genus they have a diversity of requirements. However, most will grow in a fertile garden soil, especially if it is moisture retentive. Most, but not all, prefer an open, sunny position. Celandines, *R. ficaria*, do well in both sun or shade, but open better in the former. They can become a menace in that they quickly form large colonies, however they do die back below ground before spring is over and are no trouble for the rest of the year. If you do decide to rid any part of the garden of them either use a weedkiller, or carefully remove every piece of their tuberous roots, not the easiest thing to do. The common native plants such as *R. acris* and especially *R. repens* can spread like wildfire, both by runners and seed. The double forms of both tend to be better behaved. They should be clearly marked as they can accidentally be weeded out. The turban ranunculus, *R. asiaticus africanus*, should be planted out in spring with 'claws' downwards. It prefers a very free-draining soil and should be surrounded by sharp sand or grit to prevent it rotting. However, it should not be allowed to become too dry in the growing season and should be watered if necessary. Lift in the autumn and store in dry sand in a frost-free place. *R. asiaticus* itself is even more tricky and is best grown in pots under glass. *R. lingua* can be grown in shallow water. They can become very rampant and need to be reduced to a small patch each year otherwise they will take over the muddy margins of the pond and beyond. The foliage of *R. gramineus* seems to be a delicacy for either pheasants or partridges, and whole plants can be stripped in spring. *R. aconitifolius* prefers a light shade. It can get congested, so to maintain vigour lift and divide every few years. The sap from *R. acris* can cause blistering on sensitive skins. Mildew may be a problem for many species but this is usually late in the season. One of the worst affected is the large-flowered *R. rupestris*. Fortunately this dies back below ground soon after flowering so it is not too much of a problem. As there is no sign of this plant after early summer it is worth marking it to make certain that it is not disturbed or overplanted. There are a lot of low-growing species that make good plants for the rock garden or peat bed. All plants benefit from a winter mulch of leafmould or other well-rotted organic matter.

Ranzania (Berberidaceae). *R. japonica*, the sole representative of this genus, being a woodlander likes a moist, lightly-shaded position. The soil should be a leafy moisture-retentive one. Although hardy it can be burnt by late frosts, so protect if early growth is threatened. There is no need to lift and divide unless for propagational reasons. As they are rarely moved make certain that the soil does not become impoverished. Remove old stems and foliage when the plant dies down. Try to save any seed that may be produced as this is a rare plant.

Ratibida (Compositae). Mexican Hat, Prairie Coneflower. *R. columnifera* is the species normally grown from this small genus of annuals and perennials. They are closely related to *Rudbeckia* and are treated in the same way. They need a well-drained soil but one that is moisture-retentive. They prefer a sunny position, but will grow in light shade. They are likely to require staking, especially in exposed areas.

Rehmannia (Gesneriaceae/Scrophulariaceae). Tender and marginally tender plants from China, but it is wet conditions that cause as much death as the cold. In the wild they inhabit cliffs, old walls and rock crevices, all of which provide them with sharp drainage. They are perennial but often act as biennials, dying after flowering. They should be planted out in spring, having been raised and overwintered in pots. If, in warmer areas, they are planted out in their first year, protect them against winter wet with a sheet of glass or polythene light. No special feeding required. No particular pests and diseases.

Reineckea (Convalariaceae/Liliaceae). *R. carnea* is the only species in this genus. It is closely related to the Lily-of-the-valley, *Convallaria*, and is treated in the same manner. It likes a woodland-type soil and light shade. It is not completely hardy and in cooler areas it may do better where it can get some summer and winter warmth, such as being planted near a wall.

Reynoutria (Polygonaceae). See *Fallopia*

Rhayza (Apocynaceae). This genus has only two species of which *R. orientalis* is the one normally grown. They will grow in any well-drained, but fertile garden soil. Preferably provide a sunny position but they will tolerate light shade. These plants are clump-formers but they are slow to increase in size. Wait until the autumn/winter clear-up before cutting back unless the foliage is looking too tatty. Slugs can be a nuisance, especially in the spring when growth commences.

Rheum (Polygonaceae). Rhubarb. A medium-sized genus of plants. They like a deeply-cultivated fertile soil with plenty of organic material added to it. The leaves of many of the rheums suffer from sun scorch, so plant them in light shade or in a position where they will be protected from the fiercest of the sun. They like to have a deeply-cultivated soil, well furnished with organic material to keep it moist and to provide nourishment. *R. alexandre* seems to pine for its cloud-shrouded mountains if it is grown in dry areas. It does best in areas such as the west of Scotland, where the air is cool and moist. The foliage of *R. palmatum* generally dies back from about mid-summer, so place another plant in front of it.

Rhexia (Melastomaceae). Deer Grass, Virginia Meadow Beauty. This is a genus of about 10 or 11 species of which *R. virginica* and *R. mariana* are the main ones in cultivation. These are plants from swampy areas that like nothing better than a bog garden or to be next to water. However, they can be grown in ordinary sandy soils as long as they are moisture-retentive. They prefer acid conditions. They should be given a sunny position. Cut back after flowering or during the autumn clear-up. They are not completely hardy and may need to be given a winter mulch of bracken or straw.

Rhodiola (Crassulaceae). Roseroot. Being very closely allied to *Sedum*, this genus is treated in the same way. They will grow in any garden soil, as long as they are reasonably well-drained. *R. rhodantha* does not like a limy soil. Once the plant has finished flowering and seeding it begins to look rather tatty and should be cut to the ground.

Rhodochiton (Scrophulariaceae). Purple Bells. *R. atrosanguineum* is the only species in this genus. It is tender in many areas and is treated as an annual. However it can be overwintered under glass. In warmer areas treat as the perennial it is. It likes to have a well-drained soil but one that is moisture retentive. It is a climber and will need some form of support, possibly through another plant.

Rigidella (Iridaceae). A genus of bulbous plants that are somewhat tender and can only be left outside in warmer areas. Grow in a light, sandy soil and a warm, sunny position, preferably against a wall. Although they like a well-drained soil, they appreciate sufficient moisture during the early part of the growing period. Plant about 4.5cm (3in) deep. The leaves only develop after flowering is over. Lift in the autumn after the leaves have died down and store in a frost-free place. Replant in mid-spring. Feed with a potash-rich fertilizer in late spring.

Rindera (Boraginaceae). This is a moderately-sized genus of short-lived perennials. The plants are happy in well-drained even dry soils. A rock garden may be ideal. They need a warm, sunny spot to help them survive the winter. Winter wet also plays a part in their demise, and some form of protection may be needed in wet areas.

Rodgersia (Saxifragaceae). A small genus of very garden-worthy plants. They are all moisture-lovers and soon begin to look sad if the soil is too dry. Deeply-cultivated soil with plenty of organic material added to it is the ideal. They will also grow in boggy areas, but avoid planting them in standing water. They will grow in full sun if the soil is moist enough (the leaves will scorch if they become too dry). They will tolerate drier conditions in shade. They do not need support. The flower spikes can be removed once they fade but the leaves should be left until the winter clear-up. They gradually spread to form a large colony so either plenty of space should be allowed or the questing shoots should be dug out. Apply a winter top-dressing of organic material.

Romneya (Papaveraceae). Californian Tree Poppy. These are strictly speaking shrubs but are usually treated as herbaceous plants. Even if they come through the winter unscathed it is still a good idea to cut back the stems during late winter or early in the spring before growth recommences. If frosted they will need to be cut off at ground level, but if still green they can be shortened by about half. However, plants usually only flower on stems during their first year. In colder areas it may be necessary to give it a winter mulch of bracken or straw. The stems may remain for a second year before dying but they carry no flowers, so cutting all stems to the ground causes no loss of flowers. They like a warm, sunny position with a light, free-draining soil that has plenty of humus added to it. They will tolerate dry conditions but if they are kept moist the foliage colour will be bluer. They can be very invasive with roots travelling long distances, so it is usually necessary to dig round them once a year to remove questing roots. Avoid disturbing the main plant unnecessarily as it may not settle down again. In spite of it being a running and spreading plant, it resents being divided. If you need to move or transplant it, start a new plant from root cuttings rather than attempt to move the existing plant which is likely to fail.

Roscoea (Zingiberaceae). This is an increasingly popular genus of plants. They like a deep moist soil with plenty of added humus, such as leafmould. They will grow in either a sunny or lightly-shaded position. Plant out the fleshy roots in autumn at about 20cm (8in) deep. They are late in appearing above ground, often not before early summer, so mark their position to prevent them being overplanted or accidentally dug out during border maintenance. Deadhead where necessary, but leave the leaves until the plant dies down. Mulch in the autumn with organic material, partly as winter protection and partly as food and soil improvement.

Rudbeckia (Compositae). Coneflower. Although rudbeckias are usually planted in the open border, many, R. 'Goldsturm' for example, prefer a slightly shady position with a moist soil. They will tolerate a sunny position if the soil never completely dries out. Like so many of the composites some of the rudbeckias, R. 'Goldsturm' for example, can be moved from a reserve bed into a position vacated by another plant that has finished blooming just before it flowers. Soak it well before the move and again afterwards. Rudbeckias are not all that long-lived and can begin to decline after a few years. Either split up the plants using the younger growth for replanting, or start afresh with new plants. They need a lot of water and can be used as a general drought indicator; if rudbeckia starts flagging it is time to water the whole border. Cut down in the winter clear-up. They may need staking in exposed positions, especially the taller forms such as *R. nitida*. Give a winter top-dressing of well-rotted, organic material.

Rumex (Polygonaceae). Docks. Most gardeners regard this genus as a pernicious weed, and rightly so for many species. However, there are one or two that have a place as ornamental plants; *R. hydrolapathum* (the giant water dock), for example, is a good plant for the water garden. They generally grow in any soil, although the one just cited prefers a moist, even wet soil. Although the seed stems of the docks can be spectacular they are best avoided as they will sow everywhere. When removing or transplanting docks make certain that every little piece of root has been removed or they will sprout to form new plants.

Ruta (Rutaceae). Rue. *R. graveolens* is the main species grown from this genus. It will grow in any fertile soil, but preferably one that is well-drained. It will tolerate quite dry conditions. A sunny position is to be preferred. It needs to be clipped back hard each spring to prevent the growth from becoming too leggy. However, clipping back does mean the sacrifice of the flowers which appear on the older growth, so a decision will be required between a neat foliage bush or a loose flowering plant. Be careful when pruning or handling as the sap can cause problems for those with sensitive skin.

Saccharum (Gramineae). Previously known as *Erianthus*, this is a genus of tall grasses of which *S. hostii* is one of the hardiest. *S. ravennae* is also sometimes seen but this is tender and can only be reliably grown in warmer areas. Both like a light, well-drained soil and a warm, sunny position. Leave the dead leaves and flower stems to help protect the plant, cutting back towards the end of winter.

Sagittaria (Alismataceae). Arrowhead. A small genus of water plants that are suitable for ponds. Arrowheads can be grown in water up to about 40cm (16in) deep. Alternatively they will grow in any muddy soil. A sunny position is required. They do not begin to emerge until the water warms up in spring. The plants overwinter as turions, or winter tubers. Unfortunately ducks like these and can devastate the stock, so protection may be required. These plants are hardy unless the pond freezes right to the bottom.

Salvia (Labiatae). Sage. This is a very large genus of which an increasing number is in cultivation. Not all salvias are hardy and may need overwintering under glass, either as cuttings or whole plants. However, many are hardier than previously thought and do come through milder winter. The more tender varieties include *SS. azurea, blepharophylla, coccinea, confertiflora, discolor, farinacea, fulgens, grahamii, greggi, hierosylmitana, indica, interrupta, involucrata, leucantha, microphylla, patens* and *rutilans*. Salvias seem to do best on light soils and grow well in alkaline conditions. Add grit to lighten heavier soils as drainage is one of the keys to growing salvias; it is the damp as much as the cold that they dislike. *S. uliginosa* takes a moister soil than the others. A light, sunny position is required by all salvias. Many, particularly most of the new introductions, need a warm situation, especially if you hope to overwinter them outside. Many of the softer-stemmed salvias suffer from attacks by slugs and snails in the spring when the shoots are just emerging. They can severely maim the plant so take evasive action. Some are inclined to self-sow thus, although short-lived, *SS. sclarea* and *haematodes* can easily be perpetuated. Some of the modern varieties are prone to produce inferior forms from seed, *S. verticillata* 'Purple Rain' is an example of this, so be certain to deadhead on time. *S. x superba* on the other hand is sterile and if clipped back will reflower. *S. nemorosa* will also flower again if clipped over after its first flush. For those plants that overwinter as a rosette, such as *S. argentea*, remove any dead leaves to prevent them infecting other leaves and to improve the plant's appearance. This plant especially likes a well-drained soil and even does well on walls. *S. patens* and *S. farinacea* are usually treated as annuals but they form a tuberous root which can be lifted and stored over winter like a dahlia in just-damp peat or sand. Those that form rounded humps, such as some of the varieties of *S. x superba*, are in need of support except in well-sheltered areas. Any wind seems to open up the middle of the clump. Pea-sticks are good for this.

Sambucus (Caprifoliaceae). Dwarf Elder. A medium-sized genus of shrubby plants of which one, *S. ebulus*, is herbaceous, dying back to the ground in winter. This will grow in any garden soil. It prefers a sunny position although it will grow in light shade. Cut to the ground during the autumn/winter clear-up. Given the right conditions it can become a bit invasive, so keep an eye on it.

Sanguinaria (Papaveraceae). Canadian Bloodroot. *S. canadensis*, the single species of this genus, needs an acid or neutral soil, preferably a moist one with a high leafmould content. Being a woodlander it also likes light shade, but looks its best where it receives spring sunlight through the bare branches of deciduous trees. The roots are spreading but rather brittle and cultivation in the area should be minimal, top-dressing rather than digging. The red sap of its vernacular name should not cause problems if you get it on the skin. Its flow can be staunched by dipping the broken root in silver sand. It slowly spreads to form large colonies but is not invasive. Top-dress with leafmould in winter. Other than drought it does not seem to have any specific pests or diseases.

Sanguisorba (Rosaceae). Burnet, Salad Burnet. A small genus of plants of which several are grown in cultivation. They will grow in most garden soils but prefer them to be on the moist side, so add plenty of humus when preparing the site. They like an open sunny position. Most creep and can become a bit invasive if not watched. Some, such as *S. officinalis*, also self-sow which can be a nuisance as they are deep-rooted, so remove seedlings as soon as they are seen. Top-dress in winter with organic material. The taller species are likely to require staking, especially in exposed areas. Remove flower heads after flowering and cut back to the ground during the autumn/winter clear-up.

Sanicula (Umbelliferae). Sanicle, Snakeroot. This is a medium-sized genus of which one, *S. europaea* is sometimes grown in woodland gardens. It will grow in any moist, woodland-type soil which contains plenty of humus. It also likes to have a shady position, often growing in quite deep shade. Some of the other species can be invasive so treat with care.

Santolina (Compositae). Lavender Cotton. These plants are really shrubs but they are often treated along with other perennials. They must have a well-drained soil and should be given a sunny site. None of them are particularly happy with wet conditions and some can become rather messy and sad in wet summers. *SS. chamaecyparis* (*incana*) and *neapolitana* should be sheared over in spring (early April) reducing the plants to a framework of old stems only 10–12cm (4–5in) high. Do not cut back after early summer or the wood may not have ripened sufficiently to get the plant through the winter. Some gardeners like to remove the yellow flowers before they open from the grey-leaved forms as they feel they spoil the silvery effect.

Saponaria (Caryophyllaceae). Bouncing Bet, Soapwort. The soapworts consist of a medium-sized genus of which quite a number are suitable for the rock garden, and a couple for the open border. The border forms do best in a light, humusy soil. Many rock species form tight clumps but *S. officinalis* can be very invasive and should only be planted with this in mind. The stems of this plant tend to flop and are difficult to support in any attractive manner. The best plan is to grow it in a wild garden where it can ramp at will and be supported by other vegetation. Cut back the stems in autumn after flowering. Top-dress with organic material in winter.

Sarracenia (Sarracenaceae). Pitcher Plants. This is a small genus of insectivorous plants that are generally too tender to be grown in colder districts. Only *S. purpurea* is hardy enough to be grown outside, and even this only in milder areas. It must be grown in wet soils, and a bog garden with plenty of sphagnum moss makes an ideal home. A sunny position is required. Do not let them dry out.

Sasa (Gramineae). Dwarf Bamboo. These are invasive bamboos that rapidly form great thickets. Only for growing where there is space. Once installed they are difficult to eradicate, so think about it carefully. It is possible to grow in a sunken container which will hold back their territorial ambitions, but they will become congested and need replanting after a few years. If possible try and remove any dead or sickly canes to improve the appearance and to enhance the remaining ones. Top-dressing with fibrous organic material will also help keep the clumps looking healthy. They are not particularly worried about type of soil, but prefer a slightly acid one.

Satureja (Labiatae). Savory. This is a genus of aromatic annual and perennial herbs and sub-shrubs. They like a dry, often poor soil, preferably on the limy side. Whatever it is it must be free-draining. A sunny position is required. Some may self-sow so clip over after flowering. Shear over the plants tightly in spring.

Saururus (Saururaceae). Lizard's Tail. This is a small genus of aquatic plants that can be grown in shallow water or in boggy areas that never dry out. They need a sunny position. They are hardy.

Sauromatum (Araceae). Monarch of the East. Only one species, *S. venosum*, of this genus of tropical aroids is hardy enough to be grown outside, and that only in very mild areas. It requires a moisture-retentive soil and a lightly-shaded position in hotter climates but a warm, sunny one in cooler conditions. It is usually sold as a curiosity as the tuber can be placed on an indoor surface without compost or water and it will come into flower. But be warned, they have a revolting smell.

Saussurea (Compositae). These curious plants occasionally crop up in seed lists, usually in the form of some of the Himalayan species. They are often clothed in a downy cotton wool which is a protection against cold and wet weather. They are difficult in cultivation and it seems that they may be better suited to pan culture than the open garden. Certainly attempts to grow them in areas of high rainfall and moist atmosphere, that resembles their native habitat, might stand the best chance. The soil should be gritty but contain well-rotted humus (peat might be best as the medium should not be too rich).

Saxifraga (Saxifragaceae). Saxifrages. A large genus of which the majority are best suited to the rock garden, but there are a number that will go in the front of the border or woodland garden. The border forms all like to have moisture-retentive soil. They nearly all like a cool, lightly-shaded position, some will even take full shade. They are all gently spreading but not fast enough to become a nuisance. They are evergreen, so just remove the flowering stems after flowering and any dead leaves. A light top-dressing of leafmould in winter is advantageous but avoid covering the plants.

Scabiosa (Dipsacaceae). Scabious. This is a large genus of annuals and perennials, several of which are grown in the border. They like a light soil and a place in the sun. The soil should be well drained and preferably alkaline, although they will grow on neutral ones. Although most will also grow on acid soils they are likely to be short-lived. Lime if necessary. Plant out in the spring. They do not like disturbance so try to avoid transplanting, but should it be unavoidable do so in the spring. They have a long flowering period, but this is improved if they are regularly deadheaded. There is no need for staking.

Schizostylis (Iridaceae). Kaffir Lily. A popular autumn-flowering genus, the most difficult thing about which is the pronunciation of its name. It dislikes dry soil and should be planted in one that is moisture-retentive. It will even grow in shallow water. The advantage of planting them near water is that the air is usually moist, which is something else that schizostylis like. They should be planted in a sunny position. Cut off the dead stems in late winter; cut, do not pull, otherwise part of the plant will also come up. A winter mulch may be needed in colder areas to protect the plants from the frosts. Top-dress with well-rotted organic material in winter. Dig up every few years, rejuvenate the soil, and replant in order to keep them healthy and vigorous.

Scilla (Hyacinthaceae/Liliaceae). Bulbous plants that grow in any good garden soil, but it should not be one that dries out during their growing season, ie spring. They are quite happy in a lightly-shaded position under deciduous shrubs. Plant out in the autumn at about 5–7.5cm (2-3in) deep. They are not too invasive although *S.*

152

bithynica does self-sow quite freely. Remove seed heads before they ripen if this is likely to become a problem.

Scirpus (Cyperaceae). Bulrushes, Rushes. This is a large genus of rhizomatous plants that are suitable for the muddy margins and shallow water of ponds. Split up every four years or so to keep the plant neat, and to prevent it getting too vigorous. The popular *S. tabernaemontani* 'Albescens' may not be fully hardy in very cold districts. In such areas they might be better planted in shallow water as this will insulate the creeping rhizomes as long as the water does not freeze solid. Most grow in water up to 45cm (18in) but the zebra bulrush, *S. tabernaemontani* 'Zebrinus', wants no more than a maximum of about 20cm (8in) and will even grow in ordinary soil as long as it does not dry out.

Scoliopus (Trilliaceae/Liliaceae). This is a two-species genus of which *S. bigelovii* is the one normally grown in gardens. They are closely related to the trilliums and like a similar woodland-type situation with a moist, humusy soil and light shade. They spread slowly to form a clump but are never invasive. Top-dress with leafmould during winter.

Scopolia (Solanaceae). This is a small genus of which *S. carniolica* and *S. lurida* are sometimes grown in cultivation. They will grow in any fertile garden soil including quite dry ones. They like a shady position. The fleshy rhizomes tend to creep widely forming large drifts of plants. These plants are poisonous.

Scorzonera (Compositae). Salsify. Although this is a large genus, *S. purpurea* is virtually the only one grown in cultivation, and that usually as a vegetable. However, it has fine purple flowers and is sometimes grown solely for these. It likes a deeply-cultivated, light sandy soil to perform of its best but it will grow in most fertile garden soils. Usually they are sown where they are to flower, but if they have been raised elsewhere transplant while they are still young as salsify is tap-rooted and resents disturbance. Do not let them run to seed as they self-sow everywhere.

Scrophularia (Scrophulariaceae). Figwort. This is a very large genus although few are grown in cultivation. The main one is *S. auriculata* in its variegated form 'Variegata'. This has previously also been known as *S. aquatica* and *S. nodosum*. It likes a moisture-retentive soil and either sun or light shade. It is prey to a few pests. Plants are often attacked by figwort weevil that seems specific to this plant (and to *Phygelius*). The leaves are covered with nasty, slimy grubs which eat off all the flower buds and make holes in the foliage. Spray with a permethrin-based chemical as soon as the grubs or adults are seen. Another predator is the mullein moth which will eat the leaves, reducing them to tatters. Hand pick these as they are reasonably visible. Slugs can also have the same effect. The flowers are of not much importance on the variegated form and they can be removed before they open; if left cut back before they start seeding. Cut back to the ground as soon as the foliage begins to look tatty. Top-dress with organic material in winter.

Scutellaria (Labiatae). Skullcaps. These plants like a light, well-drained soil but many will grow in any fertile garden soil although they may be short-lived in heavier or damper ones. They also like a sunny position. *S. altissima*, by contrast, is a woodlander and likes a moist soil and light shade. Deadhead after flowering to keep them neat and to prevent them self-sowing, particularly in the case of *S. altissima*.

Sedum (Crassulaceae). Stonecrops. This is a very large genus with many species in cultivation, although the majority are more for rock garden or pot culture. The border forms will grow in most soils but will become over-tall on richer, heavier soils necessitating staking. They are generally more compact on lighter soils. On the whole they prefer light, well-drained conditions. A sunny position is to be preferred but some will put on some sort of show in light shade. Some of the larger sedums such as *S.* 'Autumn Joy' turn a very good rusty brown in the late autumn, and it is worth not cutting back these until spring, so allowing them to add colour to the winter garden. Some of the taller autumn-flowering forms, such as *S.* 'Autumn Joy', splay open. They can be staked to prevent this or they can be lifted with a fork in spring to break their roots before replanting them in the same position. This retards their growth making shorter and stronger plants. An alternative is to dig them up each spring or autumn and then divide and replant them. They should be divided at least every three years to keep them vigorous. Vine weevil and cock chafer, together with slugs and woodlice, all make their dormitories and dining rooms amongst the roots of the bigger species. If any plants appear to be stunted, lift them and investigate. There is currently no successful chemical with which to attack vine weevil. Sifting through the soil and picking them out is the only solution. Sometimes the flower colour may be disappointing in some varieties. This may be because they are newly planted, the true colours often not coming out until their second year. Some of the smaller forms spread quite quickly and can become a nuisance if not kept in check.

Selinum (Umbelliferae). In this small genus *S. tenuifolium* (*S. candollei*) is the species that is normally grown. They will grow in any deep, fertile garden soil, although they prefer a well-drained one. They will grow in heavier ones but may be short-lived. A sunny position is required. Slugs can be a problem for emerging shoots in spring. Cut back all old stems in the winter clear-up.

Semiaquilegia (Ranunculaceae). A small genus closely related to aquilegia and requiring the same treatment.

Sempervivum (Crassulaceae). Houseleeks, Hens and Chickens. A large genus of succulent plants that is popular with collectors. They will grow in any well-drained soil, including quite poor ones. They will even grow on walls and roofs. They like a sunny position. Once they have flowered they die, but the flowering plant is usually surrounded by new offsets so there is continuance. Remove the dead rosettes. Most are hardy but there are some species that suffer from winter wet and require protection or pot culture.

Senecio (Compositae). Ragworts. A very large genus of plants with around 3,000 species, only a few of which are in cultivation. Some, such as *S. jacobaea* (Ragwort) and *S. vulgaris*, are outright weeds and should be avoided, mainly because they seed everywhere but also because the latter harbours various rusts which it can pass on to other plants. Those that are garden-worthy will grow in any fertile garden soil. They like a sunny position. Most garden senecios grow on dry land but the white-flowered *S. smithii* will grow in several inches of water as well as growing in damp soil. *S. aureus* also prefers a damp soil and is suitable for growing in a bog garden. It is a plant much beloved by slugs. *S. tangutica* is terribly invasive and should be avoided in smaller borders. Elsewhere it should either be dug up regularly and replanted, or dug around to remove questing rhizomes. Some of the smaller species are short-lived. Most species produce copious amounts of seed and are best deadheaded immediately after flowering. They can be cut to the ground during the autumn or winter clear-up.

Seriocarpus (Compositae). This is a small genus from North America that is similar to asters. They can be grown in any good garden soil and like a sunny position. Cut to the ground after flowering or during the winter clear-up. They are clump-forming and need to be divided every few years to keep them vigorous.

Serratula (Compositae). Saw-worts. This large genus of plants is almost unknown in cultivation except for *S. seoanei* (*S. shawii*) and *S. tinctoria*. They will grow in any good garden soil and prefer a sunny position. They flower late and should be cut down during the winter or early spring. They slowly form clumps so seem to be best left undisturbed although they can be lifted and divided for propagational purposes. Lightly top-dress with well-rotted organic matter or bonemeal to keep them vigorous.

Sesleria (Gramineae). Moor Grass. A large genus of grasses of which quite a number are in cultivation. The majority come from alkaline soils of various kinds and do best in similar conditions in the garden. The majority prefer an open, sunny situation, although *S. heuffleriana* is a woodlander and prefers light shade and a moist, humusy soil. *S. caerulea* also likes a moist, even boggy soil, but should have an open position. They are clump-formers and those that die back in winter should be cut back in late winter. Those that remain evergreen usually flower in the spring and should not be cut back, although dead leaves should be carefully combed out.

Shortia (Diapensiaceae). These are plants that will grow best in areas of high rainfall. In spite of their love of moisture they must have a free-draining soil. The ideal is a gritty soil with plenty of leafmould in it. It should be acidic or neutral. They do best in a sunny position where they will flower better, but the soil must be moisture-retentive. They will grow in light shade, but, from the gardener's point of view, they will not do so well. However, they will tolerate a slightly drier soil in such situations. Plant out in spring. They slowly spread but never become a nuisance. Preferably do not disturb them unnecessarily. Top-dress with leafmould in winter. The leaves are evergreen so just remove old flower stalks and any dead leaves. They do not seem to suffer from any specific pests and diseases.

Sidalcea (Malvaceae). This is a small genus of plants that grow in any good garden soil, but prefers them to be reasonably well-drained as they can be killed off if the soil is too damp during the winter. They also do better if it contains a certain amount of organic material. Sidalceas should be planted in full sun. They are not all that strong and often require staking, especially if in exposed positions. Cut back after flowering to get a second flush. Do not remove the basal foliage in the autumn. Some sidalceas are attacked by the same rust that attacks hollyhocks. Spray with a fungicide. A top-dressing of organic matter in the winter may be of benefit.

Sideritis (Labiatae). A large genus that has hardly any species in general cultivation. They like well-drained soils, especially in areas where winter wet is likely to be a problem. Most come from alkaline soils and so this may help to prolong their lives as they are generally short-lived in cultivation. They are reasonably drought-resistant. A hot, sunny position is a suitable location for them. Shear over after flowering.

Silene (Caryophyllaceae). Campions. Although this is a large genus the majority of plants in cultivation are mainly grown on rock gardens. The larger border forms will grow in any garden soil, although many prefer it to be well-drained. They will grow in either sun or light shade. Most tend to be short-lived but do produce copious amounts of seed and so vouchsafe their continuance. *S. dioica* 'Flora Pleno' benefits from being dug up every second or third year and divided. Spring is the best time for doing this. It seems to do best if replanted in new soil. Most will produce a second flush of flowers if deadheaded as the first fade. They are best cut almost to the ground but leave any basal foliage. This will also help to prevent too much self-sowing. Cut back during the winter clear-up, again leaving any overwintering basal leaves. Some silenes are susceptible to rust diseases. *S. vulgaris* occasionally suffers from a smut that effects the centre of the flower, giving it a sooty appearance. For both problems spray with a fungicide.

Silphium (Compositae). Compass Plant, Cup Plant, Prairie Dock, Rosinweed. Several of this genus are grown in gardens. They all need a deep, fertile soil, but one that is reasonably free-draining. However, *S. perfoliatum* prefers a moist humus-rich soil. It will also tolerate a little light shade whereas the rest prefer an open, sunny position. They flower late in the season, so that by the time they have finished flowering it is time to cut them to the ground in the autumn/winter tidy-up. Although tall they do not normally need staking.

Silybum (Compositae). Of the two species in this genus only *S. marianum* is commonly grown. Although they are best in any garden soil they will grow in quite spartan conditions. If grown in organic-rich soil they can become gigantic, sometimes 2.5m (8ft) or more across. It is grown mainly for its foliage effect so the flowers may be removed before they open. If left on, deadhead immediately flowering is over, otherwise they are likely to self-sow vigorously.

Sinarundinaria (Gramineae). A genus where many of the *Arundinaria*, such as *A. nitida*, have found refuge. This plant could do with a light shade as the leaves curl in overhead sun. They will grow on a wide range of soils but prefer it slightly acid. Cut out any of the older, tatty canes as low down as possible to rejuvenate the clump. Thinning and top-dressing also helps produce a healthier clump with thicker, more vigorous canes.

Sisyrinchium (Iridaceae). Blue-eyed Grass. These can be grown in any well-drained garden soil. They need a warm, sunny position. Sisyrinchium are notorious self-sowers and the flowering stems should be removed before they start to shed seed. Do not destroy all the seedlings as a few are sometimes needed to replace plants that have suddenly died. They are not all that long-lived and need regular dividing and replanting. *S. striatum* tends to accumulate black leaves and these really need to be removed, especially in the form 'Aunt May' which is grown for its cream-striped leaves. Blackening of the leaves may indicate that the plant has become loose in the soil, perhaps having had its roots chewed through, so check before the plant is lost. *S.s.* 'Aunt May' also benefits from being lifted every three years and divided and replanted in a new position. Frequent dividing and replanting in rejuvenated soil tends to encourage much better flowering. In hot areas 'Aunt May' benefits from a little light shade.

Smilacina (Convallariaceae/Liliaceae). False Solomon's Seal. Like the true solomon's seal these plants like to have a moist, woodland-type soil. They generally do not like alkaline soils, but they can occasionally be seen growing on mildly chalky soils where they have been given plenty of humus and kept moist. They perform best in a light shade, but can be grown in more open areas as long as it is not too hot and the soil remains moist. This is a spreading plant, eventually forming large clumps, but it is slow enough not to be invasive. The best time to lift and split congested plantings is in autumn, so that they are ready to perform again the following spring. In some areas where the plants will not have time to re-establish themselves before winter sets in it will be necessary to leave division until spring, but this means that a year's flowering is likely to be lost. Give the soil a good top-dressing of organic material during the winter. They are strong enough not to require supporting.

Smyrmium (Umbelliferae). This is a small genus of biennial plants of which *S. perfoliata* is grown in shady borders and woodland areas. It will grow in any good garden soil and likes a lightly-shaded position. It normally produces more than enough self-sown seedlings to keep it going. If you do not wish it to seed remove the plants after flowering. *S. olustratum*, alexanders, is a British native found flowering in coastal regions, particularly in hedgerows. Although it is an attractive plant in a coarse kind of way it is a very vigorous self-sower and should not be grown in formal positions unless deadheaded.

Solidago (Compositae). Goldenrod. These will grow in any garden soil, even quite poor ones. However, they will do best in reasonably fertile soils that are well-drained. They will grow in light shade but always look best in sun. Cut back as soon as they have finished flowering otherwise they are likely to self-sow throughout the garden. However, if you can bear weeding them all out they can be left to feed the birds. They all tend to spread and make clumps, but some quite aggressively do so and need to be kept in check with regular division. Goldenrod often suffer from mildew, especially late in the season after a dry period. They can be sprayed if necessary with fungicide or, if they have finished flowering, cut down and burnt. They are generally strong enough to stand without support.

X *Solidaster* (Compositae). This genus consists solely of X *Solidaster luteus* (also known as X *S. hybridus*), which is a bigeneric hybrid between a *Solidago* species and *Aster ptarmicoides*. The cultivation is the same as for *Solidago*.

Sonchus (Compositae). Sow Thistles. Not all of this large genus are weeds although a lot are, and pestilent ones at that. However, there are a few that are deliberately grown in gardens of which *S. palustris* is one. This is a plant that likes damp areas and can be grown next to water features. Others can be grown in any garden soil. All like an open position. Be warned though, they can all spread very vigorously from seed. Deadhead or cut back once the flowers fade.

Sophora (Leguminosae). This is a medium-sized genus of woody plants that contain a few herbs and sub-shrubs that can be treated as herbaceous plants. They will grow in a well-drained soil, and need a warm, sunny position. It is likely to be cut to the ground in the winter. Cut off the dead stems in early spring, or earlier if you want to apply a winter mulch of straw or bracken.

Sorghum (Gramineae). This is a small genus of grasses, most of which are annuals, although the perennial *S. halepense*, Johnson grass, is sometimes seen in cultivation. It is rather a vigorously-spreading plant and should only be planted in areas where there is space to take it. It will grow in any garden soil and, like most grasses, prefers an open position. Any planting or replanting should take place in spring. Cut over during the late winter.

Sparaxis (Iridaceae). Harlequin Flower, Wandflowers. A small genus of species that like a well-drained soil and a warm, sunny position. Plant out in the spring at about 5–7.5cm (2–3in) deep. These bulbs are tender in most areas and should be lifted and overwintered in a frost-free place. They have a habit of breaking into growth far too early to be planted out. This can possibly be solved by either leaving in the ground and mulching well with bracken, fern fronds or masses of chipped bark, or they can be stored in a cool place such as a cellar, which is immune to the fluctuations of winter temperatures, thus avoiding the warmer periods. Alternatively new bulbs can be purchased each spring.

Sparganium (Sparganiaceae). Bur-reeds. This is a small genus of rush-like plants for the margins of ponds and lakes. They can be grown either in the mud at the edge of ponds or streams, or in shallow water. An open position is required. They are all rather rampant and could be well take over the whole pond unless they are kept in check by annually reducing their numbers. Think twice about introducing them into ponds lined with plastic as the questing root tips of some species (*S. erectum* for example) are sharp enough to penetrate them.

Spartina (Gramineae). Prairie Cord Grass. *S. pectinata* 'Aureomarginata' is about the only form generally grown in gardens as the others are a bit weedy. The species from which it derives is very invasive and this form is moderately so, but not so bad. It can be grown on the edge of ponds and lakes, but is too vigorous for small pools. It does self-sow so either deadhead before seed is formed, or be certain to remove all seedlings, especially any of the green-leaved ones which will probably form the majority.

Speirantha (Convallaria/Liliaceae). *S. convallarioides* is the only member of this genus. It is closely related to the Lily-of-the-valley and likes the same treatment. It likes a moist, woodland-type soil in a cool, lightly-shaded position. The rootstock is running like the lily-of-the-valley, but it does not travel as fast and is less invasive. It is not reliably hardy and benefits from a winter mulch of leafmould both to keep it warm and to add humus to the soil. Planting is best done in spring.

Sphaeralcea (Malvaceae). Desert Mallow, Globe Mallow. Increasing in popularity, this is a large genus of plants of which most are on the tender side. However, there are several that can be grown particularly in warmer areas. In a gritty, well-drained soil and a warm, sunny position they will even grow in cooler areas, but it is a good idea to take cuttings as insurance against a stiff winter. Winter protection will also help to bring them through mild frosts.

Spigelia (Loganaceae). Indian Pink, Pinkroot. In spite of there being about 30 species in this genus, it is only *S. marilandica* that is normally grown in gardens. It is a woodlander and likes a deep, humusy soil and light, shady conditions, although it will grow in the open if the soil is not too dry. Deadhead after flowering, and cut back during the autumn/winter clear-up. It is a poisonous plant.

Stachys (Labiatae). A very large genus of which only a relatively few are in cultivation. Most will grow in any fertile garden soil but they prefer it to be well-drained. Many gardeners grow *S. byzantinum* (*lanatum*) for its silver leaves rather than its flowers. In fact it is often the stems that are disliked as much as the flowers as they upset the carpeting effect of the foliage. Either way many gardeners remove the flowering stems on sight. Those that enjoy the pale pink flowers that contrast well with the foliage, leave them on until after flowering. It is then essential to remove them. Partly because they soon become rather ugly and partly because they are liable to seed everywhere. If left on, the stems soon become wet and flabby and rather unpleasant to handle. It needs dividing every few years to prevent the centre from dying out and becoming ugly. In some gardens it may be beneficial to support *S. macrantha* with short sticks. *S. coccinea* is on the tender side and it is a good idea to produce some young plants each year to overwinter as an insurance. It may be that the winter wetness is as much to blame as the cold, so make certain that the plant has a well-drained soil.

Stanleya (Cruciferae). Prince's Plume. Any good garden soil will suit these plants. They prefer a well-drained one and will even take moderate drought conditions. An open, sunny position is needed. Deadhead after flowering unless you wish to leave them for their decorative seedpods and cut back during the autumn/winter clear-up.

Statice (Plumbaginaceae). See *Limonium*

Stellaria (Caryophyllaceae). Stitchworts. In this genus the majority of species are considered weeds, although possibly fit for the wild garden. They will grow in any good garden soil and generally like an open position. They do travel like mad and an eye needs to be kept on them.

Stenanthium (Melanthiaceae/Liliaceae). Featherbells. Of the two species grown in gardens, *S. gramineum* will grow in any soil, while *S. robustum* prefers a more moist condition. They are stoloniferous, forming clumps, but are not invasive. Remove flowering stems after blooming.

Sternbergia (Amaryllidaceae). Crocus-like bulbs of which *S. lutea* and *S. sicula* are grown in the open garden, the former being the most frequently seen. They like a well-drained soil in a warm, sheltered position, such as at the base of a wall, where they can get a reasonable baking from the sun. Do not plant amongst other perennials as the ground needs to be open to the sun. The flowers appear in the autumn or even early winter. They will grow in any light soil and do well under alkaline conditions.

Stipa (Gramineae). Feather Grass. This is a large genus of clump-forming, non-invasive grasses. They will grow in any fertile garden soil and need an open, sunny position. Plant out or transplant stipa in the spring. It will take up to four years for *S. gigantea*, and many of the others, to make a decent clump. Cut back all leaves and stems in the spring before the new growth begins, but do not cut too close to the ground otherwise the following summer's flowering buds will be removed. Sparrows can be a nuisance in that they strip the flower heads. There is no real solution to this problem, although using the plant away from any buildings where sparrows congregate sometimes helps. Do not cut down too early as they make attractive winter decoration in the garden. However, cut back before the new growth starts in spring. Top-dress around the plants with organic material in winter.

Stokesia (Compositae). *S. laevis* is the only species in this genus. It will grow in any garden soil as long as it is well-drained. Drainage is particularly important during winter. They need a sunny position. Deadhead after flowering.

Stratiotes (Hydrocharitaceae). Water Soldier. A single-species genus with *S. aloides* being the sole member. It is a marginal plant for still or slow-moving water. Shallow water on the edge of a pond or stream is the ideal position, but it will also grow in the verging mud. It can also be grown in bog gardens but it must not be allowed to dry out. During the winter it retires to the bottom of the pool where it survives as a resting bud. In a bog garden it might need to be given a protective mulch in colder areas, but under water it will survive as long as the water itself does not freeze.

Streptopus (Convallariaceae/Liliaceae). Twisted Stalk. This is a small genus of woodland plants related to *Polygonatum*. They like similar conditions with a cool, moist, humusy soil and a light shade. Top-dress in the winter with leafmould or other organic material. Like Solomon's seal its rhizomatous roots travel quite a bit, making a decent sized clump, but it is not invasive. Do not cut back until the foliage dies down, at least not on *S. amplexifolius* as it has beautiful red berries in autumn.

Strobilanthes (Acanthaceae). They will grow in any good garden soil, preferably a well-drained one. They are reasonably drought tolerant. Plant or transplant in spring. A warm, sunny position is required. Cut back after flowering in the late autumn or early winter.

Stylomecon (Papaveraceae). *S. heterophylla*, the only member of this genus, is a woodlander that relishes moist, leafy soils and light shade. Like most members of the family it spreads around, in this case by seed, but is not so invasive as its relatives and is much easier to control.

Stylophorum (Papaveraceae). A small genus of woodlanders of which *S. diphyllum* and *S. lasiocarpum* are the most commonly seen in cultivation. They like moist, humusy soils and light shade. Top-dress with organic material during the winter.

Succisa (Dipsacaceae). This small genus is closely allied to *Scabiosa*. It likes a moist soil and would even do well in a bog garden. A sunny position is required. Cut back in the autumn/winter clear-up.

Symphyandra (Campanulaceae). A genus that very closely resembles *Campanula*. They will grow on any fertile garden soil, but prefer a well-drained one. Most do best in full sun but will also grow in light shade. Although they are perennials they do tend to be short-lived, often only lasting one year. Fortunately they produce masses of seed and usually self-sow prodigiously. If you want to be certain of a succession do not cut down until they have seeded.

Symphytum (Boraginaceae). Comfrey. Many gardeners have a love-hate relationship with this genus. They are rather coarse and can grow like weeds and are difficult to eradicate. However, quite a number are grown in gardens, often in wilder parts. Apart from problems with any bits of roots that are left in the ground, which always reshoot, the main problem is that they spread invasively both underground and by seed. They will grow in most garden soils, including both damp and dry ones, although they are probably happiest in the former. Either sun or light shade is appropriate. The taller forms such as *S.* x *uplandicum* may need to be supported in a more formal position. Cut back after flowering to prevent them self-sowing and to get them to produce a fresh crop of leaves to replace the somewhat ungainly flower stems. To get the best out of them, top-dress with organic matter during the winter.

Symplocarpus (Araceae). Skunk Cabbage. *S. foetidus* is the sole representative of this genus. It likes a damp, boggy soil and a sunny position. Any top-dressing with organic material should be done early in the winter as it can start emerging around mid-winter. It also retires early and is gone by late summer.

Synthyris (Scrophulariaceae). This is a small genus of woodland plants that are usually grown in the peat garden. They like a moist, humusy soil and light shade. Remove the flower spikes once they have gone over, unless you want seed, and any dead leaves. They are not keen on being moved so plant out while they are young and avoid transplanting.

Tanacetum (Compositae). Pyrethrum, Tansy. A medium-size genus that has recently had an influx of new species from *Chrysanthemum* and *Pyrethrum*. They are not too fussy about soil and will do well in most good garden conditions as long as they are reasonably well-drained. Naturally they will do best in well-fed soils. Some gardeners feel that *T. herderi* does better on alkaline soils. They all like an open, sunny position. Cut pyrethrums hard back after flowering. Tansy, *T. vulgare*, can spread rather rapidly and can be too vigorous for borders or even herb gardens where it is usually grown. Dig it up each year and replant it, or dig around it, removing questing roots. Feverfew, *T. parthenium*, can suffer badly from black fly gathering around the top of the young shoots in early spring. Use an insecticide aimed at aphids, but do not use one that is labelled as not being suitable for chrysanthemums as this might have adverse effects on the plants. The golden form *T.p.* 'Aurea' naturally grows greener as the season progresses; there is nothing wrong with it if it does. It will also seed around very freely and should be deadheaded or, preferably, cut to the ground so that a fresh clump of leaves is formed. Not all seedlings will bear golden foliage and some have reverted to green. It is not a very long-lived plant and it is often best to replace it with one of the seedlings each year. The pyrethrums, *T. coccineum*, like a rich soil, which, although well-drained, should be watered during dry weather. They are likely to need supporting. Cut back immediately after flowering to obtain a second flush of blooms. Many gardeners, especially those on heavy soils, find that planting or transplanting in autumn is a bad time as the plants often die or languish. Late summer, after flowering, or spring are the best times.

Tanakaea (Saxifragaceae). *T. radicans* is the only member of this genus. It is a creeping woodlander that likes a cool, moist, humus-rich soil and a lightly-shaded position. It is not completely hardy and a winter mulch of leafmould will help protect it as well as maintain the health of the soil.

Telekia (Compositae). This genus only contains a couple of species of which *T. speciosa* is the one usually grown in gardens. It will grow in any garden soil but prefers one that is on the moist side, and will happily grow beside water. It will grow in either sun or light shade. This plant is an inveterate runner so avoid it unless you have space to let it have its head, or can contain it in some way. It will also self-sow unless it is deadheaded soon after flowering. The spent flowers look tatty anyway so this task is doubly worth doing. *T. speciosissima* has similar requirements although it prefers a sunny position.

Telesonix (Saxifragaceae). *T. jamesii* has now moved back to Boykinia.

Tellima (Saxifragaceae). Fringecup. *T. grandiflora*, the only species, is basically a woodland plant and needs the kind of soil that you would find there; cool, moist and humusy. They naturally also like shade, varying from the light to quite dense. They tend to spread quite rapidly but are not too difficult to control. Remove any dying or dead leaves from tellimas at the beginning of winter to enhance their appearance throughout that season. The best time to lift and split congested plantings is in autumn, so that they are ready to perform again the following spring. In some areas where the plants will not have time to re-establish themselves before winter sets in it will be necessary to leave division until spring, but this means that a year's flowering is likely to be lost.

Teucrium (Labiatae). Germander. This is a surprisingly large genus considering that it has only a relatively few species in cultivation. Most will grow in any fertile garden soil although they prefer it to be well-drained. *T. canadense* is the exception as this likes a moist, humus-rich soil. This plant also likes light shade, although it will grow in the open. The rest prefer a sunny position. One reason for the lack of species in cultivation is possibly that many are not reliably hardy and may require winter protection. This should not take the form of anything that will prevent air circulating around the plants so that they lie damp as this will surely kill them. Hardier forms with winter appeal, such as *T. scorodonia* 'Crispum', need to be tidied up in the autumn, removing all dead leaves. This species will also tolerate some shade and is also one of the species that needs an acid or neutral soil.

Thalictrum (Ranunculaceae). Meadow Rue. Although there are only a relatively few in cultivation this is quite a large genus with about 140 species or so. They will grow in most garden soils that are reasonably well-drained, but should also be rich in organic material. Most will grow either in full sun or light shade. The taller species need some form of support, such as tying the lower (unseen) part of the stems to a cane. Some, *T. minus* being the main one in cultivation, spread quite rapidly by stolons and need to be kept in check. Others such as *T. aquilegifolium* self-sow prodigiously. The way to prevent this of course is to deadhead after flowering, but the seedheads are so attractive that one can be loathe to do it. The thing to do is to time it right and cut them back just as the seeds turn brown, before they are dispersed. The other thing about this plant is that if it is given a good soaking before and after, it can be moved from its flowering position to a reserve bed so that other plants can take over once it has served its purpose. One or two, *T. diffusiflorum* for example, are difficult to satisfy and experiments must be made both in soil and position before they are happy. This plant also tends to be short-lived. Top-dress during the winter with well-rotted, organic material.

Thelypteris (Polypodiaceae). Beech Fern. A few of this very large genus are in cultivation. They all like a moist, humus-rich soil, some, such as *T. palustris*, will grow in very damp conditions, even shallow water in the case of this species and one or two

162

others. Cut back before the new fronds appear and top-dress with organic matter during the winter.

Thermopsis (Leguminosae). False Lupin. These prefer a well-drained soil, preferably in a warm, sunny position. Most are quite able to cope with dry weather conditions. They are all inclined to be a bit invasive so either plant where this does not matter or take evasive action by digging round the clump each year, restricting its advances. Cut back to the ground once it begins to look tired and ragged. In cooler, moist conditions the foliage may well last until autumn.

Thladianthia (Curcubitaceae). These are climbing plants that can be vigorous, not only in their ability to climb but also to spread. They will grow in any good garden soil but require a warm, sunny position. As well as being interesting in flower they produce attractive red fruit, but since the species are dioecious both male and female plants will be required to achieve them. Although it can be used as ground cover it is best as a climbing plant, when it will require tall supports (up to 3m (10ft) or more). This can be trellis or a strong woody plant, such as a tree.

Thymus (Labiatae). Thymes. Although strictly shrubby, these plants are often grown in the front of borders, particularly if they abut a path. They all prefer a light, well-drained soil and a sunny position. Shear over after flowering to keep them tight and compact. Bald patches often occur in the centre of the carpeting forms. The plants need to be lifted, the soil rejuvenated, and the rooted younger parts replanted.

Tiarella (Saxifragaceae). Foamflower. This small genus of woodlanders likes a cool, moist, humus-rich soil and light shade. *T. cordifolia*, *T. lanciniata* and *T. polyphylla* spread by stolons forming large colonies but they are easy to control so are not invasive. *T. wherryi, T. trifoliata* and *T. unifoliata* are clump-formers. Tiarella are evergreen and make a good contribution to the winter scene but they will look better if any dying or dead leaves are removed at the beginning of that season. Top-dress with leafmould. They can suffer from vine weevil grubs chewing through their roots, the first sign usually being the plants blowing away rootless.

Tigridia (Iridaceae). Tender bulbs that can only be overwintered in the soil in warmer districts. Elsewhere the bulbs should be lifted and stored in a frost-free place in trays of dry sand after being dusted with a fungicide. They need a well-drained but moisture-retentive soil and a warm, sunny position.

Tofieldia (Melanthiaceae/Liliaceae). They are plants that need an acidic, constantly damp soil. They can be grown in a bog garden or a peat bed that never dries out. In the former they should be carefully placed so that they are not swamped by other, more vigorous plants. Cut back the flowering stems after blooming.

Tolmiea (Saxifragaceae). Pickaback Plant, Piggy-back Plant, Young on Age. *T. menziesii* is the only member of this genus. Although this is more frequently grown as a houseplant it is also grown in the open garden. It is a woodlander and requires a cool, humusy soil and a lightly-shaded position. *Tolmiea* is rhizomatous and creeps about but is easily controlled and is not invasive. It also produces new plants on the basal leaves. Top-dress with leafmould in the winter. Can suffer from vine weevil grubs, which are likely to eat through all the roots, killing the plant.

Tovara (Polygonaceae). See *Persicaria*

Trachystemon (Boraginaceae). *T. orientale* is the best known of the two species in this genus. It is a ground cover plant that will grow in virtually any soil. If it has any preferences it would be for shade and a moist soil, but it is very adaptable. It is stoloniferous and spreads rather rapidly so give it a position where it can ramp or be contained.

Tradescantia (Commelinaceae). Spiderwort. This is mainly a tender genus of plants, but *T. virginiana* and its hybrids *T. x andersoniana* are hardy. They like a well-drained soil, and often do best in poor soils when not too much vegetative growth is put on at the expense of flowers. Cut back after flowering, both to discourage their habit of self-sowing and to promote a new flush of blooms. The best time to lift and split congested plantings is in autumn, so that they are ready to perform again the following year. In some areas where the plants will not have time to re-establish themselves before winter sets in it will be necessary to leave division until spring, but this means that a year's flowering is likely to be lost. They can become very congested so it is worth doing this at least every three years or so.

Trapa (Trapaceae). Water Chestnut. This is a small genus of annual aquatic plants. However, they produce fruit which regenerate the plant each year. *T. natans* is the species usually grown. It is a floating plant. When introducing such plants throw or lower them into the water, do not plant them in the conventional manner. In late summer each year the seed falls to the bottom of the pool and a new plant appears the following year. Some seed should be collected and overwintered in a jar of water or wet sphagnum moss to ensure their continuance. Seed that dries out will not germinate. They are hardy as long as they are covered with water that does not freeze.

Tricyrtis (Convallariaceae/Liliaceae). Toad Lilies. Plant out in a moist, woodland-type soil with plenty of leafmould or other organic material so that it does not dry out. They like to have light shade and are liable to scorch in full sun. However, they like a little sun and will flower earlier if they obtain at least some. In a darker position they may flower too late to be effective as they are cut back by the frosts. Cut back to the ground after flowering (late autumn/early winter). They are hardy as long as they are below ground but late spring frosts can turn the emerging shoots to mush, but they will usually regenerate, although repeated attacks could severely weaken them. Top-dress with leafmould or other organic material in winter. They spread under-ground by rhizomes but rarely get out of control. Slugs can be a problem, especially for the emerging growth in spring.

Trientalis (Primulaceae). This small genus of woodlanders like to have a moist, humusy soil with plenty of added leafmould or pine needles. They seem to prefer it to be acidic and not too heavy, light sandy soils are best. A lightly-shaded position should be made available to them. They are rhizomatous and will quickly creep to form a large colony but are rarely a nuisance.

Trifolium (Leguminosae). Clovers. A large genus, most of which are considered too weedy for the garden and should not be introduced as they can be difficult to eradicate. However a few are grown as decorative plants. They will grow in any fertile garden soil although the carpeting *T. alpinum* is a lime-hater and should be given acid conditions. They should be given a sunny position. Cut back once they begin to look tatty or wait until the autumn/winter clear-up. The tall species *T. pannonicum* may need some support in spite of its bushiness.

Trillium (Trilliaceae/Liliaceae). Wake Robin. Trilliums like a humus-rich, woodland soil that is on the acid side; top-dressing with pine needles may be sufficient. Most will grow in a neutral soil. *T. rivale* prefers a limy soil, while a few others, for example *TT. cernum, erectum, grandiflorum, luteum, nivale* and *sessile* for example, will tolerate such conditions as long as they are not severe. Most prefer cool, lightly-shaded conditions but the dwarf *T. rivale* enjoys a sunny position although it still requires moist soil. Avoid damaging trilliums while they are in growth. If any part of the plant above ground is damaged or removed it will not regrow during that season. It will reappear in the next, but in the meantime it has lost the chance of photosynthesis, and hence the replenishment of below-ground stores and growth. They also resent root disturbance so do not cultivate deeply around them. If the clumps become congested dig them up in autumn, carefully split them and replant immediately in rejuvenated soil. If they are lifted just for transplanting, dig up as much soil as possible so that the roots receive minimum disturbance. The various green-flowered and green-striped forms of *T. grandiflorum* with flower and or leaf distortions are diseased, the mycoplasma organism causing this can be transmitted to other species so avoid growing them.

Triosteum (Caprifoliaceae). Horse Gentian. This small genus are woodlanders by nature and require similar conditions in the garden. A moist, humusy soil and a little light shade is ideal. Do not be in too much of a hurry to cut them back as it is the berries as much as the flowers that make them attractive. These berries do eventually produce self-sown seedlings but they do not usually become a nuisance, particularly if they do grow in a wilder part of the garden to which they are more suited.

Tritelia (Alliaceae/Liliaceae). These are bulbous plants closely allied to the *Brodiaea*. They all like a well-drained soil and a warm, sunny position. The best time for planting out is in the autumn, but they may well need some form of winter protection if they are being grown in cooler areas. Plant at about 10–12.5cm (4–5in) deep, perhaps slightly deeper in lighter soils. They do not like to be disturbed but clumps become congested and need lifting every few years so that they can be split up and replanted. This is best done in autumn. They are not completely hardy and a winter mulch helps to protect them.

Tritonia (Iridaceae). A genus of bulbous plants closely related to *Crocosmia*. They like a similar treatment. They will grow in any fertile garden soil although they prefer it to be free-draining but reasonably rich in humus. A warm, sunny position is best. Plant out in autumn as the stolons that produce new corms start into growth very early in the spring. If they become congested, lift, divide and replant after rejuvenating the soil. Cut back after flowering or wait until the autumn/winter clear-up.

Trollius (Ranunculaceae). Globe Flower. This genus of plants has long been popular in gardens. Although they come from marshy areas they will grow in any fertile garden soil as long as it contains enough humus to prevent it drying out. They are particularly good in waterside plantings. Either full sun or light shade will suit them.

Deadhead after flowering, leaving the basal leaves to continue. Sometimes this induces a second flowering. Although some species are quite tall they generally do not need staking. Top-dress with organic matter in the winter.

Tropaeolum (Tropaeolaceae). Nasturtiums. *T. tuberosum* is not completely hardy and needs to be dug up and overwintered indoors for complete safety. In milder areas it can be given a warm mulch. The variety 'Ken Aslet' is much earlier-flowering than the species and is particularly worth growing in places where autumn comes early. Both will grow in any fertile garden soil as long as it is free-draining. They need a warm, sunny position. *T. speciosum* does best in moist soil although in rainy areas it grows very well in dry or quick-drying soils, such as against yew hedges and under demanding conifers. In drier areas add plenty of well-rotted, organic material to the soil to help preserve moisture. It may be slow to start but will suddenly take off, so do not give up on it too soon. Both need some form of support up which to grow. Bushes are ideal. *T. polyphyllum* needs a well-drained, hot position. It is a bit on the tender side so plant it deep, at least 23cm (9in), possibly under a rock. It often travels some distance underground before emerging sometimes a long way from where it was planted. This habit makes it difficult to transplant. Unlike the other two this one is a sprawler and looks best when it can hang down from a wall or a rock garden.

Tulbaghia (Alliaceae/Liliaceae). These bulbous plants need a well-drained, but reasonably moisture-retentive soil. They like a warm, sunny position, such as up against a wall. Do not allow other plants to shade the sun from the soil around it. Most are too tender, except in frost-free areas, but *T. violacea* is just about hardy and should survive most winters if grown against a sunny, south-facing wall. The foliage is evergreen in milder areas and should not be cut back unless damaged. If frosts catch the leaves they are liable to turn into a mushy mess smelling strongly of garlic. The plants will recover. The variegated form is not so hardy and may need winter protection, alternatively it can be grown in a container and moved indoors for the winter.

Tulipa (Liliaceae). Tulips. This large genus of bulbs grow in a wide variety of soils but they do seem to do better on heavier ones than light ones. A planting depth of about 15cm (6in) is required. They prefer a sunny site although they will happily take a little light shade. There is no need to lift tulips every year except if they are part of a bedding scheme. If they are planted amongst perennials they can be left where they are indefinitely unless they become congested. If they are not lifted each year, mark all clumps while still in leave so that they can be divided later when they are dormant, and also to prevent them being accidentally dug up or over-planted. Those that are lifted should be dug up as the leaves are dying down. They can be replanted somewhere else perhaps putting the smallest bulbs in a reserve bed to plump up, or they can be stored in a cool place in a net bag, away from where they can be attacked by mice, by hanging the bag on a shed wall, for example. Rejuvenate the soil with a top-dressing of well-rotted, organic matter during the winter and a light dressing of a potash-rich fertilizer in spring.

Typha (Typhaceae). Reedmace, Bulrush. Unless you have a very large pond or lake this is a genus to avoid. They can spread like greased lightning through shallow water. Not only do they spread by vigorous rhizomes but also by seed. Often they will arrive unbidden in a pond, and unless you have space for them they should be removed without delay. Where they are grown it should become an annual ritual to wade into the pond and reduce their numbers to manageable proportions. Wear gloves as the leaves can cut. They will not travel so fast when grown in a container in a lined pool but then a different problem arises in that the taller species is top heavy and will often topple over in the wind. The variegated form of *T. latifolia* is better behaved and does not spread so fast. Nor does the smallest of the bunch, *T. minima*. They will all grow in shallow water on the margins of ponds, preferably in full sun. They are not so keen on deep water and one way of eradicating the plants is to raise the water-level if that is possible. Although beautiful, cut back the brown seed heads before the seed starts to disperse.

Tweedia (Asclepiadaceae). Southern Star. *T. caeruleum* (*Oxypetalum caeruleum*) has become a popular plant in recent times, mainly because of its amazing blue flowers. It often crops up at plant sales so it is worth mentioning even if it is a tender shrub. It is unlikely to come through a winter except in the mildest districts, unless it is taken inside under glass. It likes a well-drained compost and should be kept in a warm, sunny position. With its weak scrambling habit it needs some support in the form of twigs or another plant. Pinch out the growing point to make it bush out, otherwise it is likely to grow only one stem. Can be prey to whitefly.

Urospermum (Compositae). *U. dalechampii* is the species normally grown. This likes a well-drained soil and a warm, sunny position.

Uvularia (Convallariaceae/Liliaceae). Merrybells. This is a small genus of woodlanders that are related to the solomon's seals. Like them they enjoy a moist, humusy soil with plenty of leafmould in it. They prefer a light shade but they will grow in the open as long as they have enough moisture. Cut back when they begin to look a bit tatty, or wait until the autumn clear-up. They spread by underground rhizomes and can become a bit invasive when well-suited. Top-dress in the winter with leafmould or other well-rotted, organic material.

Valeriana (Valerianaceae). Valerian. These will all grow in any good garden soil, although most prefer it on the moist side. Incorporating organic matter will help with this. They are happy in either sun or shade. *V. phu* 'Aurea' needs to be grown in full sun otherwise its golden leaves turn green. Many gardeners like to remove the flower stems of this plant before it blooms as they are a muddy pink and of little aesthetic value. Many often treat it as a bedding plant and discard it after its spring show. Do not be in such a hurry to deadhead the others, *V. alliariifolia*, in particular, as it has attractive seed heads. However this will usually allow them to self-sow. The taller forms usually require staking of some kind. *V. officinalis* is liked by cats which can be a problem.

Vancouveria (Berberidaceae). This is a small genus closely related to *Epimedium*. They like a moist, humus-rich soil. Light shade is generally preferred, but they will also grow in the open as long as they have enough moisture in the soil. They spread rather vigorously, especially *V. chrysantha*, and will usually swamp anything that gets in their way, so be careful with their siting. Cut off all leaves in January or early February before the new leaves or flower stems start to form. The new leaves look

167

particularly attractive if the old ones have been cut off. Their tangled web of roots can exhaust the soil so try to work in some leafmould over and around the plants during the winter.

Veratrum (Melanthiaceae/Liliaceae). Although some veratrums grow in the open in the wild they seem to do best in a lightly-shaded position and if planted in a typical, moist woodland soil, full of humus. Some, such as *V. album*, will grow in the open as long as there is enough moisture in the soil. Veratrum, *V. nigrum* in particular, are sheer martyrs to slugs. Unless they are controlled in some way they will reduce the pleated leaves to tatters. They will self-sow but take several years to reach flowering size. Do not cut back immediately after flowering, as they can look very attractive while in seed. Cut back in the winter or after seed has dispersed. Top-dress with leafmould or other well-rotted, organic material during winter. Although they are tall when flowering they rarely need staking.

Verbascum (Scrophulariaceae). A very large genus, mostly of biennials but also including perennials and sub-shrubs. Most of the biennial forms self-sow copiously and thus count as honorary perennials. Not all the perennials are long-lived, especially if grown in damp conditions, so it is always worth-while propagating new stock each year to hold in reserve. They all like a well-drained soil and a sunny position. Transfer self-sown seedlings early in their life to any preferred positions before they put down deep tap roots. Remove any dead leaves from the overwintering rosette to prevent them infecting other leaves, and to improve the plant's appearance. They can suffer from mildew; spray with a fungicide if necessary, although the attacks often occur after flowering is over by which time they can be discarded. They are frequently attacked by caterpillars of the mullein moth, which can reduce the foliage to tatters in a bad attack. The caterpillars can be easily seen and can be removed by hand. The tall species can be blown over by the wind and so may need individual staking. The shrubby *V.* 'Letitia' needs to be sheared over after flowering to keep it compact. Remove the flowering stems of the others as soon as blooming is over to prevent too much self-sowing.

Verbena (Verbenaceae). Although this is a large genus most are too tender to be grown in most gardens. Many are used as tender bedding although quite a number of these can be kept from one year to another, even in quite cold areas, if they are covered with evergreen branches or a tomato tray filled with newspaper whenever there is a frost. There are a few perennials that will survive a winter. They all need a warm, sunny position and rich garden soil, preferably well-drained, many will tolerate quite dry conditions. *V. rigida* requires a moisture-retentive soil to grow well. A warm, sunny position is required for all verbenas. Some, such as *V. bonariensis*, self-sow prodigiously and need to be cut back after flowering to prevent this. Some seedlings are required in the case of this plant as it is often short-lived. On the other hand *V. corymbosa* spreads vigorously by underground runners and needs to be sited carefully or rigorously kept in check. Plants in containers should be watered regularly, at least once a day in hot weather. *V. bonariensis* is a very tall plant but rarely needs to be staked.

Verbesina (Compositae). Crown Beard. A large genus of coarse, weedy plants that are occasionally grown in gardens, valuable mainly for their late flowering. They like moisture-retentive soil and will grow in either the open or in light shade. They are liable to self-sow.

Vernonia (Compositae). Ironweed. This genus contains around 1,000 species and yet there are only a couple in cultivation, and these only seen rarely. These two will do well in a rich, deeply-cultivated soil. They preferably need a sunny position. They soon form quite a large clump, but are not invasive. Although the stems are quite stiff they are likely to need some form of staking, pea-sticks being best. They are late-flowering and should not be cut back until the winter clean-up. Top-dress with organic matter in winter.

Veronica (Scrophulariaceae). Speedwells. Most of the garden species are not lovers of wet conditions but the majority (the silver-leaved forms being the exception) are the first to show the signs of drought so keep well-watered in dry weather. A well-drained, moisture-retentive soil is the ideal. Nearly all do best in an open, sunny position, although they will also grow in a light shade if necessary. Some, *V. longifolia* for example, self-sow quite extensively so deadhead the flower spikes after flowering. This process also makes them look tidier and should be applied to all forms. Cut to the ground in the winter clear-up, or earlier if they begin to look tatty. Most spread steadily to form large clumps but are not vigorous enough to become invasive. Most are strong enough to stand without staking, but in more exposed positions some of the taller ones may need some support. *V. beccabunga*, brooklime, is a waterside plant and grows in the mud beside water, or in it if only a couple of centimetres deep. It needs to be constantly wet.

Veronicastrum (Scrophulariaceae). Bowman's Root. Culver's Physic. A small genus of two plants that are very closely related to the veronicas, so close it is very difficult to see the difference. From the cultivation point of view they are treated in the same manner.

Vicia (Leguminaceae). Vetch. Tare. This genus contains some terrible weeds that should not be introduced into the garden except to the wild-flower meadow, where they have a place. The few that should be admitted (*V. orobus* and *V. unijuga* for example) include plants that like to scramble up through other plants, perhaps some that have finished flowering. They will grow in any fertile garden soil and most prefer a sunny position, but will tolerate a little shade. Cut back after flowering, preferably before they shed their seed. Pea-stick support is required if there are no plants through which the vicia can scramble.

Vinca (Aponcymaceae). Periwinkle. The members of this genus will grow in any fertile garden soil, but do best in humus-rich ones. They will grow in the open but are usually grown as ground cover in light shade. *V. minor* will grow in even quite deep shade. Here it will produce a few flowers, producing most in a sunny position. The plants benefit from being sheared to the ground in the winter.

Viola (Violaceae). Pansies, Violas, Violets. This is a large genus of which the majority of species might be considered more suitable for the rock garden than the border. However, a large number of cultivars are grown as border plants. The majority of these, and the species, prefer to have a moisture-retentive soil with plenty of humus added to it. They also like to be shielded from the hottest time of the day, with most growing best in light shade. *V. laboradorica* retains its purple leaves best if they are planted in the open. Pansies and the more vigorous violas such as *V. cornuta* appreciate a trim after their main flush of flowers, when they will flower again. If left they will continue to flower but only sporadically. Do not cut back most of the species. Species of the *V. odorata* type, which produce new plants on thin runners, should have these removed in spring and replanted to keep the individual plants and the colony vigorous. *V. elatior* has an upright growth and likes to scramble through other plants or low shrubs. *V. cornuta* similarly likes to scramble through bushes, although this is generally grown in a conventional clump. Top-dress in winter with well-rotted, organic material. Slugs can be a problem, even to the extent of completely eating plants, so take evasive action. Vine weevil grubs are partial to viola roots and can chew right through them leaving the plant dead. Many violas are short-lived and cuttings should be taken regularly to insure against loss.

Viscaria (Caryophyllaceae). See *Lychnis*

Wachendorfia (Haemodoraceae). Red Root. This is a small genus of bulbous plants that are really only suitable for warmer areas. Although they should have a free-draining soil, it should also be moisture-retentive and should be kept damp during the growing season. Plant at around 7.5–10cm (3–4in) deep, slightly deeper in light soils. Grow in full sun in cooler areas, but light shade elsewhere. Remove the flower spike once the last bloom has faded, each only lasts a day. They will tolerate the short periods of light frost.

Wahlenbergia (Campanulaceae). Related to *Campanula*, this genus requires similar conditions. They like a well-drained, but moisture-retentive soil and a sunny position. *W. hederacea* is a plant for the bog garden. Since they are relatively short-lived it is a good idea to have a few replacement plants in reserve. Fortunately most self-sow thus providing ample replacements.

Waldsteinia (Rosaceae). A small genus of woodland plants that prefer a humus-rich soil, but which will tolerate quite dry conditions. They are plants for a shady place where, being rhizomatous, they make a good ground cover. Top-dress with leafmould during the winter.

Watsonia (Iridaceae). These bulbs are hardy enough to be left in the ground in the more mild areas, especially if the soil is free-draining, but they need to be lifted and overwintered in a frost-free place in colder districts. Some are evergreen but these do not like being stored out of the ground, so should only be grown where they can be successfully overwintered outside. Although they require a well-drained soil they do need moisture during the growing season and so the addition of humus helps. Plant at a depth of 10–15cm (4–6in) after the threat of frosts has passed. Cut back the deciduous forms during the autumn or winter clear-up if they are not lifted for storage.

Weldenia (Commelinaceae). *W. candida* is the only species in this genus. It is a plant that requires a well-drained soil such as a rock garden might provide. Its roots are long and it needs a deeply-cultivated soil. It also needs a sunny position. It is on the tender side and can therefore only be grown in mild areas. Elsewhere it should either be given winter protection or lifted and overwintered under glass. If possible keep it on the dry side during its dormant period.

Woodsia (Dryopteridaceae). This is a medium-sized genus of ferns. They mainly like a rocky situation where they can find moisture beneath the rocks, but are not waterlogged. Either sun or the lightest of shade is suitable. They are not easy to satisfy and a degree of experimentation may be necessary before they grow well. They are rare in the wild and should never be collected.

Woodwardia (Blechnaceae). Chain Fern. A small genus of ferns of which half a dozen are in cultivation. Some are evergreen while others are deciduous. WW. *virginica*, *fimbriata* and *aureolata* need a moist soil, the first are even happy to grow in shallow water, while all three will grow in the bog garden. They generally like an acid or neutral soil, preferably the former. W. *radicans* is tender and only suitable for sheltered spots in milder areas. This will grow in any enriched garden soil. They have creeping rhizomes which quickly form quite large colonies.

Wulfenia (Scrophulariaceae). This is a small genus of rhizomatous plants that like a moist, humusy soil that is not too heavy. They are lime-haters and should be given an acid soil. W. *baldacci* is the exception to this. A lightly-shaded position should be provided and a sheltered peat bed is the ideal as they must not be allowed to dry out. Top-dress with leafmould during winter. Cut off flowering spikes after blooming, unless seed is required.

Xerophyllum (Phormiaceae/Liliaceae). Bear Grass, Turkey Beard. A small genus of two species that are not too easy to cultivate. They need a lightish acid soil that is moisture-retentive, a peat bed is ideal as long as it is not too heavy. If possible it should be kept on the dry side over winter. Try planting them near evergreens or conifers that will extract some of the winter moisture from the soil. They like a partially-shaded position. You will need patience as they often take as many as seven years before flowers are produced. Any transplanting should be avoided if possible, but if necessary move them during the spring. Planting should be at the same time of year. The main species in cultivation is X. *asphodeloides*, but X. *tenax* is also grown. This needs almost similar conditions but might need to be given a slightly drier soil and a bit more sun.

Yucca (Agavaceae). Adam's Needle, Palm Lily, Spanish Dagger. This is an increasingly popular genus of plants. They like a well-drained soil and a sunny position. Drought conditions are tolerated but they dislike the wet hanging around the roots, especially during the winter. Do not try to overfeed to get quick growth. They may take several years to reach flowering size, but once they have flowered the plant dies. Fortunately there are nearly always several offsets growing around the main plant to continue its presence. Yuccas are evergreen but the leaves still die from time to time and should be removed. This is facilitated by a twisting movement as well as a pulling one. If the dead leaves are not removed they will hang around for years making the plant look tattier and tattier. Wear leather gloves when doing this.

Zantedeschia (Araceae). Arum Lily, Calla Lily, Lily-of-the-Nile. This small genus of plants are generally too tender for the open garden, but Z. *aethiopica* will survive in most. The form Z. *a.* 'Crowborough' is the one that used to be quoted as the hardiest but it is now generally thought that nearly all forms of this species are as hardy as one another. As well as being able to grow this species in moist soil it can be grown in water. Indeed, it may be safer here as ponds rarely freeze completely, keeping the arum safe in the mud. A little light shade helps to prevent the flowers scorching, but as long as the soil is moist they will grow in a sunny spot. The yellow Z. *elliottiana* is more tender but can be grown in milder gardens, although it may still need a mulch to protect it. This must have a drier soil, especially during the winter. Slugs love these plants and can prevent any shoots appearing in spring. If grown in the border top-dress with organic material at sometime during the winter.

Zauschneria (Onagraceae). California Fuchsia. Strictly speaking these plants have all been taken under the wing of *Epilobium canum*, but in gardening terms they are sufficiently distinct to retain their own genus. It is a small genus of woody plants that like a well-drained soil and a warm, sunny position. Z. *californica* is the hardiest and most freely flowering in cooler areas. When happy it can be invasive, spreading underground, and needs to be kept in check. All are evergreen and should be sheared over to keep them compact.

Zephyranthes (Amaryllidaceae). Flower-of-the-west-wind, Rain Flower. The main member of this bulbous genus that is grown in the open is Z. *candida*. This is a plant of damp fields in Argentina and does best in moist, but free-draining soils. They do like a dry summer prior to flowering. Make certain that the soil has had a good soaking around the time they are due to start flowering which is in late summer or early autumn. It does best in a warm position with plenty of sun. Plant the bulbs in spring at a depth of about 7.5–10cm (3–4in). Lift and divide when congested which often shows up when the bulbs become shy flowering. A light dressing of potash in spring is beneficial.

Zigadenus (Melanthiaceae/Liliaceae). The species of this small genus of rhizomatous bulbous plants require a lime-free, free-draining soil, but it should be both moist and moisture-retentive for best performance. Z. *nuttallii* should have a drier soil. They will grow in either sun or light shade. Planting out is best carried out in the autumn, but spring will do if the bulbs cannot be obtained before then. Plant at a depth of about 5–7.5cm (2–3in). Divide the clumps, in autumn, when they become congested. These are poisonous plants, both to man and animals, and have several vernacular names with the word 'death' in them.

Zizania (Gramineae). This is a very small genus of creeping grasses that are mainly annual and that need to be planted by or in water. An open position is to be preferred. They will tolerate up to about 20cm (8in) of still water, but will also grow in the mud beside the pond as long as it does not dry out. The perennial species are invasive, so do not plant in a small pond unless you can contain it in some way.

Bibliography

Armitage, Allan M. *Herbaceous perennial plants*. Varsity Press (Georgia), 1989

Bird, Richard. *Border pinks*. Batsford (London), 1994

Bird, Richard, *Complete book of hardy perennials*. Ward Lock (London), 1993

Bird, Richard, *Lilies*. Apple Press (London), 1991

Bird, Richard, *The Propagation of hardy perennials*. Batsford (London), 1993

Bird, Richard, *Woodland gardening*. Souvenir Press (London), 1992

Clausen, Ruth Rogers, and Ekstrom, Nicolas H., *Perennials for American gardens*. Random House (New York), 1989

Cobb, James, *Meconopsis*. Helm/Batsford (London), 1989

Cribb, Philip, and Bailes, Christopher, *Hardy orchids*. Helm/Batsford (London), 1989

Davies, Dilys, *Allium*. Batsford (London), 1992

Grenfell, Diana, *Hosta*. Batsford (London), 1990

Grounds, Roger, *Ornamental grasses*. Helm/Batsford (London), 1989

Jellito, Leo, and Schacht, Wilhelm, *Hardy herbaceous perennials*. 2 vols. Batsford (London), Timber Press (Portland), 1990

Lewis, Peter, and Lynch, Margaret, *Campanulas*. Helm/Batsford (London), 1989

Lloyd, Christopher, *The well-tempered garden*. Collins (London), 1970

Mathew, Brian, *Hellebores*. Alpine Garden Society (Pershore), 1989

Mathew, Brian, *The Iris*. Batsford (London), 1981

Perry, Frances, *Collins guide to border plants*. Collins (London), 1957

Pesch, Barbara, *Perennials: a nursery source manual*. Brooklyn Botanic Gardens (Brooklyn), 1989

Phillips, Roger, and Rix, Martin, *Perennials*. 2 vols. Pan (London), 1991

The Plant finder. Headmain (Whitbourne), annual

The Plantsman. Royal Horticultural Society (London), quarterly.

Rice, Graham, and Strangman, Elizabeth, *Hellebores*. David & Charles (Newton Abbot), 1993

Swindells, Philip, and Mason, David, *The complete book of the water garden*. Ward Lock (London), 1989

Thomas, Graham Stuart, *Perennial garden plants*. 3rd ed. Dent, 1990

Yeo, Peter, *Hardy geraniums*. Helm/Batsford (London), 1985

Index of Common Names

175

General Index